IMAGES
of Rail

Rail Depots of Eastern North Carolina

ON THE COVER: Atlantic Coast Line passenger excursion train stopped at Ahoskie in 1959. By that date, the line from Rocky Mount to Norfolk was freight service only, the last regular passenger train ended service on November 30, 1954. (Photograph by D.M. Humphrey; David Lloyd Humphrey collection.)

IMAGES
of Rail

Rail Depots of Eastern North Carolina

Larry K. Neal Jr.

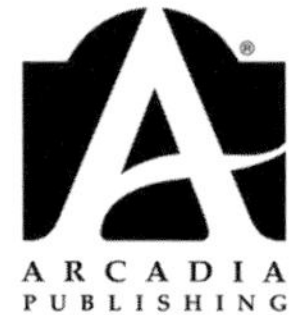

ISBN 978-1-4671-2622-9

Published by Arcadia Publishing
Charleston, South Carolina

Printed in the United States of America

Library of Congress Control Number: 2017931484

For all general information, please contact Arcadia Publishing:
Telephone 843-853-2070
Fax 843-853-0044
E-mail sales@arcadiapublishing.com
For customer service and orders:
Toll-Free 1-888-313-2665

Visit us on the Internet at www.arcadiapublishing.com

This book is dedicated to all the local historians, rail, and architectural enthusiasts who actively photographed and recorded railroad depots and stations through the past 100 years. Because of their time and effort, this part of railroad history can and will be preserved for future generations.

Contents

ACKNOWLEDGMENTS

There are several people I have met over the last 20–30 years that have helped me with my interest in photographing and documenting railroad depots of North Carolina. First, I would like to mention the volunteers who worked at the Wilmington Railroad Museum during the mid- to late 1980s. I volunteered there while in high school and college, and some of the older volunteers had actually worked for the railroad and knew where some of the depots still stood across the eastern part of the state. One of my good high school friends, Steven Somberg, would ride with me as we followed the old rail lines to research and photograph what we found along the way. Another friend, Ben Brantley, who also volunteered at the museum, would help me explore as well from time to time. Another friend and volunteer, Charles Kernan, researched about the Atlantic Coast Line buildings in Wilmington, which most were merely ghosts by the time he published his findings. I would also like to thank my brother Kelly for grabbing a few depots for me around Jacksonville.

I had compiled a fairly accurate depot list by the late 1990s and worked with Art Peterson to complete his railroad structure book, published by the Old North Chapter, NRHS (National Railway Historical Society) in 2001. Art and I exchanged our lists, and I was able to learn not only about more that still stood, but some of the background information about the buildings in general. Art's book was definitely one any serious North Carolina depot or station aficionado should be required to possess in their collection.

For this book, I reached out to several photographers who had documented depots from the 1960s to the 1980s. Of these, Tom King was the greatest help, opening his collection of several thousand depot images, which included many from C.K. Marsh, who traveled across North Carolina in the early 1970s, especially along the Norfolk Southern Railway. Without their help, this book would never have been completed. I would also like to thank Brian Ezzelle, S. David Carriker, and Robert Rosseau for their help in providing images as well. Karen Andersen from the North Carolina Department of Archives and History was a great help allowing me to look through the image collection in the North Carolina State Archives.

I would be remiss if I did not mention by parents, Larry Neal Sr. and Donna Neal, who help foster my interest in railroads by letting me borrow their car for trips or did not mind when I increased the phone bill by calling towns and cities for information before planning day or weekend trips. Their help and nurturing guidance will never be forgotten.

To my wife, Traci, and daughter, Kerstin, thank you for your patience and understanding while I worked nights and other times on this book. I love you both more than you will ever know.

INTRODUCTION

When people today are asked to describe the cultural or economic center of their community, one building that will usually not be mentioned is the railroad depot (or station). If the question was asked 70 or 100 years ago, the answer would be quite different. The railroad depot was viewed in many ways as a necessity for both travelers and businesses. From the smallest town or largest city, the depot allowed people to explore their state or the nation.

For those seeking travel, a ticket on a passenger train could be considered magical, transporting riders from one place to another. This was an experience—from gourmet food served with china and silver, Pullman sleeping cars and plenty of good conversation with fellow travelers. Trains allowed travelers to see the countryside as it snaked across plains, climbed mountains, and crossed rivers. Even the simple wooden depot acted as the perfect launching pad for these journeys, and welcomed those at their destination.

One type of business created because of the passenger train was package express. Express companies would contract with the railroads to transport packages and mail along their routes. During World War I, the American Railway Express was created from four express companies to better facilitate the movement of packages across the United States. It was later renamed Railway Express Agency in 1929 and owned by 86 railroads that participated in the company. Their fleet of green trucks would deliver the goods from the depot to homes and businesses.

Farmers and local businessmen counted on the depots to bring in rail cars full of goods to use or sell or to load with their wares to markets across the United States. Special team tracks were used for these deliveries, which could be delivering new automobiles, furniture, or the latest fabrics for the dress shop. Railroads developed less than carload services for smaller shipments that would not fill an entire boxcar but were loaded with other shipments to maximize space to a destination. Even Christmas presents were delivered to the local depots ordered from the latest mail order catalogs.

Most of this changed, unfortunately, starting in the 1940s. Railroad passenger business was down, mainly due to competition from airlines. What used to be a 20-to-24-hour train ride could now be done in a matter of hours in the air. Air Express, a division of the Railway Express Agency (REA), was flourishing during this time. Railroads began to downsize or eliminate passenger trains and subsequently closing or demolishing depots no longer needed. The depots that remained were converted strictly for freight service or sold to neighboring businesses or farmers for storage. The REA was reorganized as REA Express in 1960 but went out of business in 1975 due to the fact it only moved 10 percent of all express shipments, none by rail.

Only the long-distance trains remained, stopping at the larger cities en route. The Atlantic Coast Line and Seaboard continued to fight for passenger travel, mainly to Florida through the 1960s. Cities like Rocky Mount, Fayetteville, Raleigh, and Hamlet continued to serve passengers but mainly in the wee hours of the night. Amtrak was formed in 1971 to take over the long-distance passenger service across the United States. They continued to use several of these old depots, some which have been lovingly restored to harken back to the glory days of rail travel.

Thanks to those efforts, passengers riding Amtrak today can still experience a taste of the golden years of rail travel.

This book will explore various railroad depots that served eastern North Carolina, from both big and small rail lines. The Atlantic Coast Line (ACL), Seaboard Air Line (SAL) and Norfolk & Southern (NS) Railway were the largest, with their lines intertwined across the eastern part of the state.

The Atlantic Coast Line was the oldest, with the first line opening in 1840 between Wilmington and Weldon. Railroad construction continued through the 19th-century for predecessor lines of the ACL and SAL, culminating in the formation of each railroad in 1900. The Norfolk & Southern Railway was formed in 1881 from the consolidation of several smaller lines along the coast, eventually heading west to Charlotte. Each of these railroads has their own chapters to illustrate the multiple depots and larger stations built through the years.

The final chapter highlights union depots and those built by short line railroads. Some larger cities constructed union depots, due to several railroads serving the same location. These stations could handle multiple trains at once. There were also several smaller rail lines that offered passenger service, constructing depots for that purpose or sharing a depot with a larger railroad. Some of these were of their own design, while others borrowed from the larger lines, which had a controlling interest in some cases.

Not only are postcards and other images used to illustrate the depots, but the history of the railroads and the communities they served are explored throughout this book. While photographic documentation is important, knowing the history behind a location helps determine why a specific small depot or large station was chosen.

The goal of any historian is to continually develop knowledge of a particular subject. It is my hope that readers will not only research and explore the depots, stations, and communities shown within these pages, but seek out other remaining depots across the state.

One

Atlantic Coast Line

The Atlantic Coast Line started in North Carolina as the Wilmington & Weldon (W&W) Railroad, operating a distance of 162 miles. This was considered the longest operating railroad in the world when opened in 1840. From there, the railroad kept centralizing lines from Wilmington, resembling spokes from a wheel. The ACL name was formalized in 1900, and lasted until 1967. The railroad served a plethora of small communities along the coast, stretching from Rocky Mount and Fayetteville to New Bern, Plymouth, and Ahoskie. Many communities were barely a mile apart but had a depot to serve the community.

The amount of coverage the ACL had in eastern North Carolina can also be seen by the number of depots shown in passenger timetables and station listings. The July 1926 timetable shows 155 stations, though some smaller communities may not be listed.

The original main line through Wilmington was later bypassed with the Fayetteville cutoff, connecting Wilson and Florence, South Carolina. Although the main passenger trains no longer operated through Wilmington, this city remained the headquarters of the ACL until 1960 when it was moved to Jacksonville, Florida. Local passenger trains continued to serve the small communities into the 1950s and freight into the 1970s.

The ACL used some standard plans for their wooden depots along the line, with size determined by the amount of freight traffic. During the 1930s and 1940s, the depots were painted a light brown with dark brown trim. This was replaced in the 1950s with white siding and purple trim. Purple had been used on their timetables since 1900 and on their diesel locomotives, starting with the Champion passenger train in 1939.

Thankfully, several nice examples of ACL depots still remain today, some having been lovingly restored for community and Amtrak service.

These depots are arranged by the various routes from Wilmington, ending with branch lines.

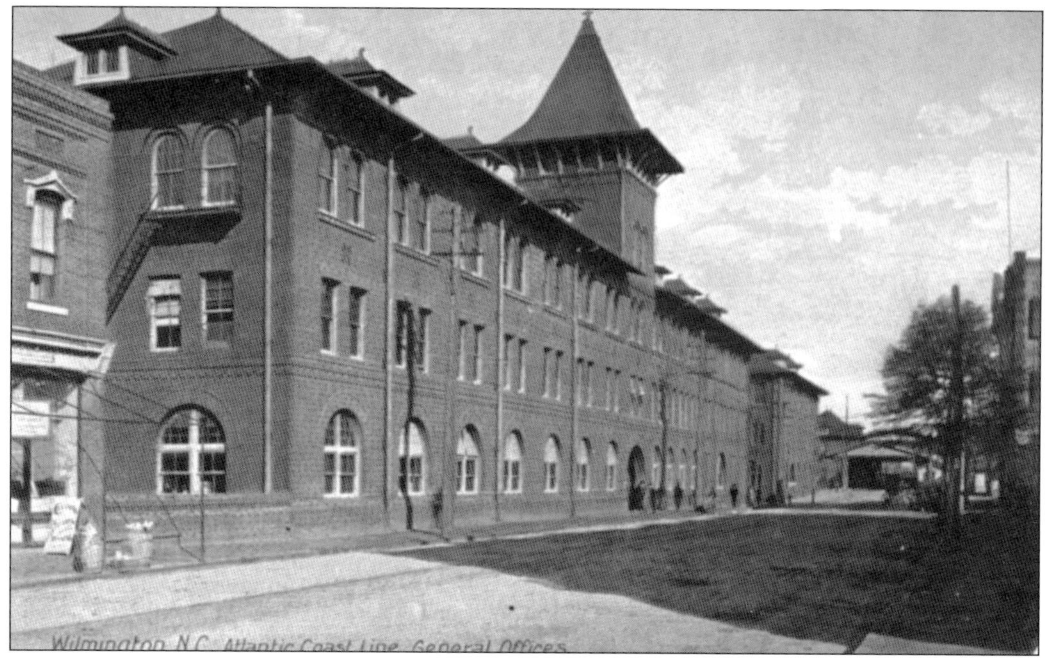

The Wilmington & Raleigh (later changed to Wilmington & Weldon) Railroad was completed in 1840, operating from Wilmington to Weldon near the Virginia border. When completed, it was the longest railroad in the world at 161.50 miles in length. The original office building was located in the first floor of Building A of the ACL office complex. Note the different style of windows compared to the added stories. (Author's collection.)

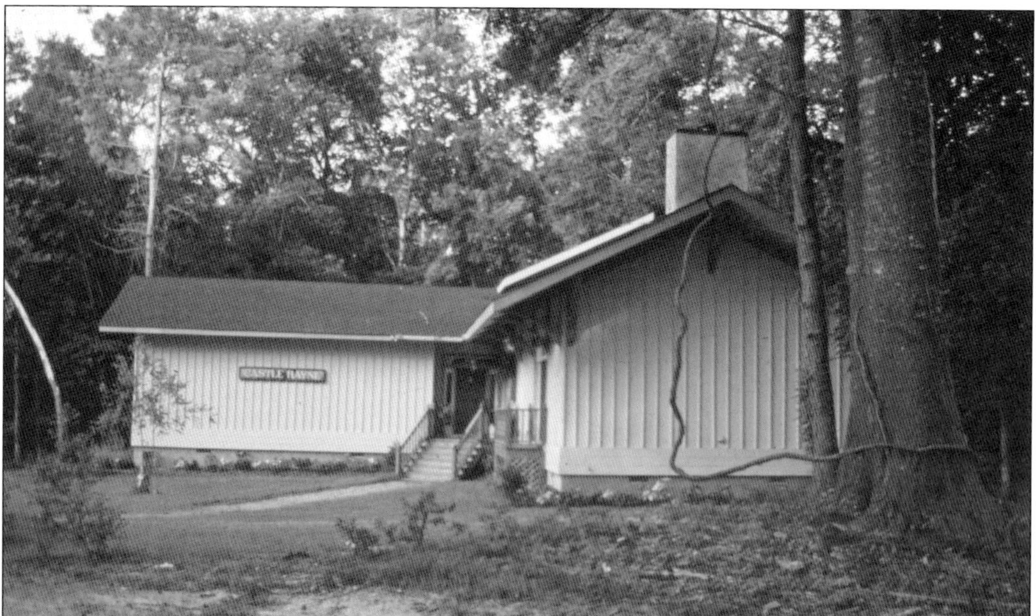

The W&W ran northward from Wilmington, crossing the Northeast Cape Fear River. One of the first depots was Castle Hayne, named for Capt. Roger Haynes. This community has never been incorporated, remaining a small rural area of New Hanover County. The depot was converted into a house, preserving the original structure. (Author's collection.)

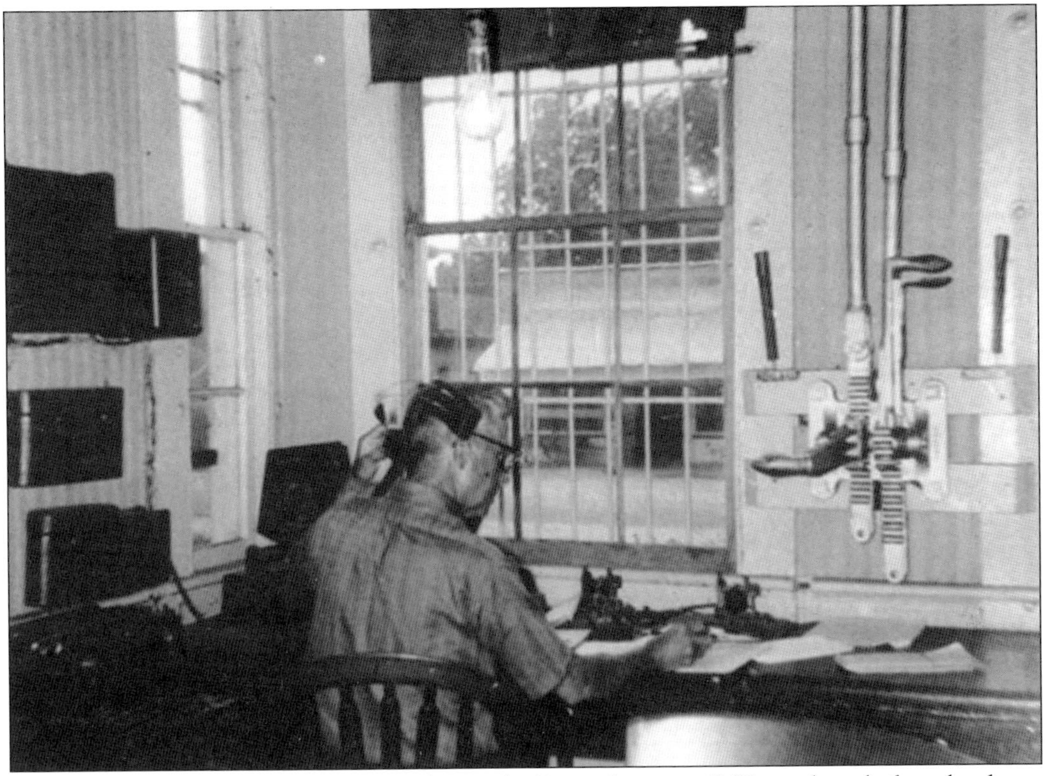

This is a view of the station agent in the Rocky Point depot in 1965, not long before the depot closed. His desk was located in the bay window, facing the tracks. From here, he could write train orders, work with area farmers for freight deliveries (passenger service had ended in the 1950s), or contact other depots along the line. The two large handles controlled the bidirectional train order board—one shows stop while the other is set for engineer to pick up new orders. (Courtesy of the Pender County Library Collection.)

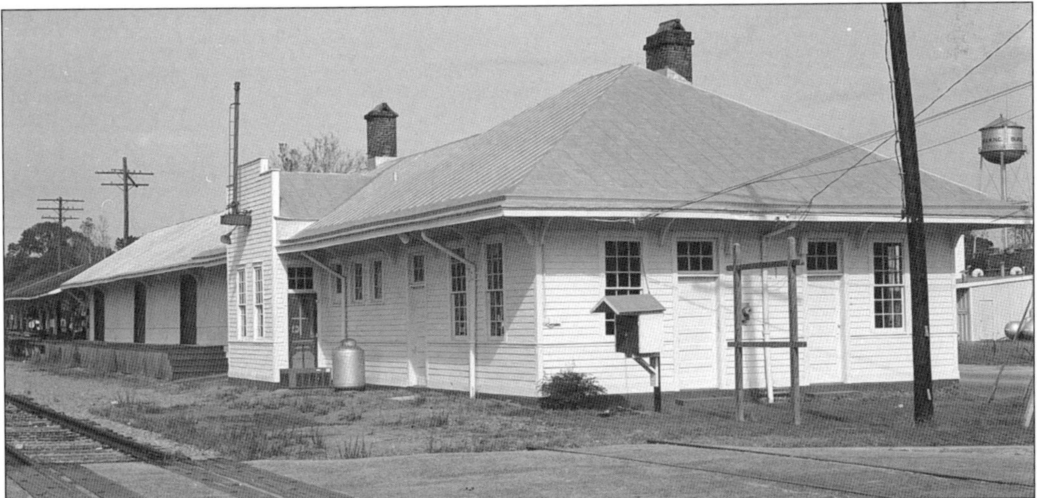

Burgaw depot is pictured here in the late 1980s. This building was restored in 2009 and is now known as the Historic Burgaw Depot and Event Center. Burgaw was incorporated in 1879 but dates back to the Wilmington & Weldon Railroad construction. (Author's collection.)

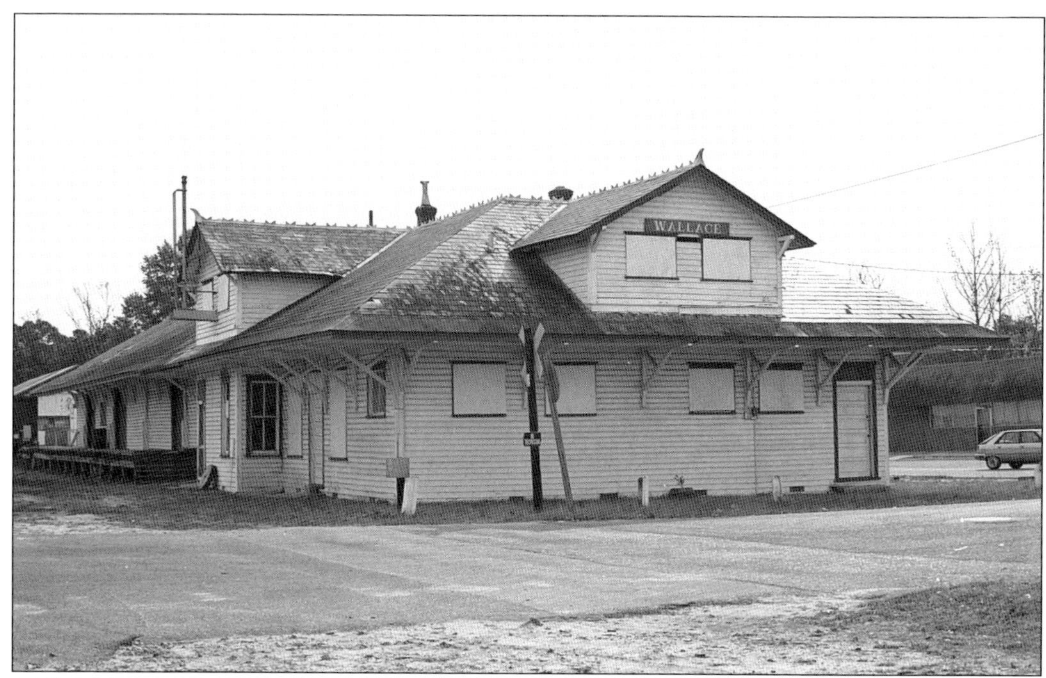

Wallace, home to the Carolina Strawberry Festival, is also where the end of track for the W&W is today. The line was cut between Wallace and Wilmington during the 1970s. The ACL built its larger standard depot here in 1920, mainly due to the higher amount of farm goods shipped out by rail. This depot was restored in 2007 and houses the local chamber of commerce. (Author's collection.)

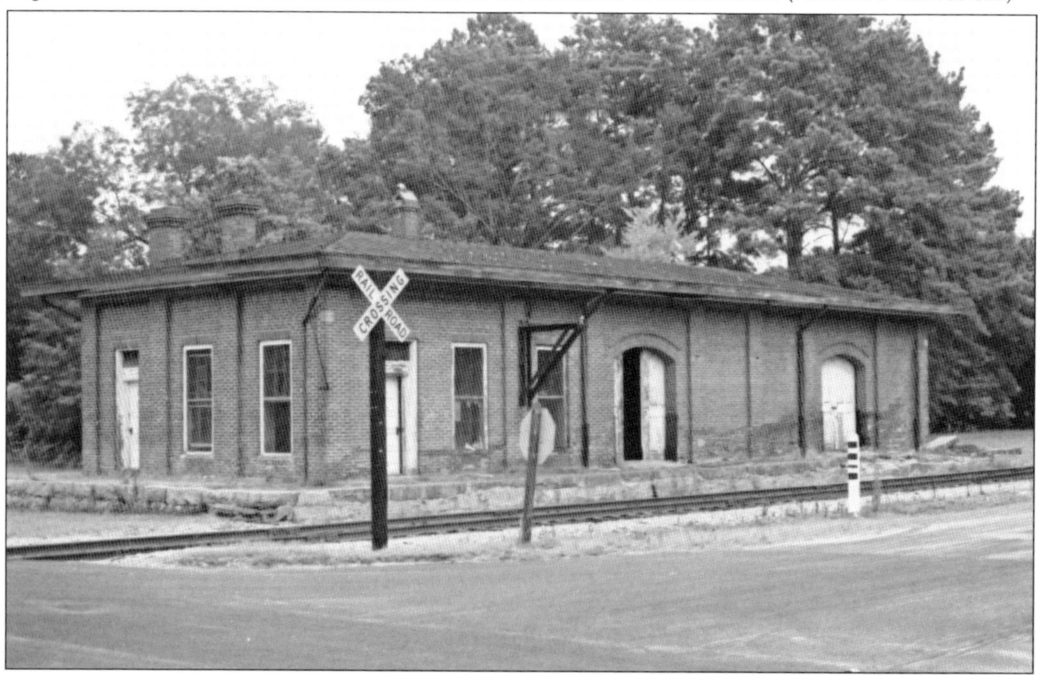

Magnolia is named for the Magnolia Grandiflora flower, which grows throughout the area. The town dates back to 1855, developed around the railroad. The depot, torn down in the mid-1980s, looks similar to railroad construction of the 1880s–1890s. (Courtesy of the Brian Ezzelle collection.)

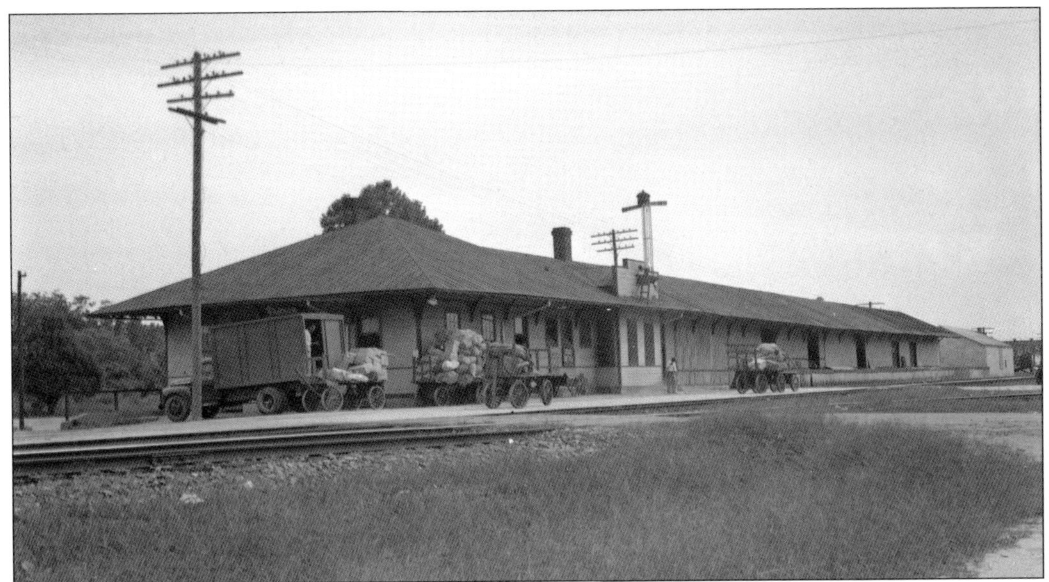

Warsaw was a busy place, as seen by the activity around the depot. The branch to Clinton also started here, bringing in more freight traffic. This view from 1948 shows baggage carts, probably loaded with mail sacks from the truck, ready for the passenger train arrival. Mail was very productive for the ACL, with a railway post office (RPO) car regularly assigned to this train to sort mail between the stops. (Photograph by Wiley Bryan, courtesy of the King-Marsh collection.)

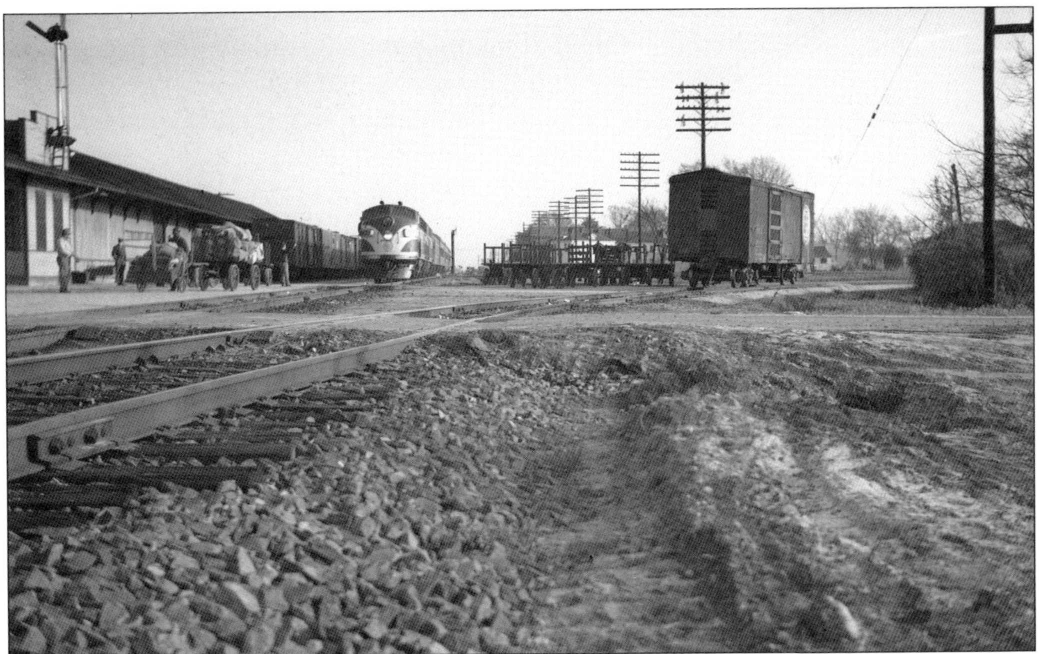

The northbound passenger train is pulling up to its stop in Warsaw. The mail carts are ready to load, while other baggage carts sit across the tracks. The wooden boxcar, probably full of produce, is sitting on the connection to the branch line to Clinton. (Courtesy of the State Archives of North Carolina.)

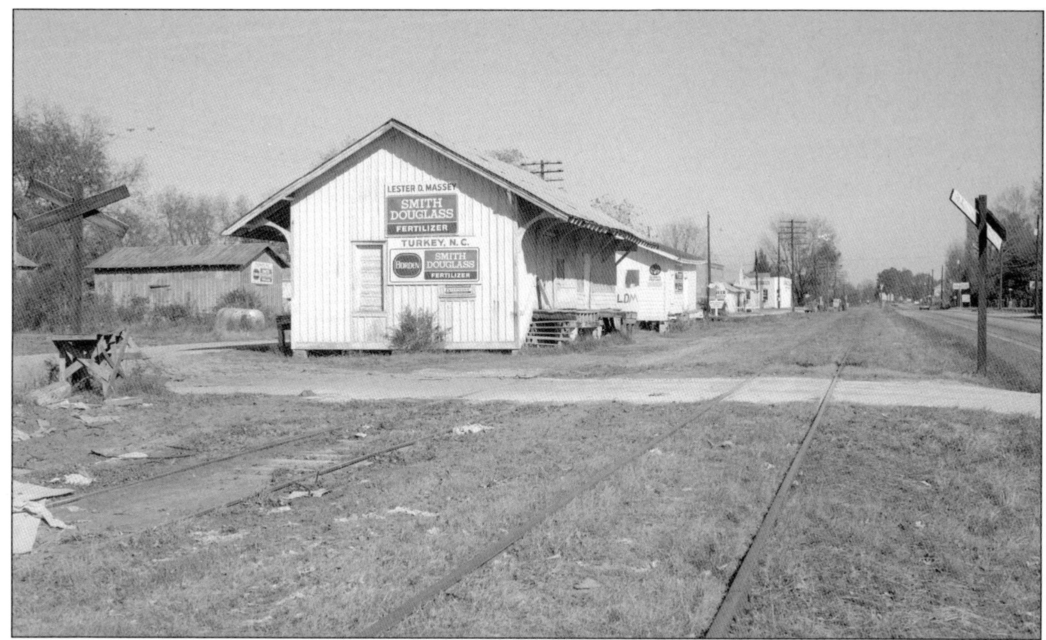

Turkey was originally known as Springville, but due to a large rafter (group of turkeys) living in the area, it was given the name Turkey Creek. The depot was used through the 1960s, when it was sold and used for storage. Today, Turkey is also known for pecans and other farm produce. (Photograph by Tom King, courtesy of the King-Marsh collection.)

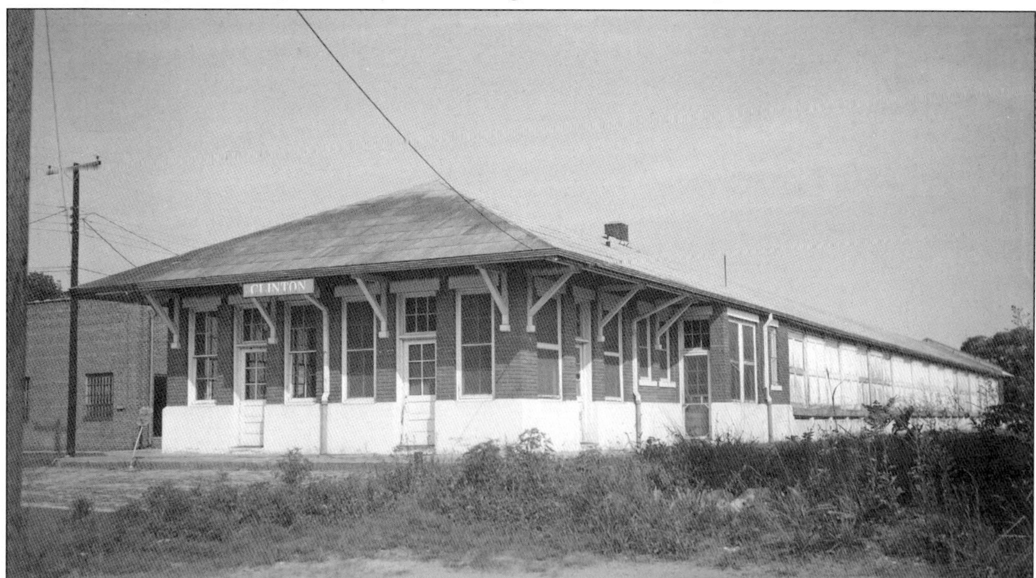

Clinton is the county seat of Sampson County and was named for Brig. Gen. Richard Clinton in 1852. Because of its location near the center of the county, Clinton grew as an important agricultural center. Note the several freight doors, which protected farm goods from the weather. Notable residents include US senator Lauch Faircloth and William Rufus King, 13th vice president of the United States. In later years, the Clinton depot was converted into Smitty's restaurant during the 1990s and is now a Hwy 55 restaurant. (Photograph by Tom King, courtesy of the King-Marsh collection.)

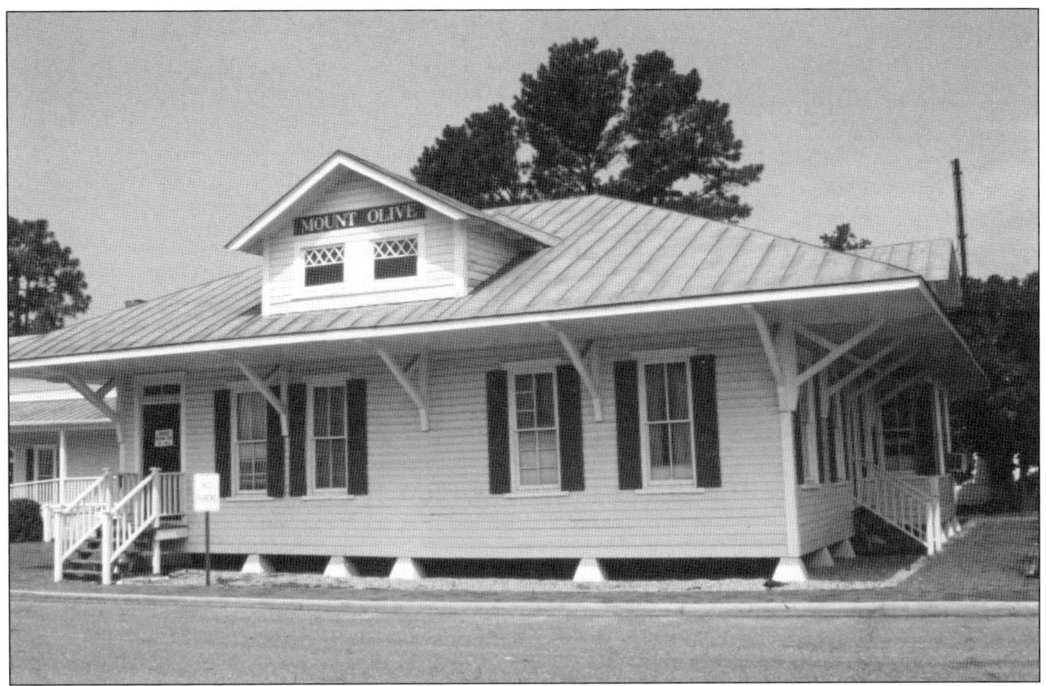

Mount Olive is best known as the home of Mount Olive Pickles, established in 1926. They also host the North Carolina Pickle Festival and celebrate New Year's Eve by lowering a three-foot pickle since 1999. This well-preserved depot still stands along the tracks. (Author's collection.)

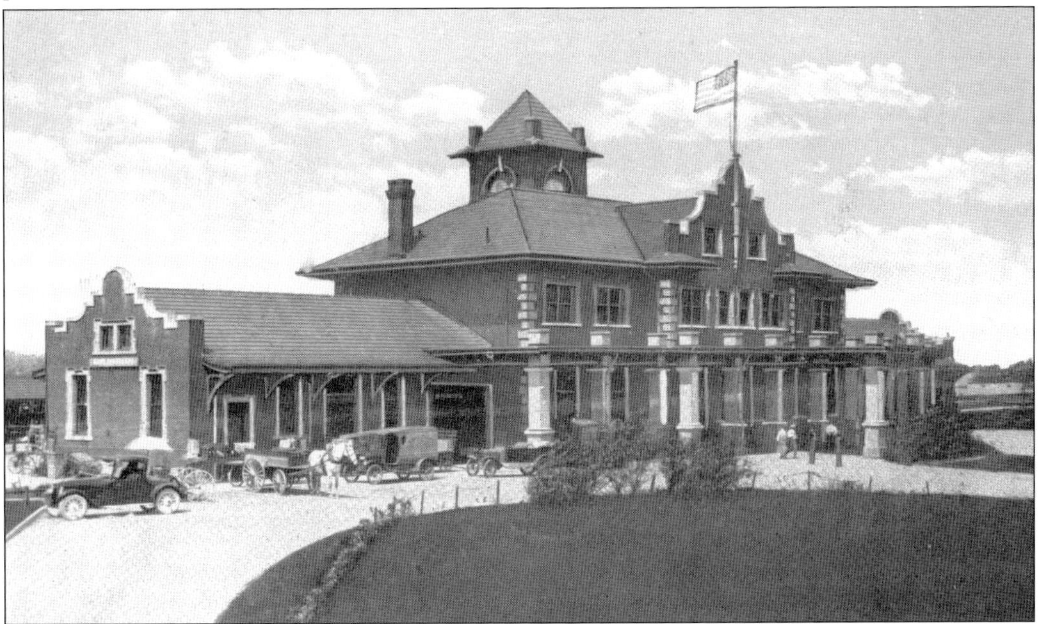

Goldsboro became the largest city along the W&W, since the ACL, Atlantic & North Carolina Railroad, and the Southern Railway all served this community. The large depot, built in 1909, showed this importance and also housed railroad offices on the second floor. In later years, this depot was used by a lumber company but is now being preserved to its former glory. (Courtesy of the State Archives of North Carolina.)

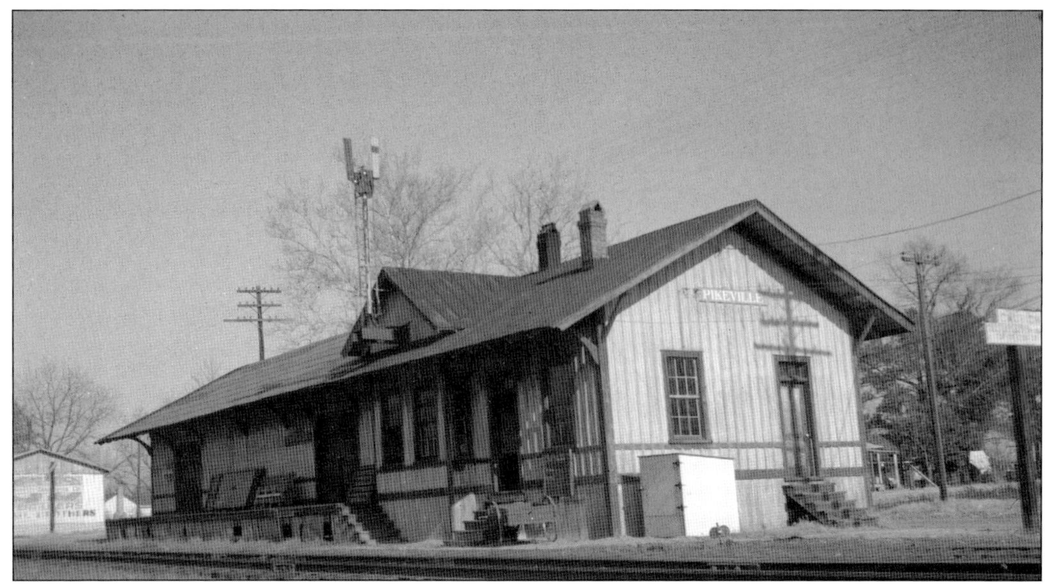

Pikeville is a small community between Goldsboro and Wilson. This view from 1963 shows the 1940s-to-1950s-era paint of beige walls and dark brown trim. This was replaced in the 1950s with white walls and purple trim to match the ACL's purple diesel locomotives. Purple had been used by the ACL since 1900 on its passenger timetables as well. (Photograph by Tom King, courtesy of the King-Marsh collection.)

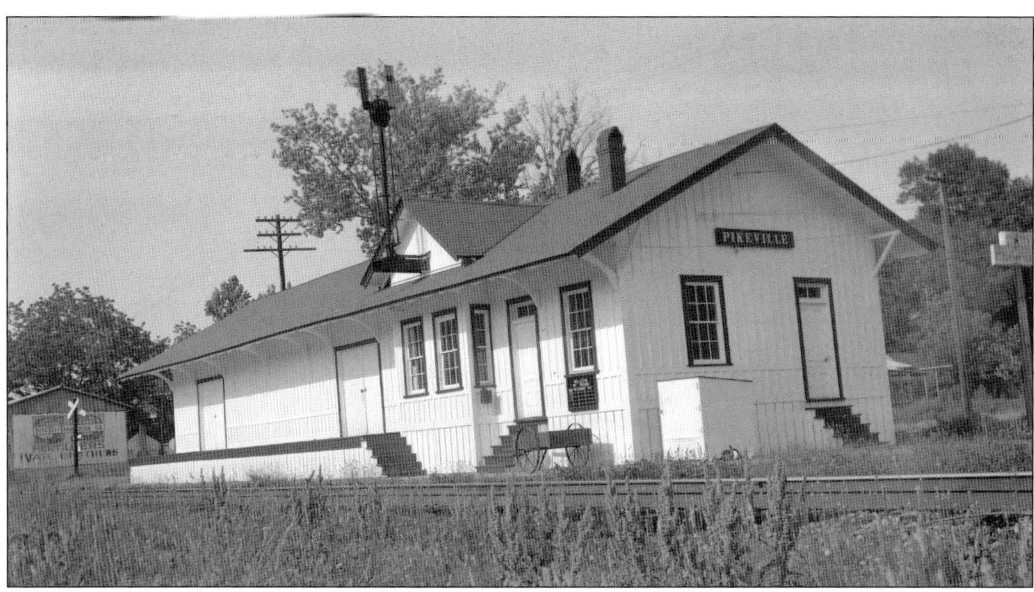

The depot was repainted in 1965 with white walls and purple trim, matching the ACL's purple diesel locomotives. (Photograph by Tom King, courtesy of the King-Marsh collection.)

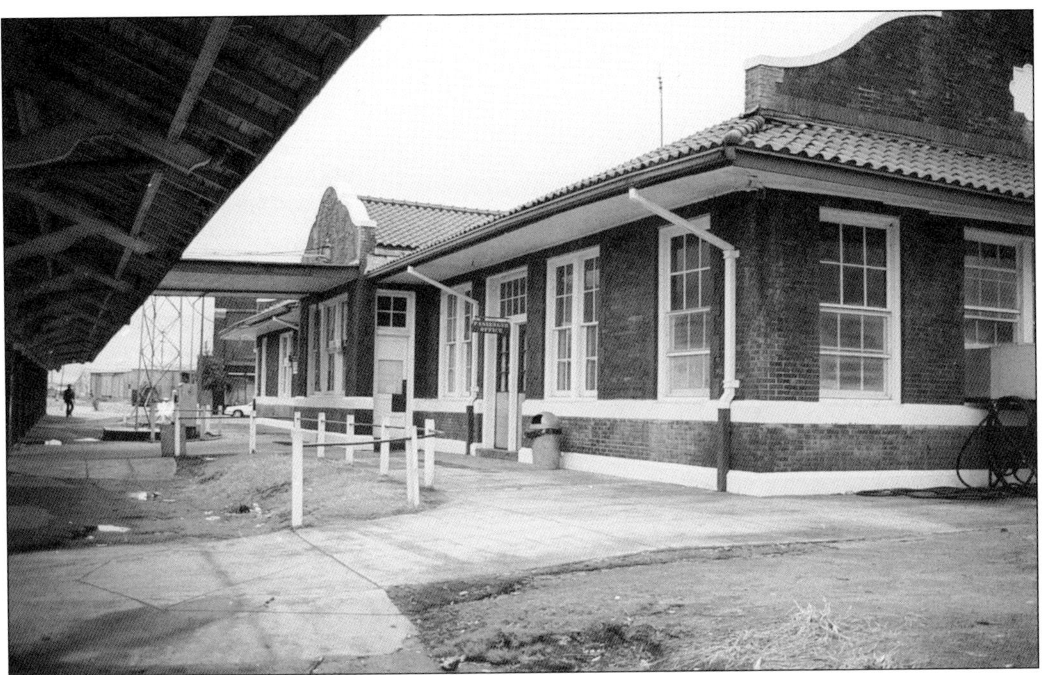

The town of Wilson dates back to 1849, and is named for Col. Louis D. Wilson, who was killed in the Mexican-American War. This depot, using Flemish style, was built in 1924 and later preserved by the North Carolina Department of Transportation. Part of the renovation included a mural depicting 100 years of railroad history in Wilson. (Author's collection.)

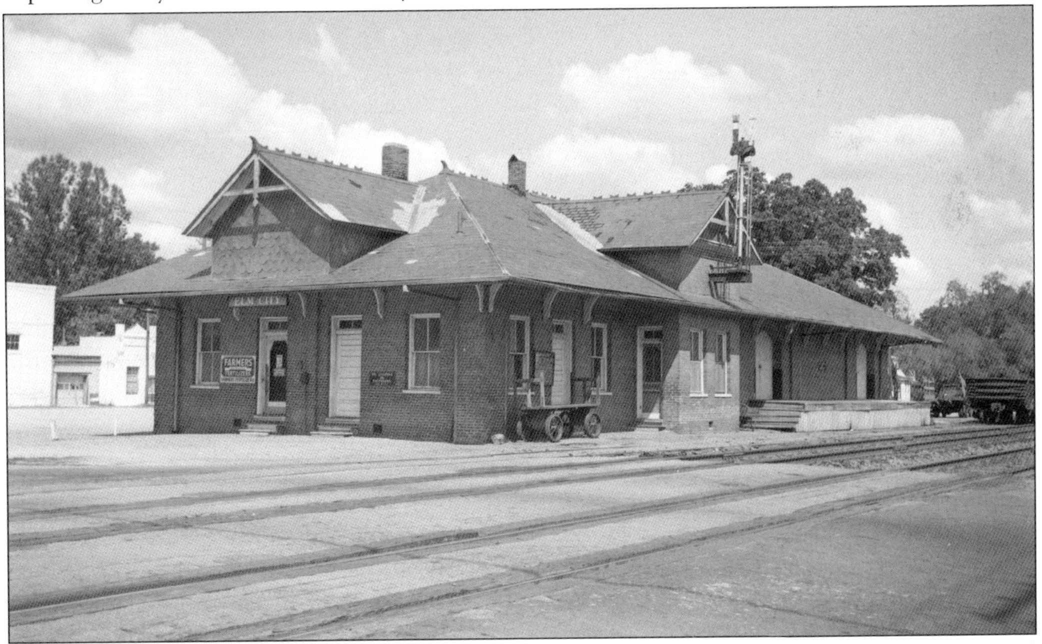

Elm City was incorporated on December 18, 1873, under the name Toisnot. It was not until October 11, 1913, that it was officially changed to Elm City. The depot, built around 1909, was moved about 100 yards so that it could be restored as a community building. This view was from September 1965. (Photograph by Tom King, courtesy of the King-Marsh collection.)

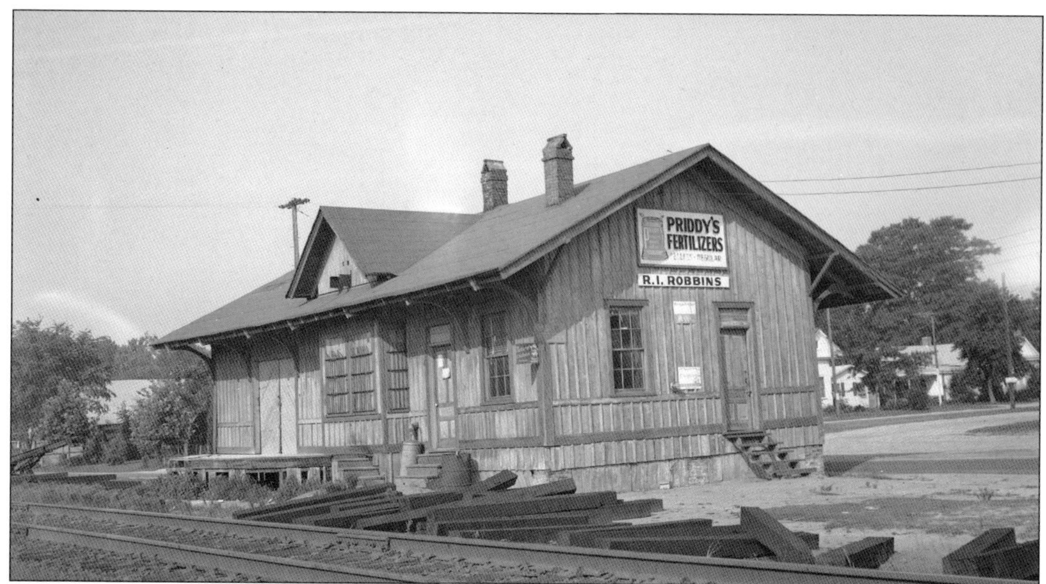

Sharpsburg is situated in three counties—Edgecombe, Nash, and Wilson—and is named for John Jacob Sharp. This depot was later moved to Rocky Mount and currently houses a restaurant. Photographed on July 2, 1967, now in private ownership. (Photograph by Tom King, courtesy of the King-Marsh collection.)

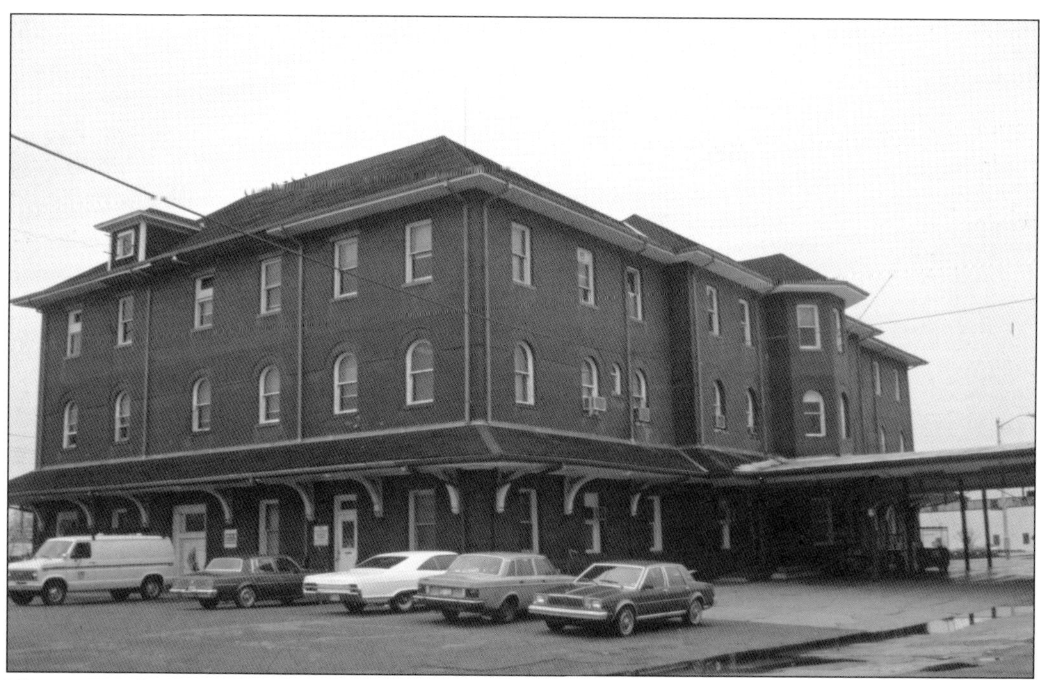

This original section of this depot started as one-story building with a center two-story section in 1903, then had the full second floor added in 1910, followed by the third floor in 1913. This building was used by the ACL as its Northern Division headquarters through the 1960s. The building, shown here in 1992, was fully restored by the North Carolina Department of Transportation in 2000, which included adding a larger train shed to the tracks. (Author's collection.)

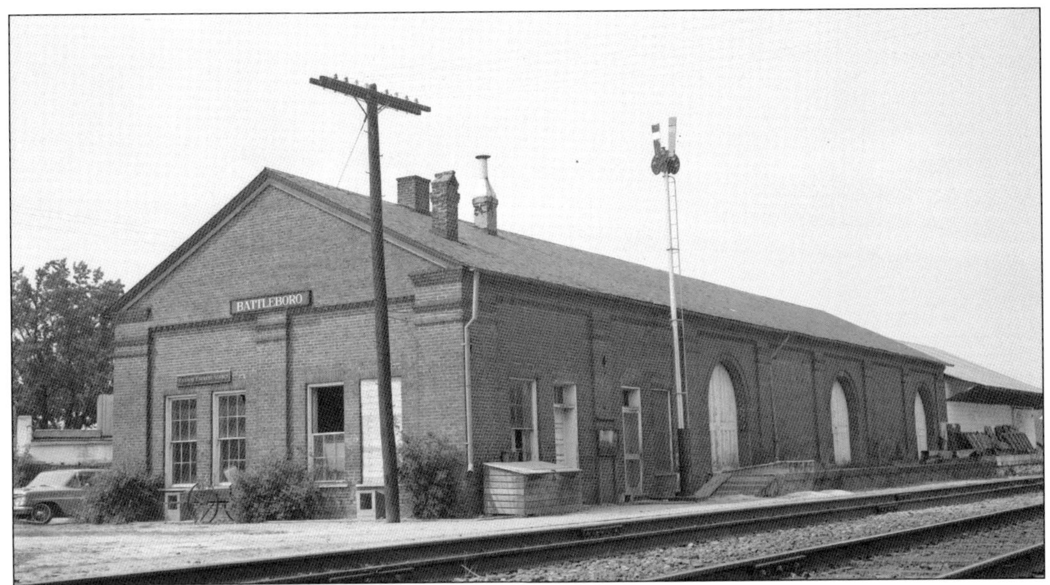

Battleboro was named for the Battle family, dating back to Elisha Battle in the 1750s. Joseph Sumner Battle was contracted to build eight miles of roadbed through the area, and it became known first as Battle Station and then Battleboro in 1873. Battleboro was the original site chosen for the railroad shops, but they were eventually built in Rocky Mount. (Photograph by Tom King, courtesy of the King-Marsh collection.)

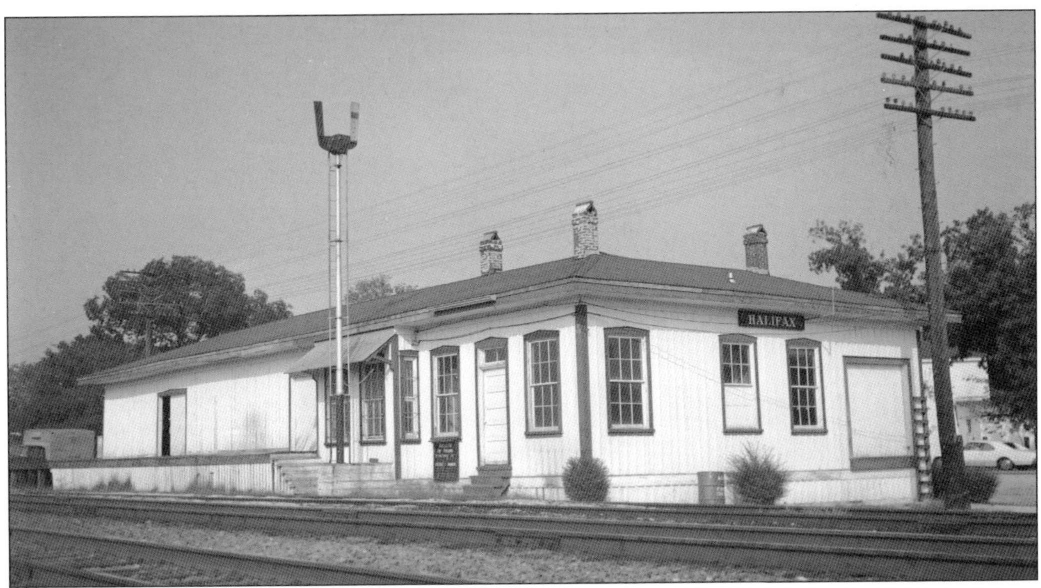

The town of Halifax dates back to 1757 and is named for George Montague-Dunk, second earl of Halifax. North Carolina's Fourth Provincial Congress met in Halifax during the spring of 1776, adopting the Halifax Resolves on April 12, 1776. The depot is shown still watching over the tracks in 1967. (Photograph by Tom King, courtesy of the King-Marsh collection.)

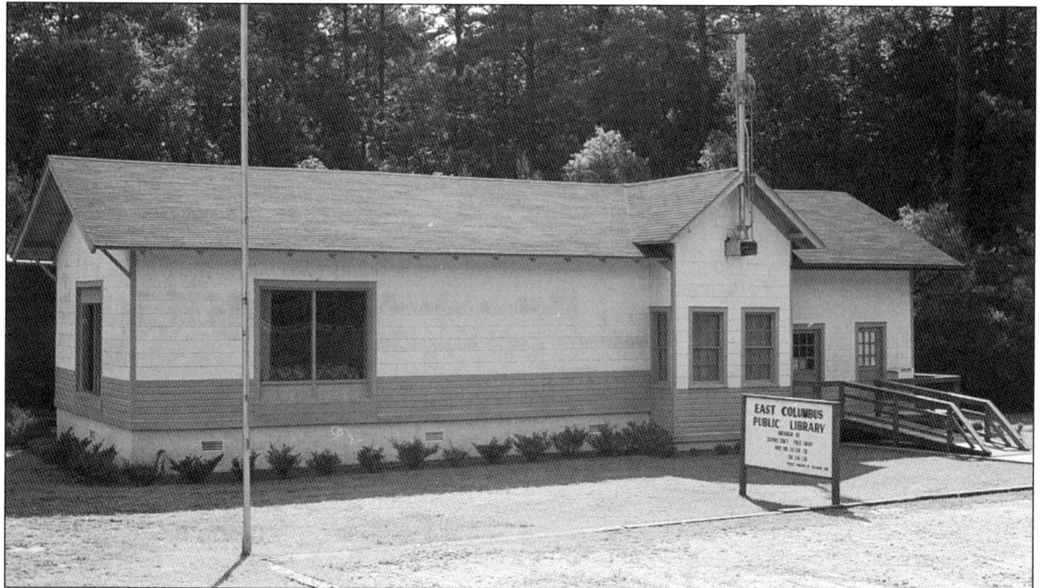

This depot was originally located in the unincorporated community of Delco but was moved in the 1980s for use as a library in Riegelwood for Columbus County. This depot was located on what was the Wilmington & Manchester Railroad, later known as the Wilmington, Columbia & Augusta, before 1900. The rail line continues through Fair Bluff before entering South Carolina. (Author's collection.)

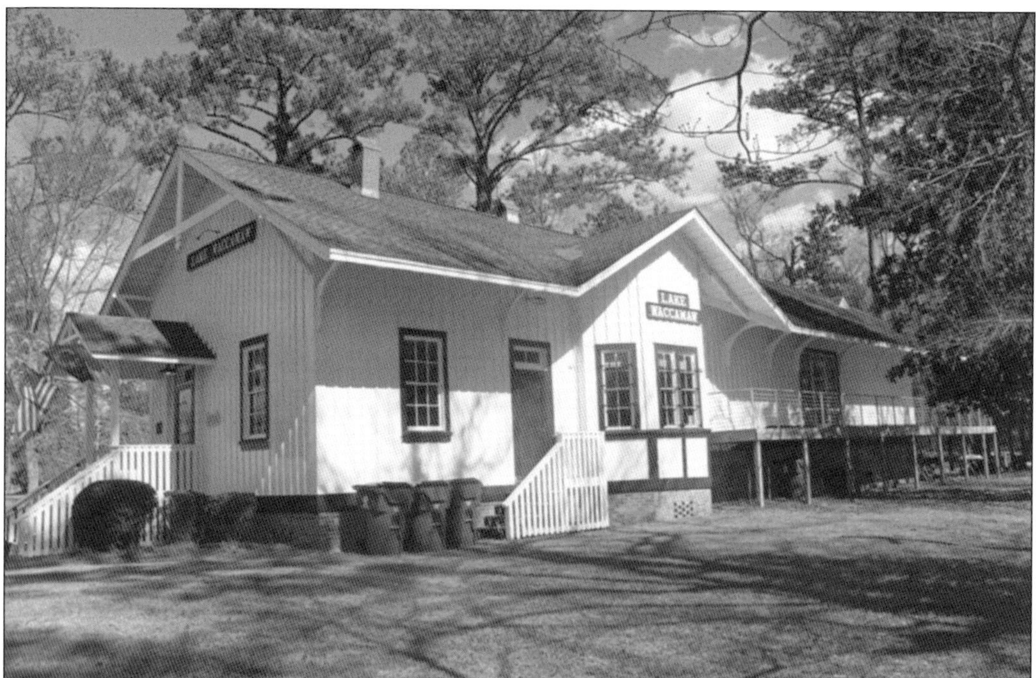

Lake Waccamaw is a freshwater lake located in Columbus County. This oval lake has an average depth of just seven-and-a-half feet and 14 miles of shoreline. Lake Waccamaw State Park administers the property today. The ACL built this station in 1904, and it houses a local museum today. (Author's collection.)

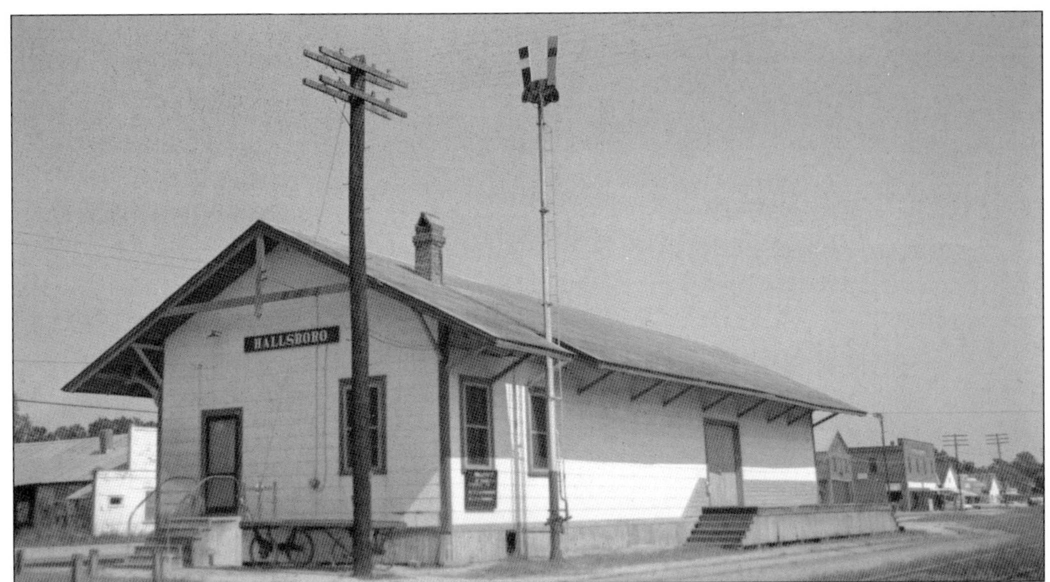

Hallsboro is an unincorporated community between Lake Waccamaw and Whiteville. Shown here in 1964, this depot closed in 1973 and was later moved to property on Lake Waccamaw and converted into a house. (Photograph by Tom King, courtesy of the King-Marsh collection.)

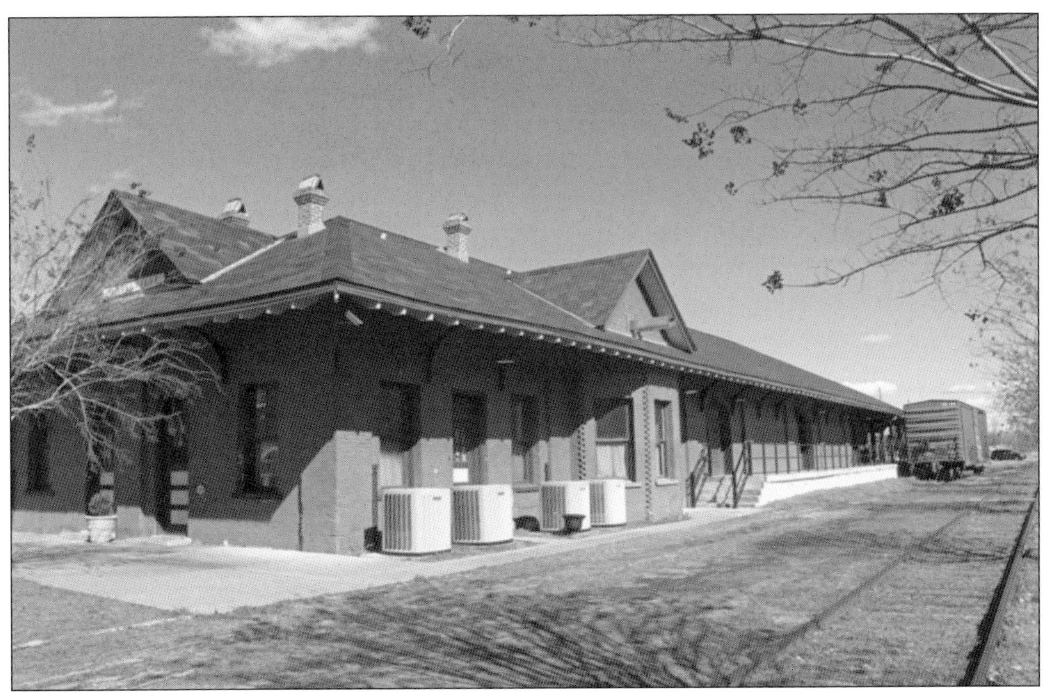

Whiteville was first named in 1810 for James B. White and originally known as White's Crossing. The railroad station, built in 1903, was also known as Vineland. The depot was recently restored and used as a community building. (Author's collection.)

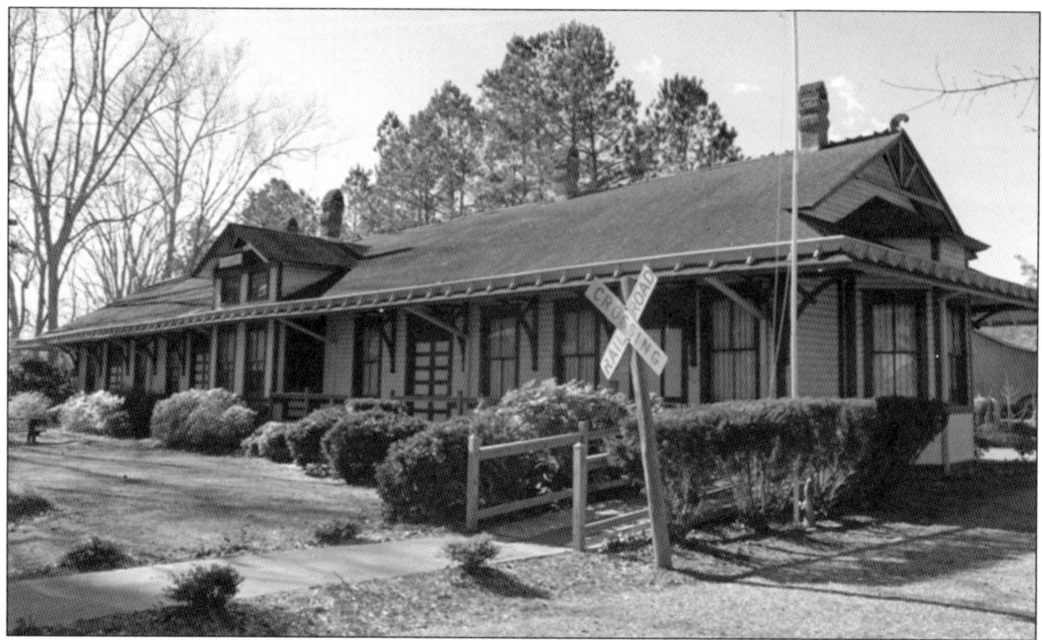

Chadbourn, named for two brothers who had a lumber business in the area, was incorporated in 1886. Chadbourn is nicknamed the "Sunny South Colony" and known for its strawberries. The North Carolina Strawberry Festival is the longest running agricultural festival in the state. This depot, the first for the town, was constructed in 1910 and serves as a local museum today. (Author's collection.)

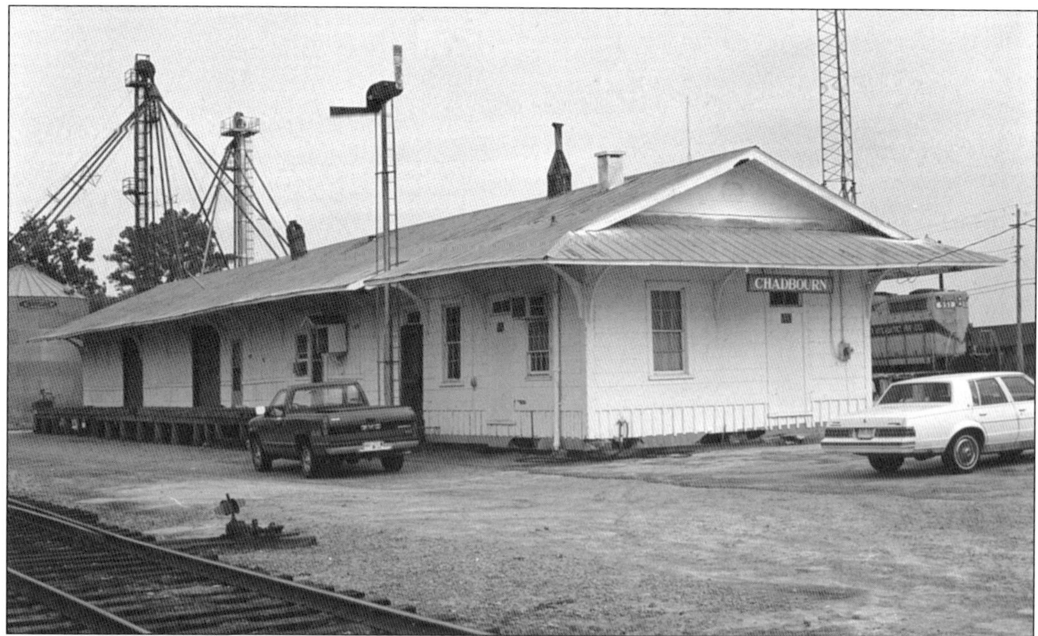

The freight station was later converted into the passenger station, as service was ended on all lines except the one to Florence. The original station was shuttered, and all railroad operations moved into this building. Today, it houses offices for R.J. Corman Railroad Group, current operator of the railroad. (Author's collection.)

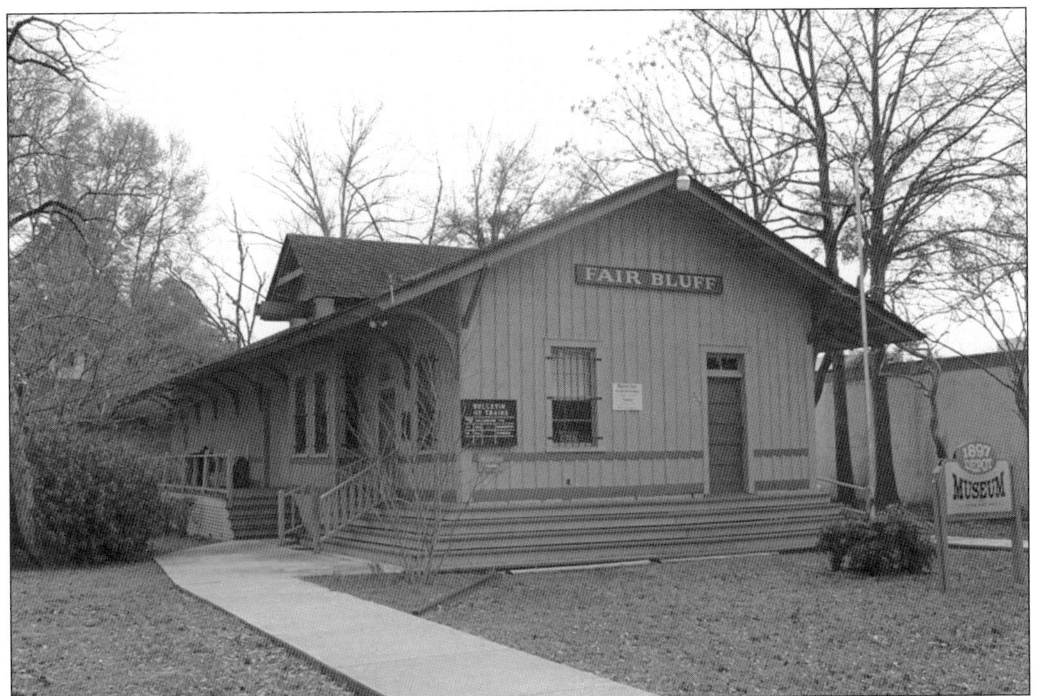

Fair Bluff was incorporated in 1873 and the last station stop in North Carolina on the line to Florence. The depot has been preserved and is now a local museum. (Author's collection.)

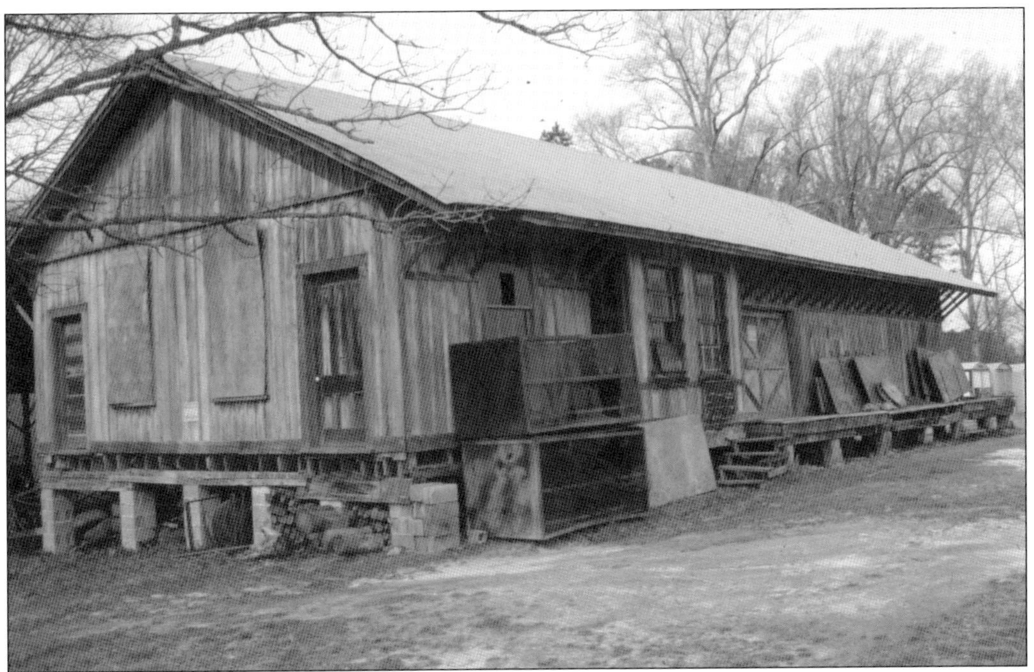

The town of Atkinson was incorporated in 1909, remaining a small farming community. This was located on the Cape Fear & Yadkin Valley (CF&YV) Railway line from Wilmington to Sanford and moved from the right-of-way when the tracks were abandoned. (Author's collection.)

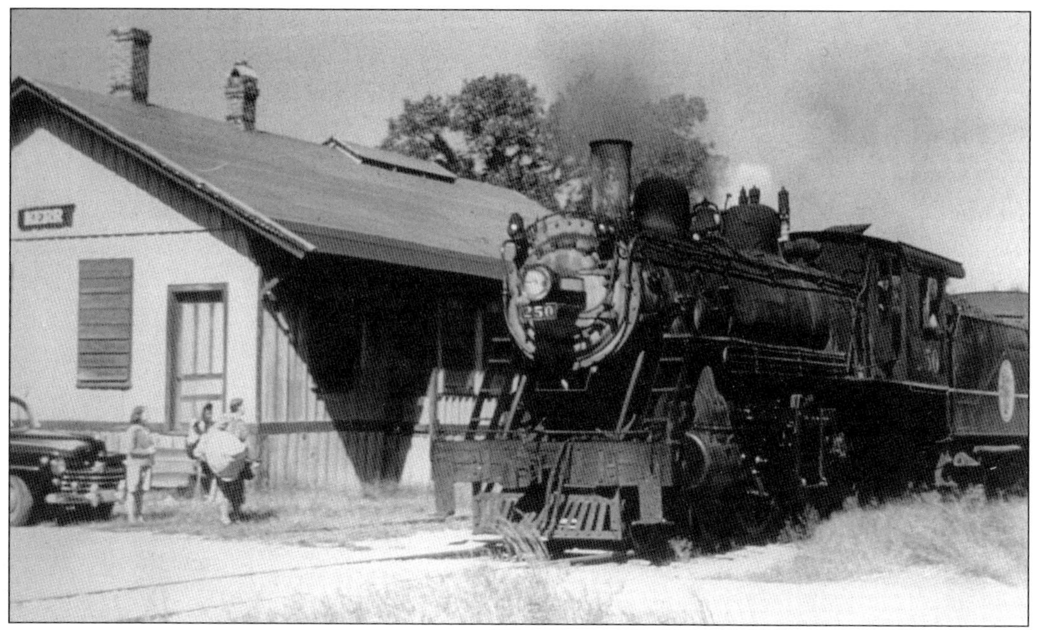

A great scene from the 1940s shows the passenger train, led by 4-6-0 250, making a station stop at Kerr. Note the station agent, or possibly the mail clerk, ready to load bags onto the train. Today, this depot is gone, but the 250 resides at the Wilmington Railroad Museum, having first been displayed in Tampa, Florida. (Author's collection.)

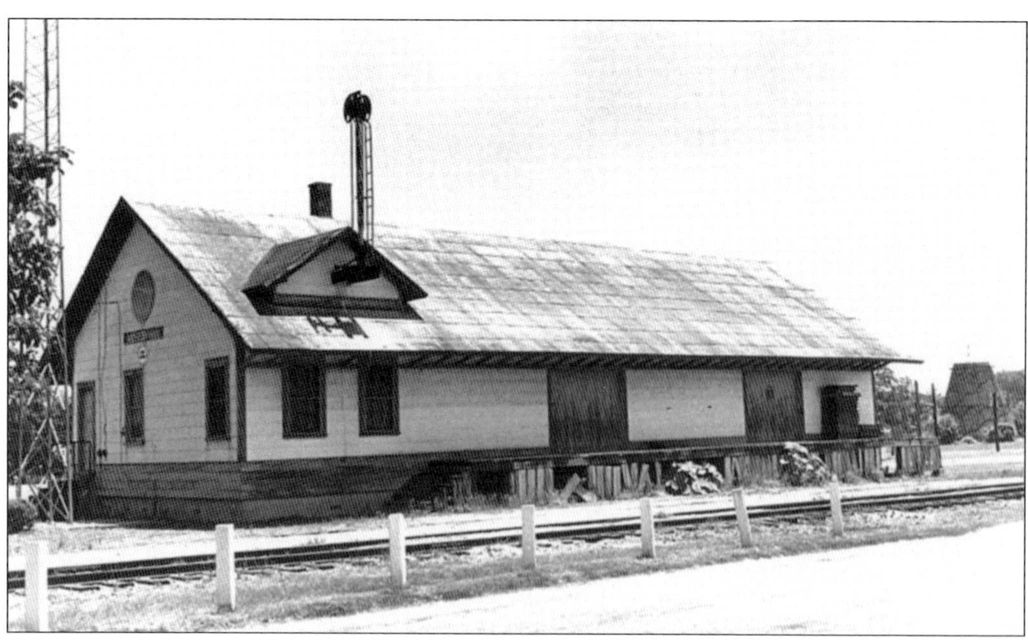

Roseboro was developed along the rail line and incorporated in 1891, named for John M. Rose, secretary of the CF&YV Railway. The building remains today and is used as a private business. (Courtesy of the Sampson County Historical Society.)

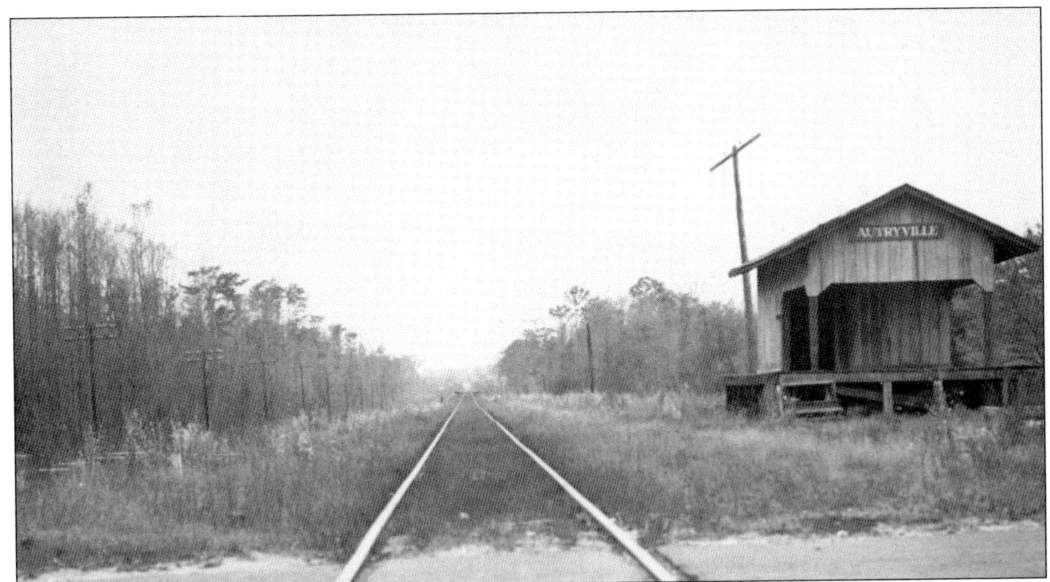

Autryville was started as Autrys in 1889, named for Julius A. Gray, president of the CF&YV Railway. The town was later incorporated as Autryville in 1891. This shelter type of depot was used for smaller communities. (Courtesy of the State Archives of North Carolina.)

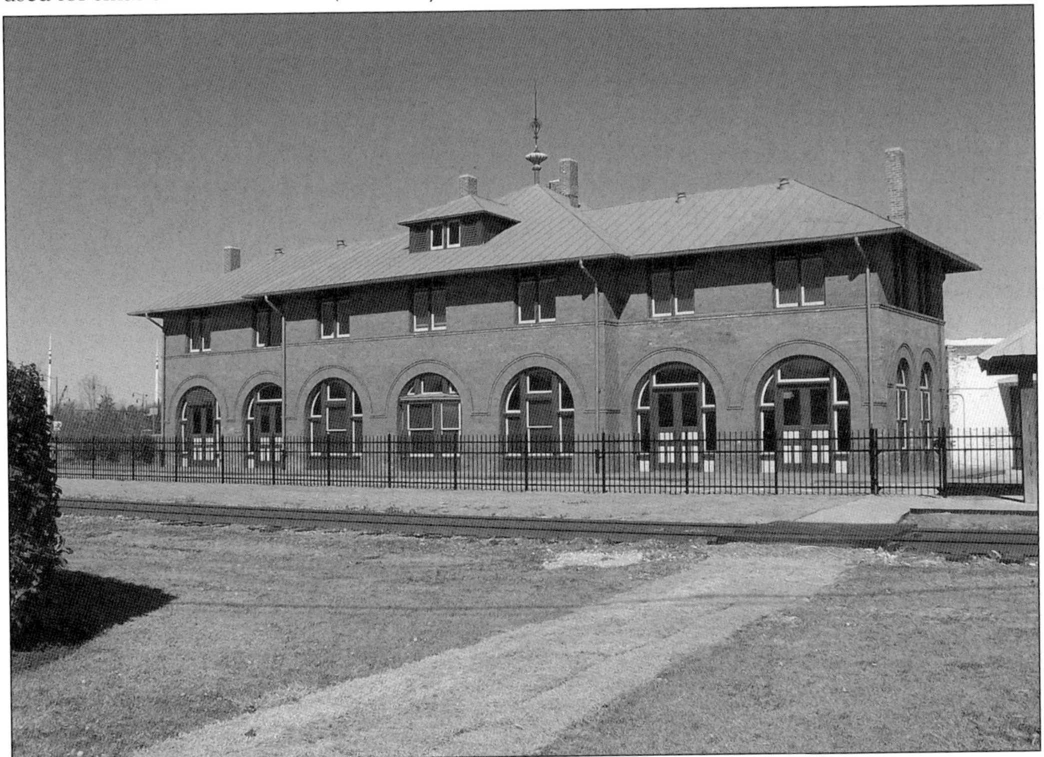

The CF&YV built this depot in Fayetteville in 1890, housing offices for the railroad. Once the ACL gained control in 1899, the passenger trains were moved to its depot on the main line. This depot today has been restored and houses the Fayetteville Area Transportation and Local History Museum. (Courtesy of the Robert Rosseau collection.)

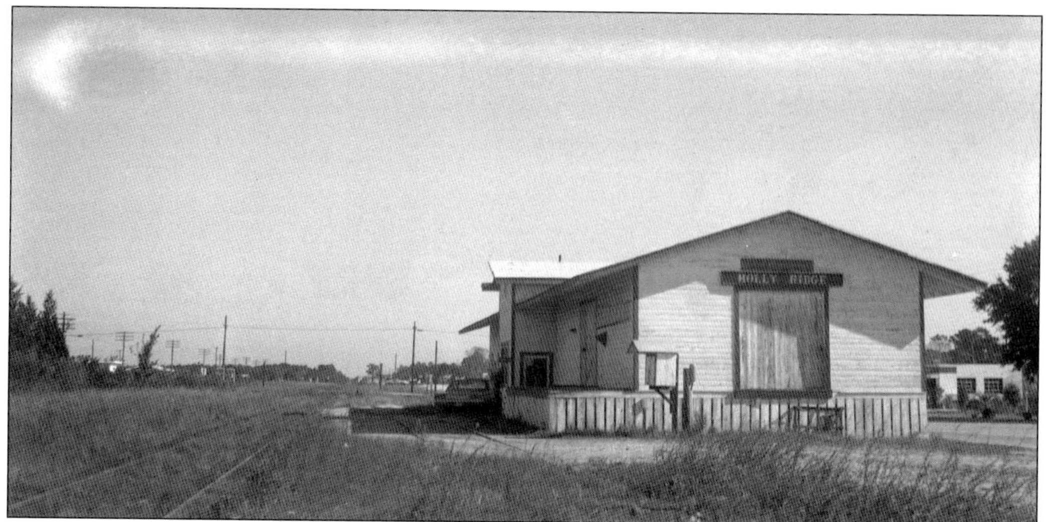

Holly Ridge is located on the Wilmington, Onslow & East Carolina Railroad line, later known as the Wilmington, New Bern & Norfolk when completed in 1891. Holly Ridge was the location of Camp Davis, an antiaircraft training base during World War II. This depot was moved to Surf City and is used as a private business. The rail line was abandoned in the early 1980s. (Courtesy of the Brian Ezzelle collection.)

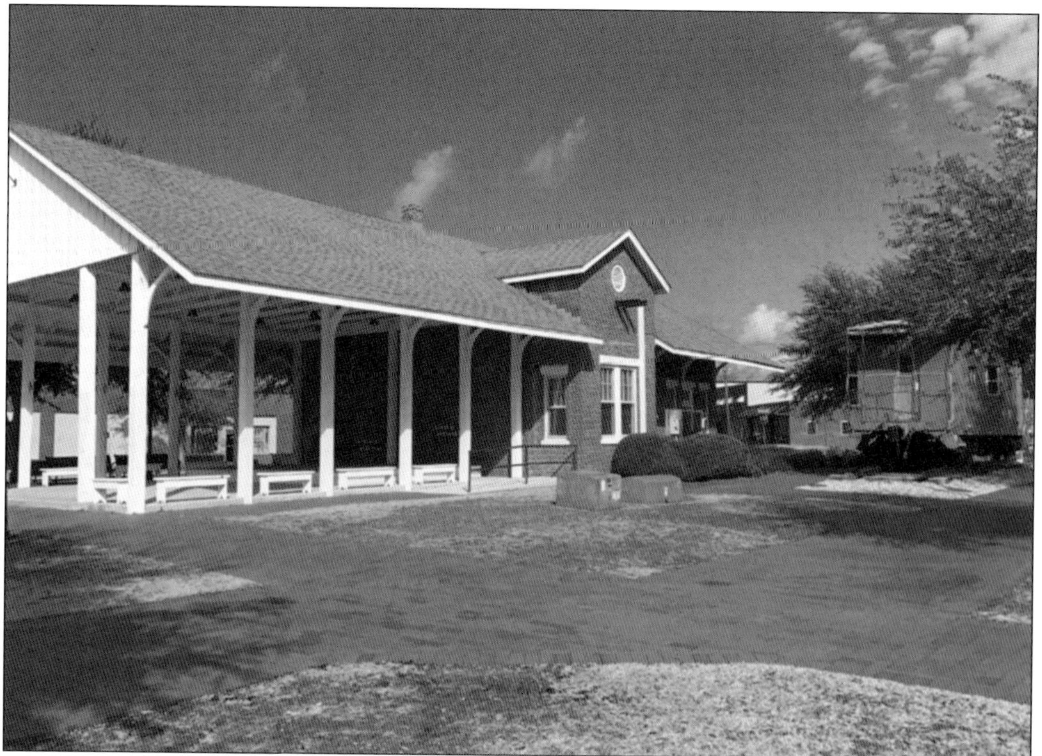

Jacksonville has history dating back to the 1700s but was officially incorporated in 1842 and named in honor of Pres. Andrew Jackson. During World War II, a Marine barracks was established there, later named Camp Lejeune Marine Corps Base after the 13th commandant of the Marine Corps, John A. Lejeune. (Photograph by Kelly Neal, author's collection.)

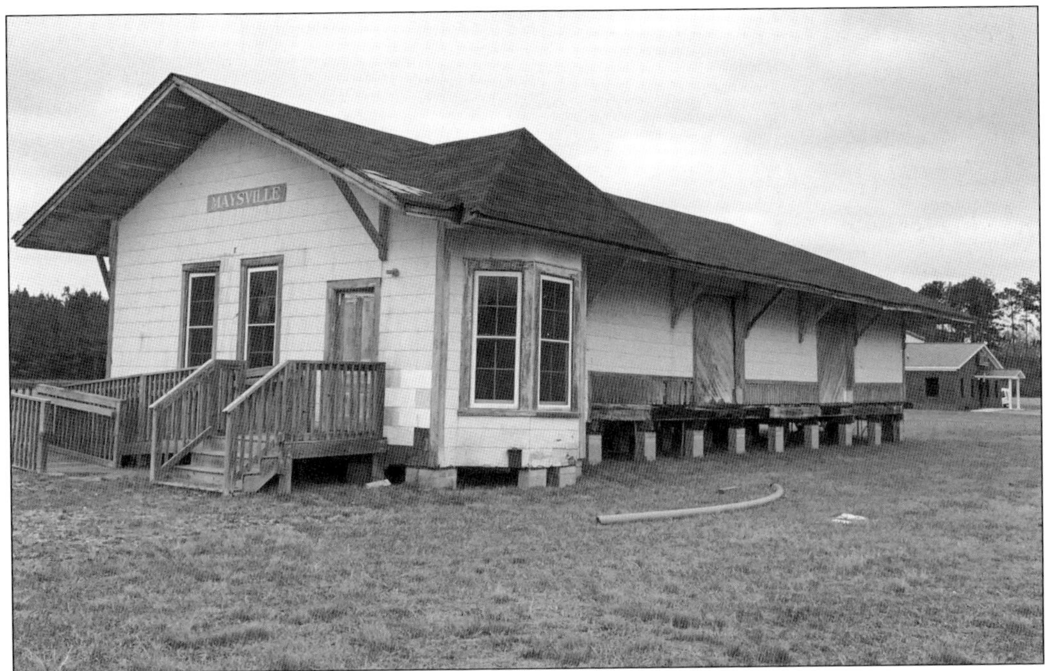

Originally known as Young's Crossroads, the name was changed to Maysville after John D. May, who was a local schoolteacher. The town was incorporated on March 9, 1897. The depot was recently moved to begin a restoration for the community. It had previously served a local business. (Photograph by Kelly Neal, author's collection.)

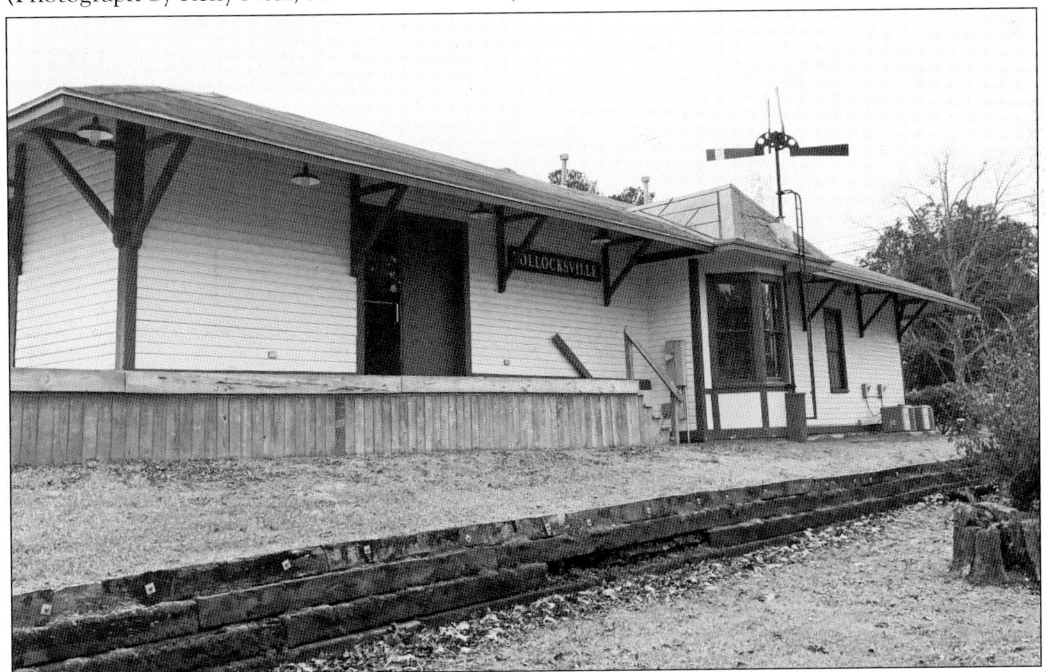

Pollocksville is the oldest town in Jones County and was first known as Trent's Bridge, but it was later named for George Pollock when it was chartered in 1834. The depot was restored and is used as a community building. (Photograph by Kelly Neal, author's collection.)

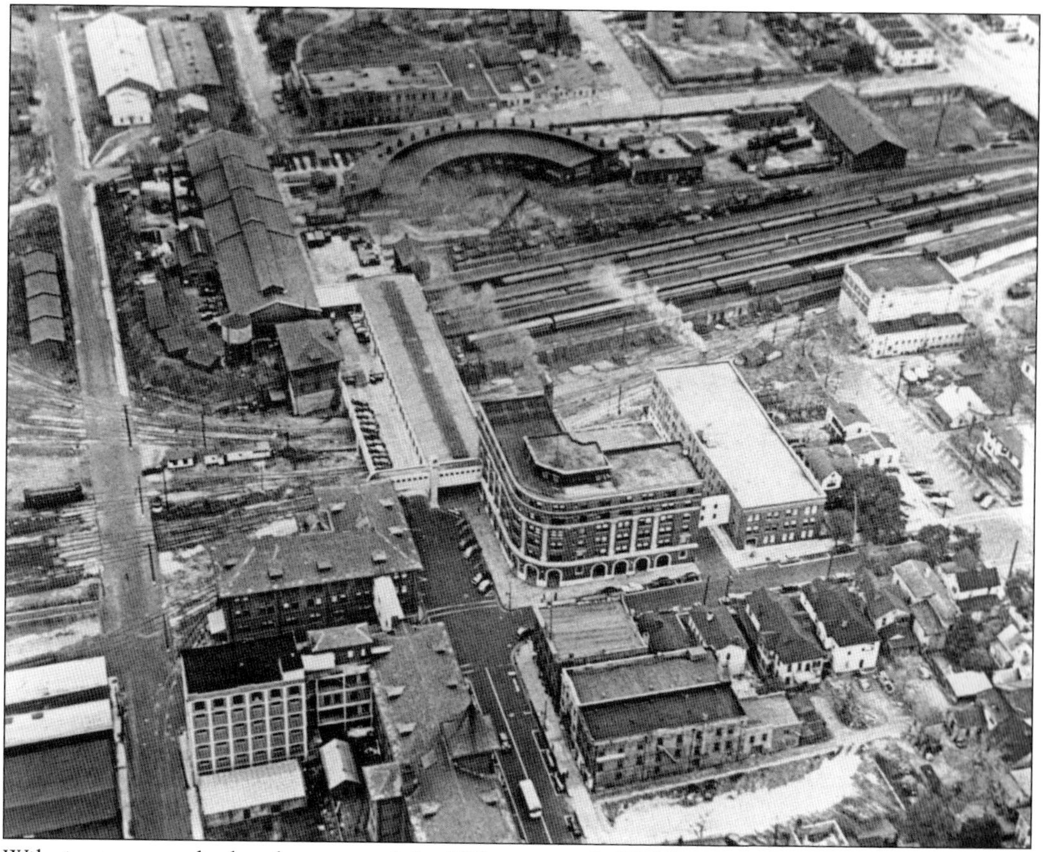

Wilmington was the headquarters of the Wilmington & Weldon and, later, the Atlantic Coast Line, the only headquarters of a major railroad located in North Carolina. The ACL built a large complex of buildings that were connected by walkways over the street. Building C, as it was known, is the curved building and houses the main railroad offices and passenger depot. Most of the buildings were torn down in 1970, since the railroad moved to Jacksonville, Florida, in 1960. (Courtesy of the New Hanover Public Library.)

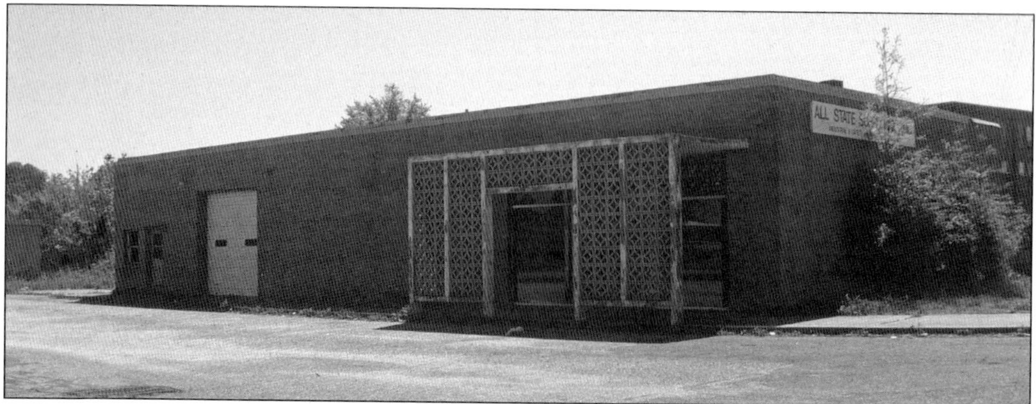

Following the move to Florida in 1960, the ACL built this new building to replace Building C as the depot. This remained in use until 1971 when Amtrak took over passenger service. Used for private business for many years, it was eventually torn down to create a parking lot for the local community college. (Author's collection.)

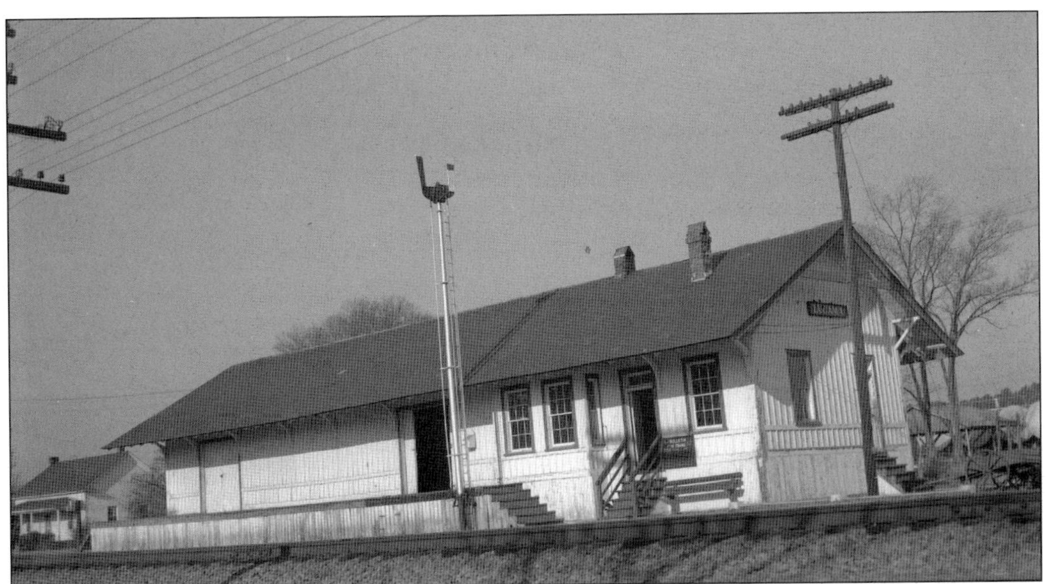

Lucama is an interesting town, since it was named for three Borden sisters: Lucy, Carrie, and Mary. This was the first town heading south on the Fayetteville cutoff, designed to bypass Wilmington for a straighter route between Rocky Mount and Florence. The depot is shown on November 19, 1965, freshly painted. (Photograph by Tom King, courtesy of the King-Marsh collection.)

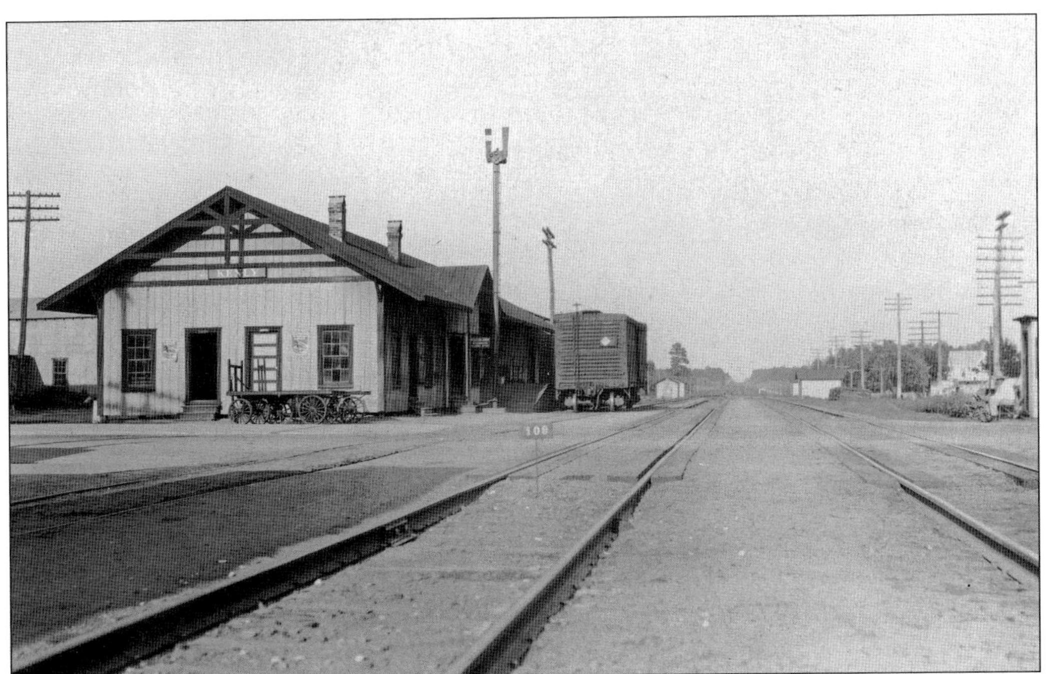

Kenly was named for John L. Kenly, superintendent of the Northern Division of the ACL and later named president of the railroad in 1913. Today, Kenly is home to the Tobacco Farm Life Museum, and this depot has been moved but preserved near the railroad tracks. (Author's collection.)

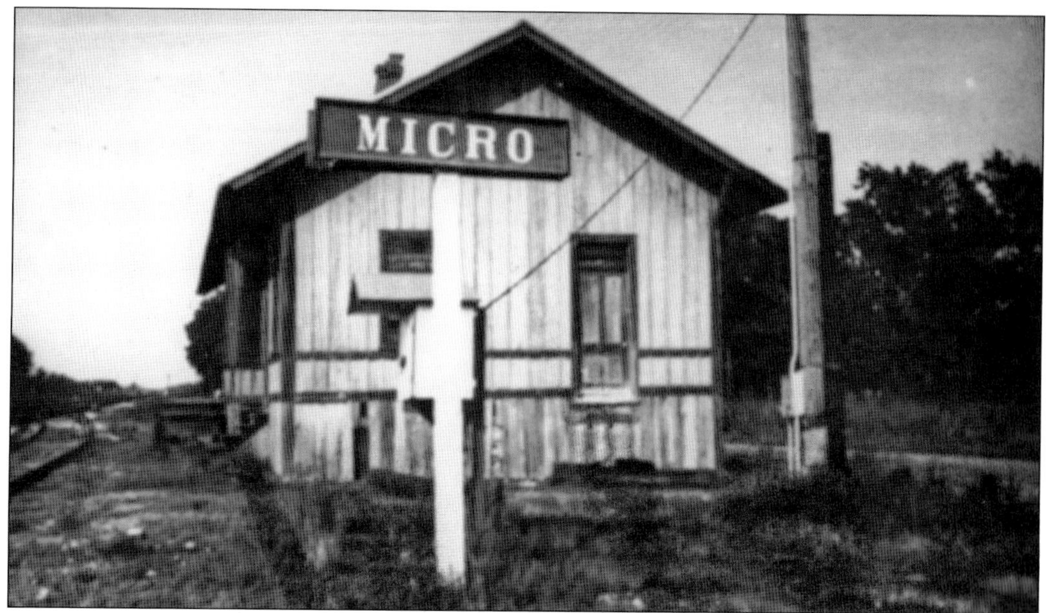

An interesting name for a location is Micro, which is located near Selma. The town is only 0.4 square miles. It was large enough, though, to have a smaller wooden depot built by the ACL. (Author's collection.)

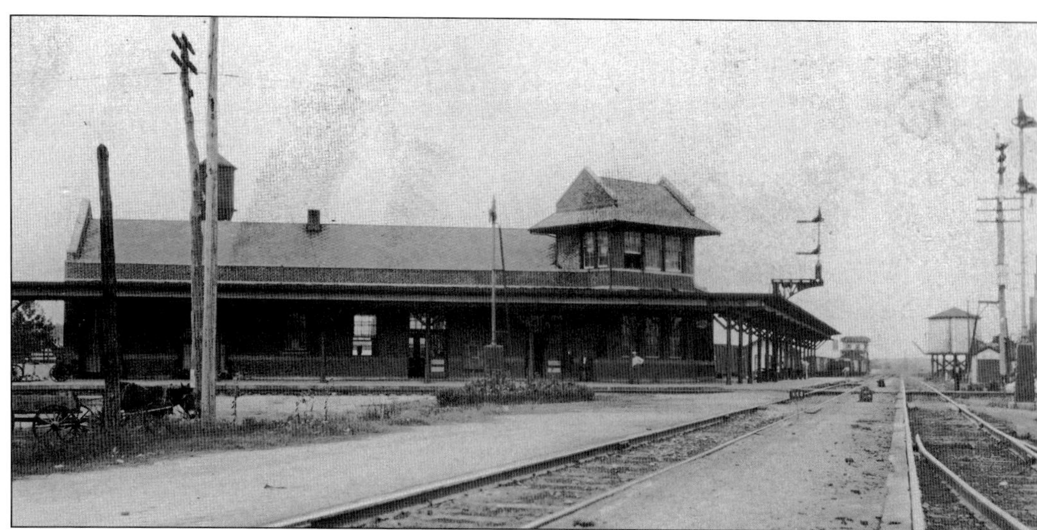

The town of Selma was first established due to the construction of the North Carolina Railroad in 1867, and later became a junction of the new ACL main line and the Southern Railway. A joint passenger station was built in 1924, which was later restored by North Carolina Department of Transportation. (Author's collection.)

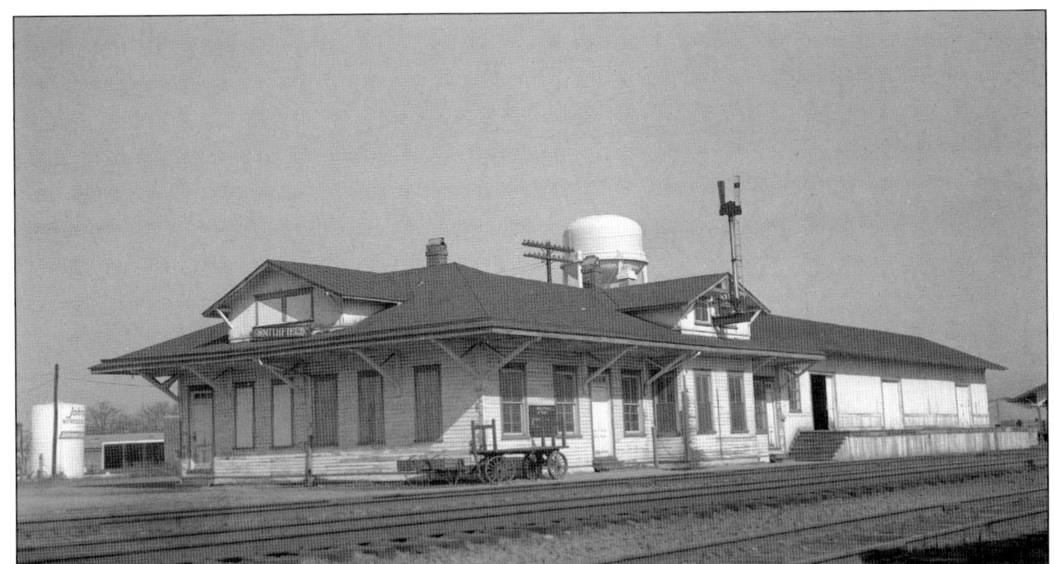

Smithfield, the county seat of Johnston County, was established in 1773. This community was also home to movie actress Ava Gardner. The town hosts the annual Smithfield Ham and Yam Festival. (Photograph by Tom King, courtesy of the King-Marsh collection.)

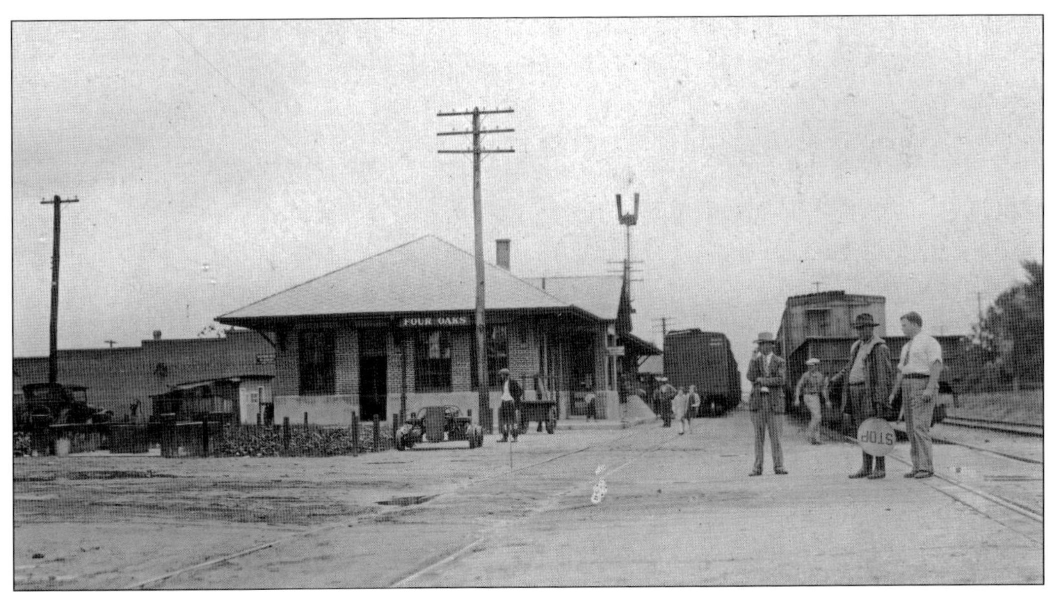

Four Oaks was named for an interesting phenomenon, an oak tree that had four trunks growing out of one base. The town was chartered in 1889, related to the construction of the railroad through the area. This 1920s-era view of the depot shows an important figure: the watchman who stopped traffic when trains came through. Unfortunately, this depot no longer stands today. (Author's collection.)

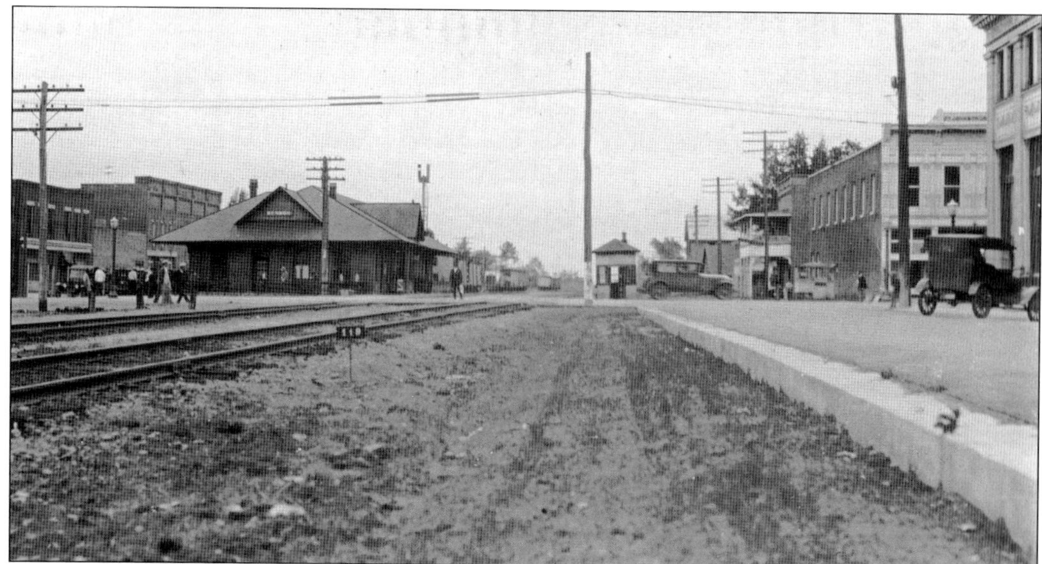

Benson was named for Alfred Monroe Benson and incorporated in 1887 as a direct result of the railroad coming through the area. An early resident, John William Hood would ride through town every day in a wagon pulled by his mule from his home near the community of Meadow. (Author's collection.)

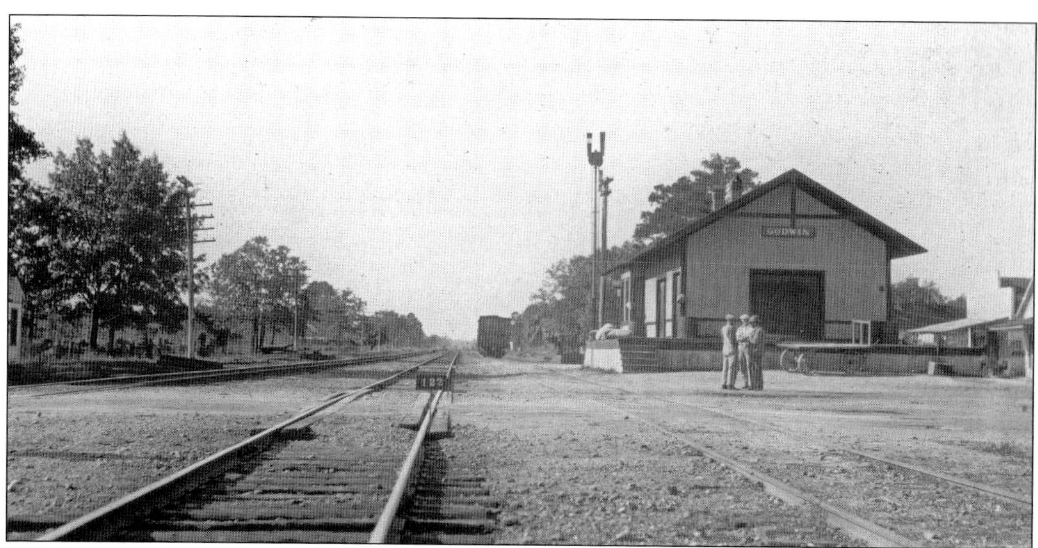

Godwin was named for William Godwin, who was an early settler to the area. The depot is shown not long after its construction. Sadly, it no longer exists. (Author's collection.)

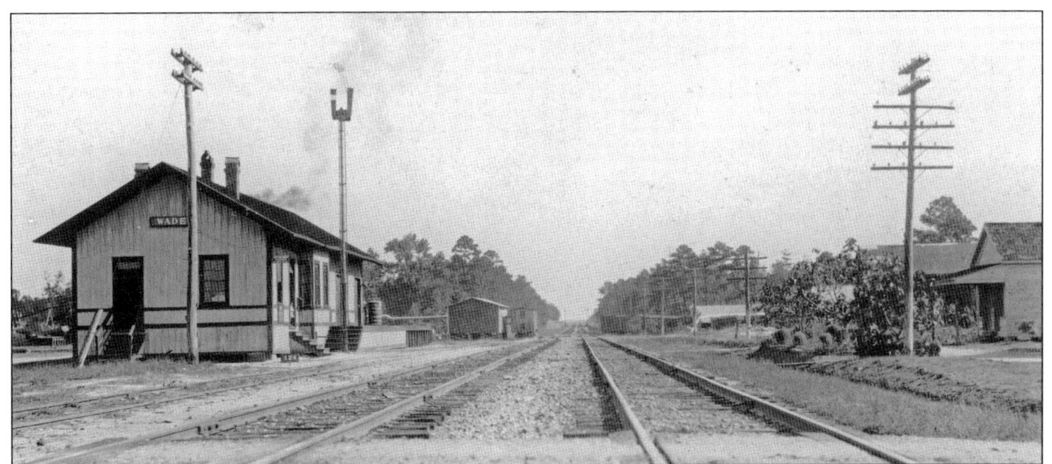

Wade was named for N.G. Wade, who sold crossties to the ACL during construction. The town was chartered on March 8, 1913. This depot was still standing in 1976 but may have been torn down. (Author's collection.)

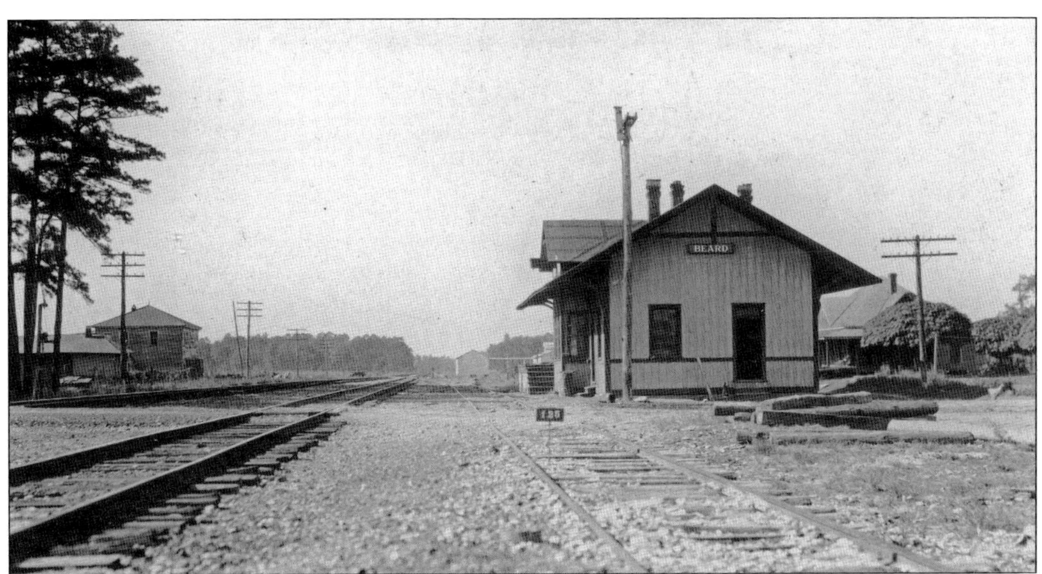

Beard was located between Wade and Fayetteville. The depot, pictured here, no longer stands. (Author's collection.)

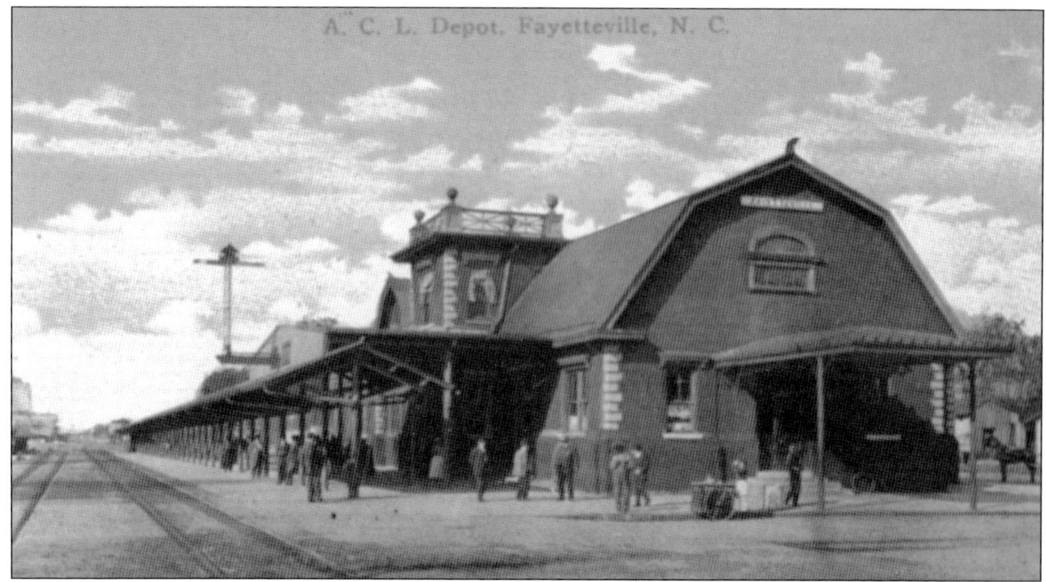

Fayetteville, originally named Campbellton, was incorporated in 1762. The name changed to Fayetteville in 1783 in honor of Lafayette. Fayetteville became a large rail center, due to construction of several railroads, including the Cape Fear & Yadkin Valley, Atlantic Coast Line, Norfolk & Southern Railway, and the Aberdeen & Rockfish Railroad. Early stations were built by the 1890s, but this is the only passenger station remaining, built for the ACL in 1911. It is still used by Amtrak today. (Author's collection.)

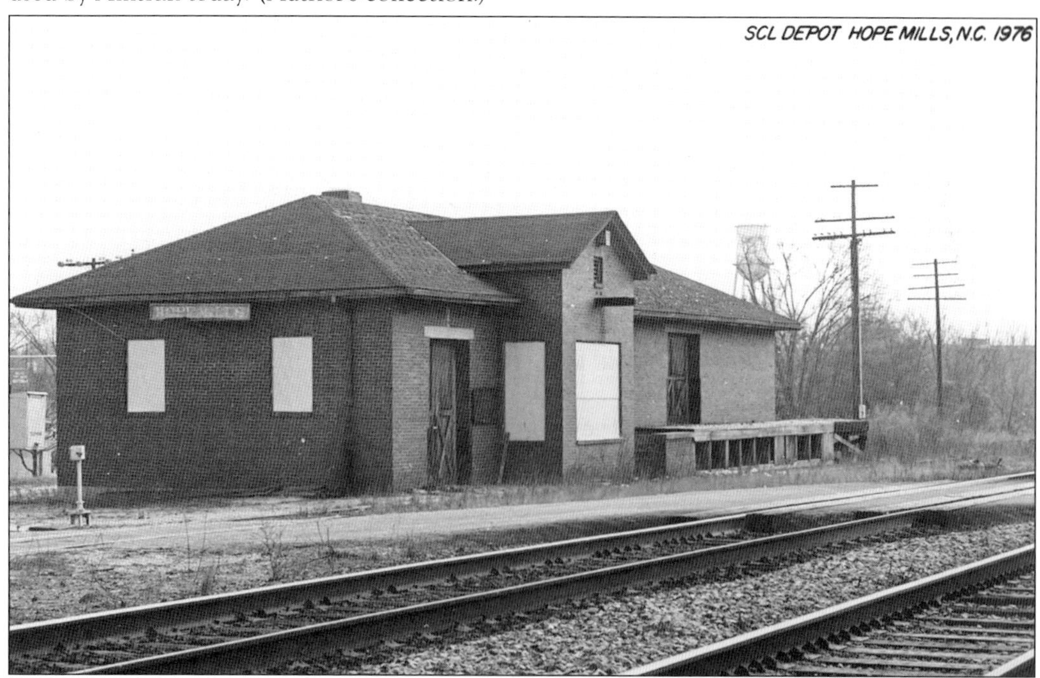

Hope Mills was incorporated in 1891, but its history dates back to the late 1700s. Cotton mills were built in the area by 1839, due to a dam being constructed on Little Rockfish Creek. The mill was later burned by Sherman on his march through North Carolina. The town name comes from Hope Mills No. 1. The depot dated back to the 1920s. (Courtesy of the Brian Ezzelle collection.)

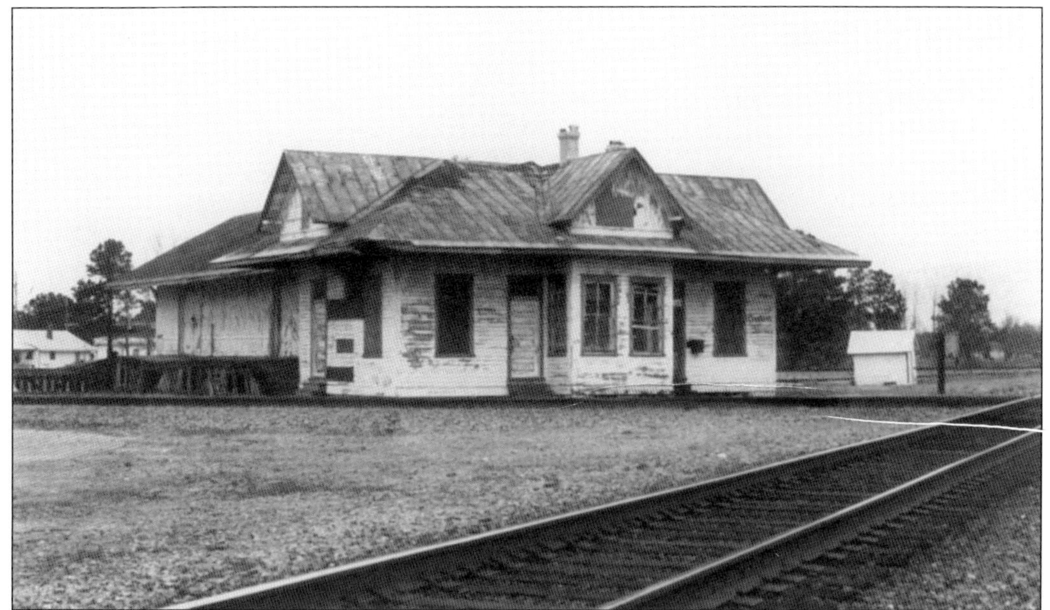

Pembroke was originally known as Campbell's Mills. This area even attracted the attention of royal governor Arthur Dobbs with reports of settlers moving to Drowning Creek, known today as the Lumbee River. The area was settled in 1789 and incorporated in 1895. Pembroke was the junction between the Atlantic Coast Line and Seaboard Air Line's route from Wilmington to Hamlet. The depot served both railroads and was located where the lines crossed. It was torn down in the late 1980s. (Courtesy of the Brian Ezzelle collection.)

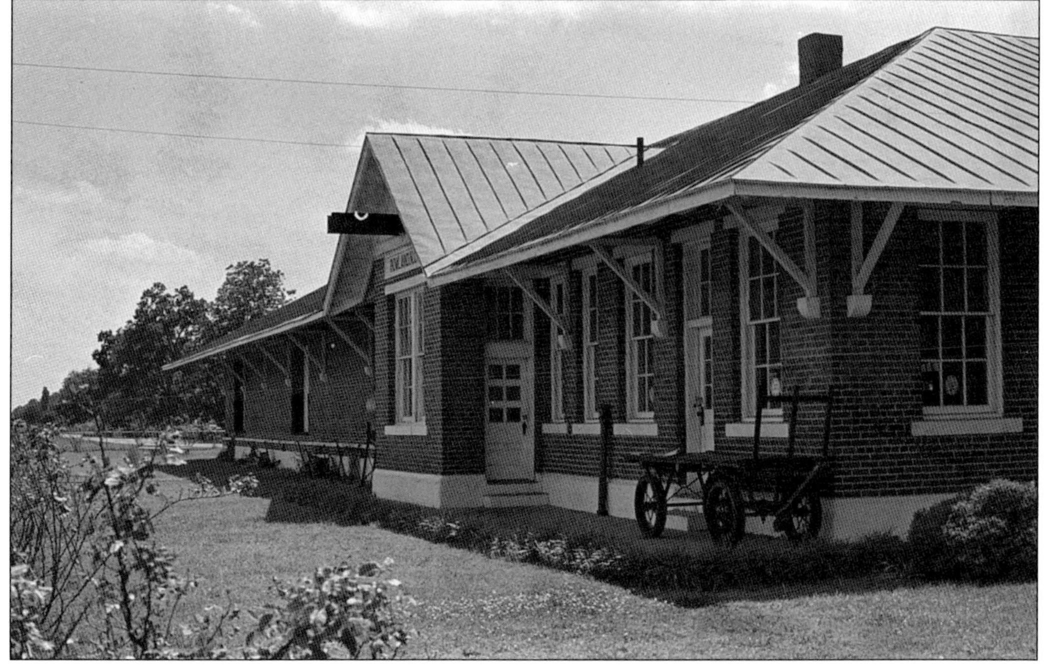

Rowland was incorporated in 1889, and the depot was built the following year as the last North Carolina stop on the main line. It was later rebuilt by the ACL in 1925. Today, the depot is a local museum. (Author's collection.)

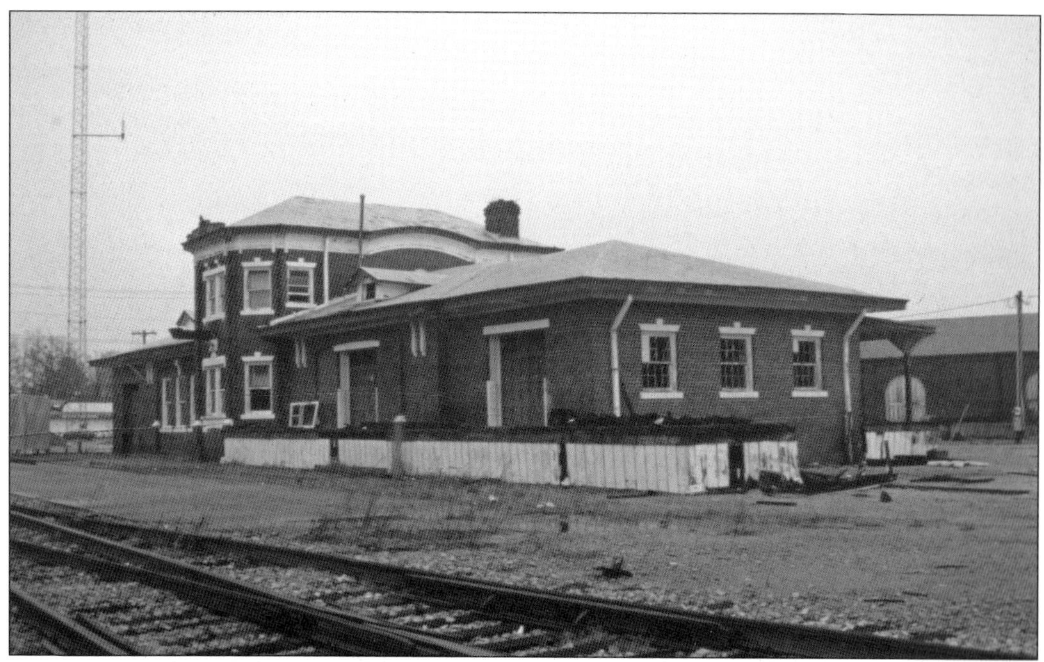

Tarboro dates to November 30, 1760, and is the ninth oldest town incorporated town in North Carolina. The Norfolk & Carolina Railroad, running from Tarboro to Norfolk, was completed on April 1, 1890. The Southern Railway had trackage rights over this line until 1974. The ornate depot, built between 1908 and 1913, was torn down in the 1990s. (Author's collection.)

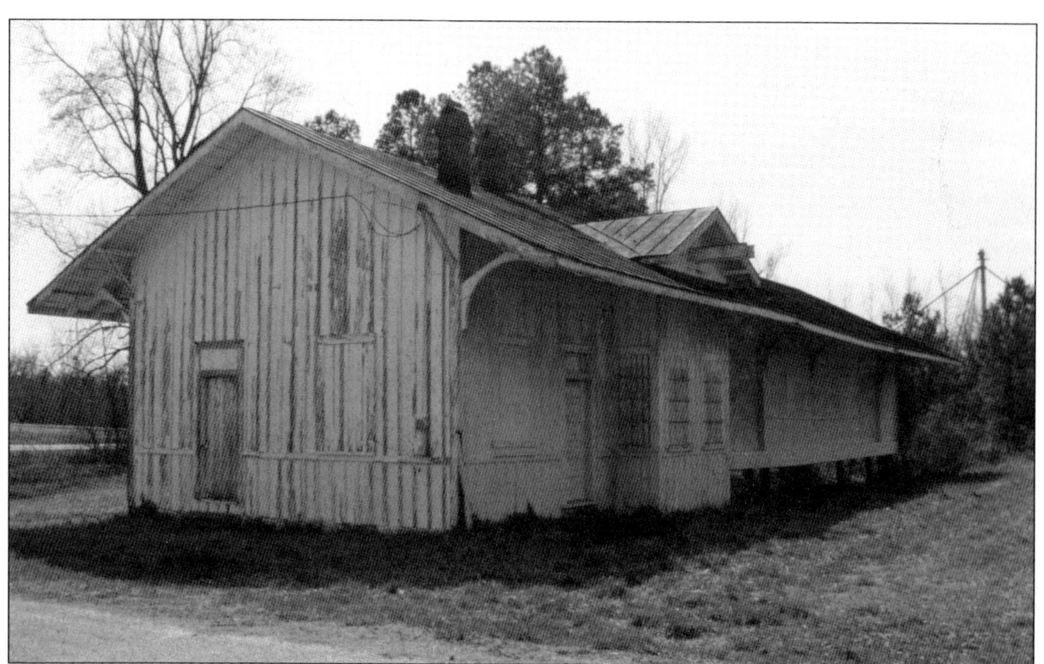

Speed was named after the town doctor, Eugene Travis Speed Sr., and founded by Andrew Jackson Parker Sr. The depot, which still stands beside the abandoned right-of-way, was built in the early 1920s in typical ACL style. (Author's collection.)

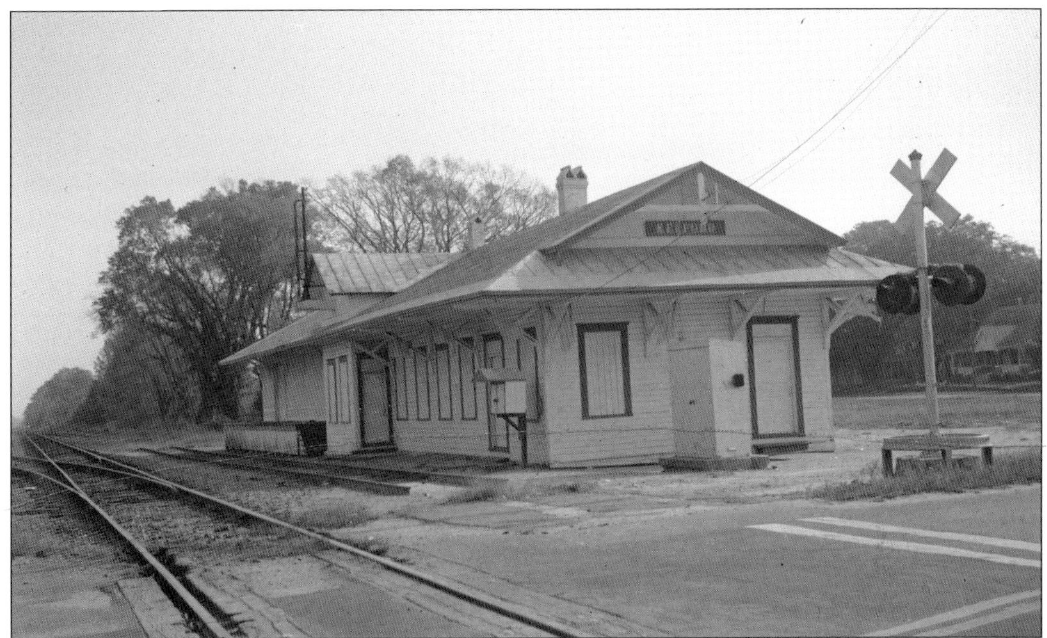

Kelford is interesting in that it was named for a fjord in Scotland by S.A. Norfleet in 1890. The depot, dating from the early 1900s, had been preserved but is now unfortunately torn down. Both the Atlantic Coast Line and Seaboard Air Line served this town. (Photograph by Tom King, courtesy of the King-Marsh collection.)

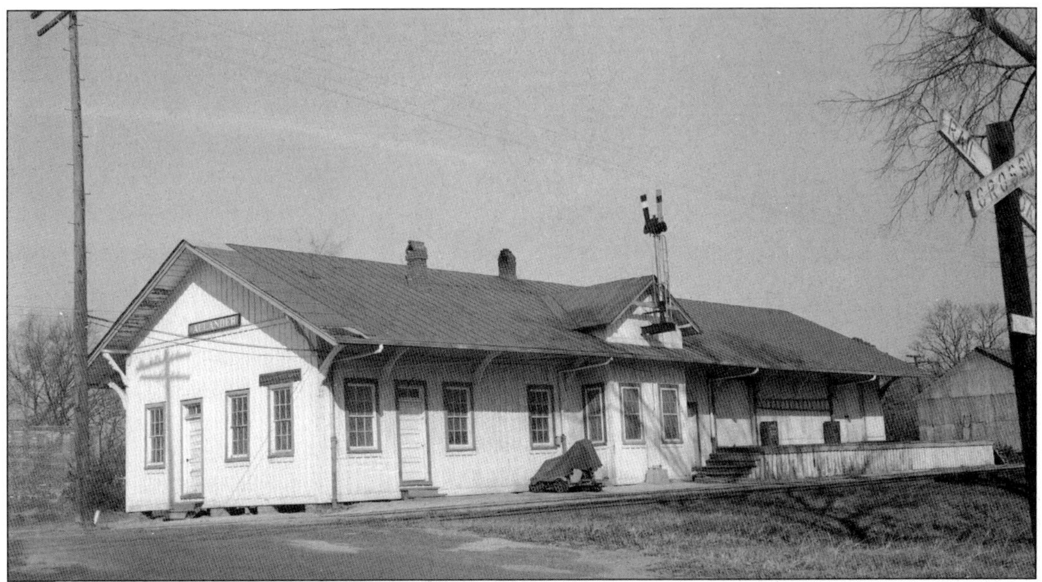

Aulander was incorporated in 1873 and was originally known as Harmon's Crossroads. One of the prominent residents wanted to change the name to Orlando but was turned down. The spelling of Aulander is pronounced like "Orlando," even today. This view shows the depot on November 29, 1965, in good condition. Unfortunately, today the depot is derelict, almost ready to fall. (Photograph by Tom King, courtesy of the King-Marsh collection.)

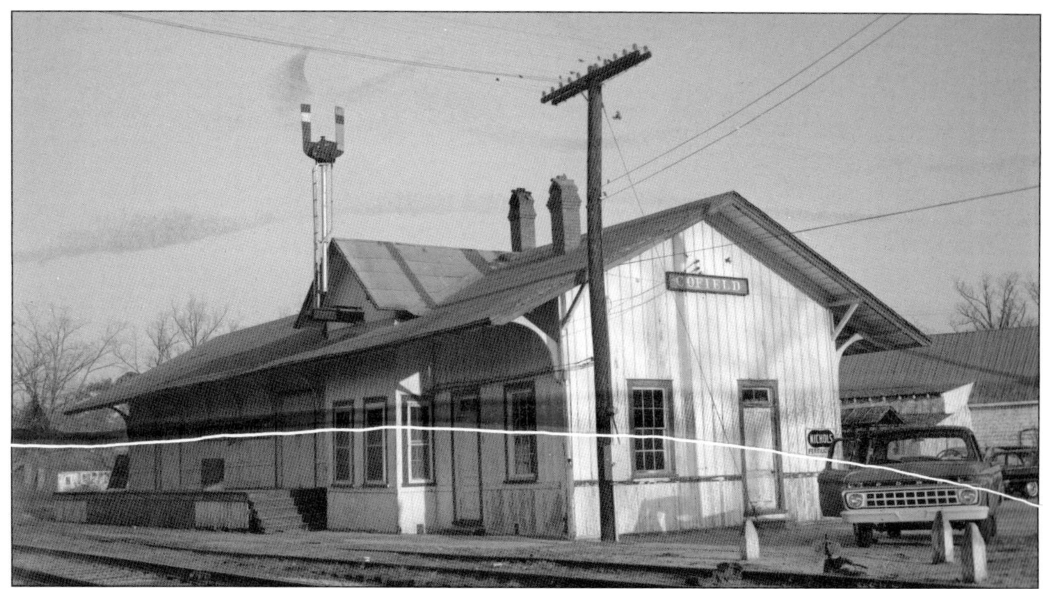

The Cofield depot is shown on December 8, 1965, ten years after regular passenger service ended on this line. (Photograph by Tom King, courtesy of the King-Marsh collection.)

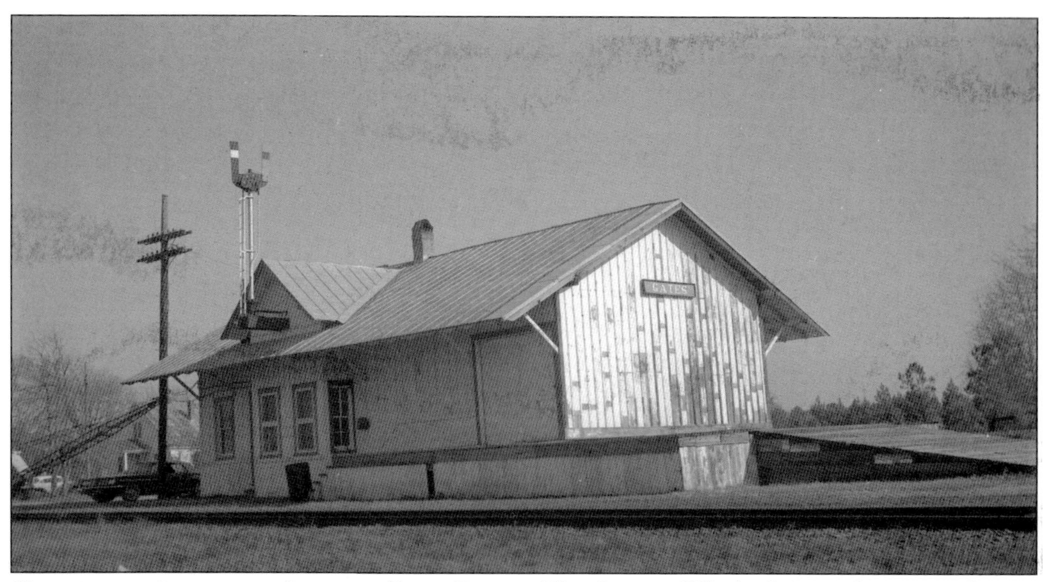

Gates is an unincorporated town in Gates County. The depot still looked pretty sharp on February 2, 1967. (Photograph by Tom King, courtesy of the King-Marsh collection.)

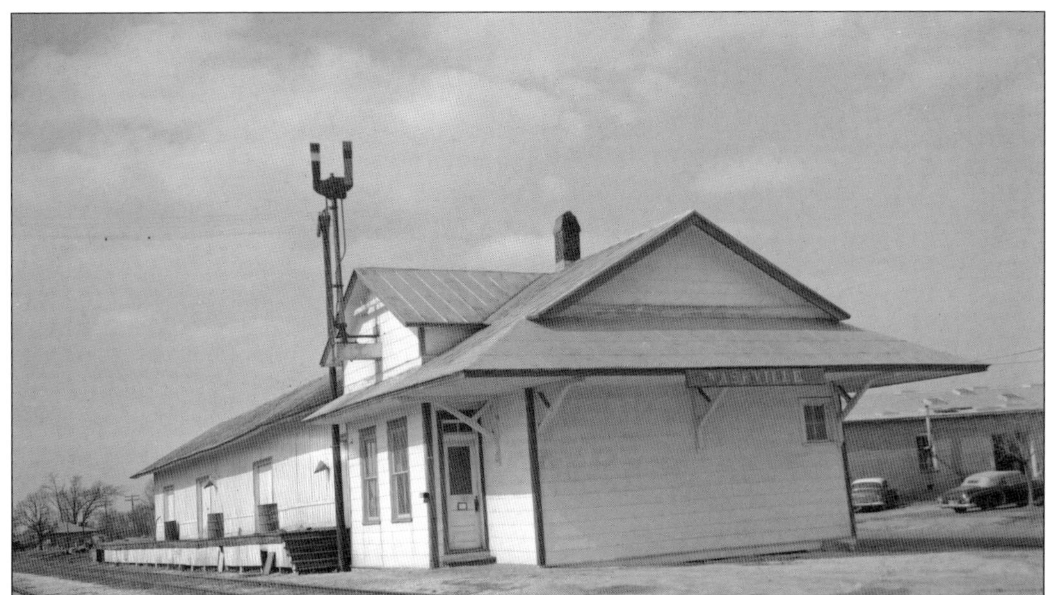

Nashville was founded in 1780 and named for Francis Nash, along with Nash County. The branch from Rocky Mount to Spring Hope and later Lassiter was opened in 1887. The depot was still looking good in 1964, even though passenger service ended before 1941. This station was later moved to Rocky Mount. (Photograph by Tom King, courtesy of the King-Marsh collection.)

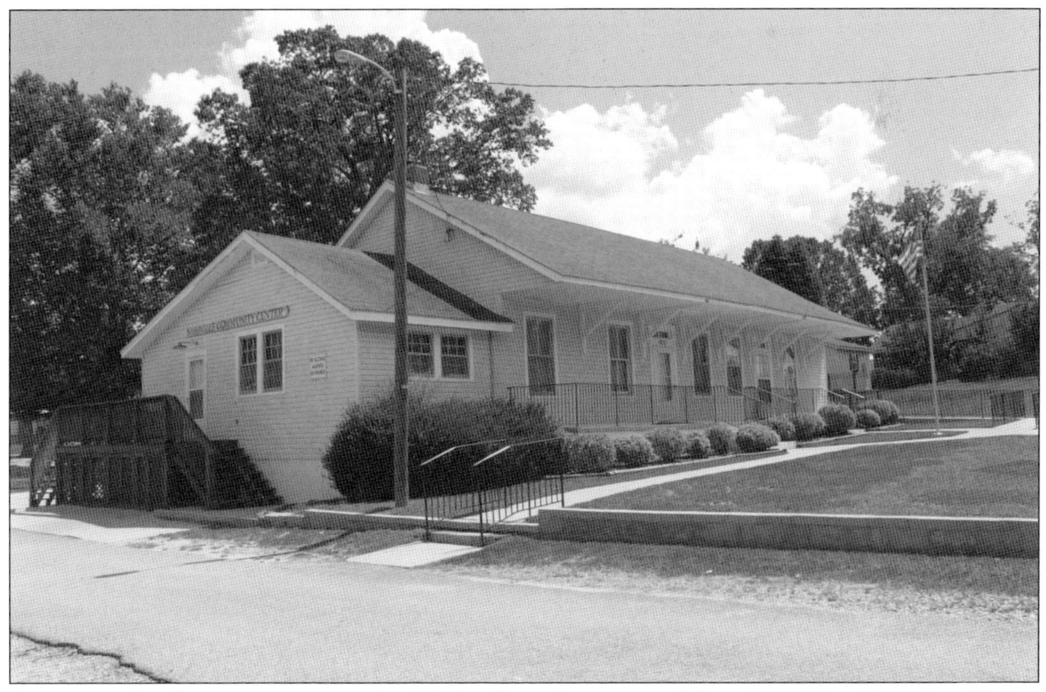

A separate freight station remained in Nashville and was moved from its original location. Today, it serves as the town community center. (Author's collection.)

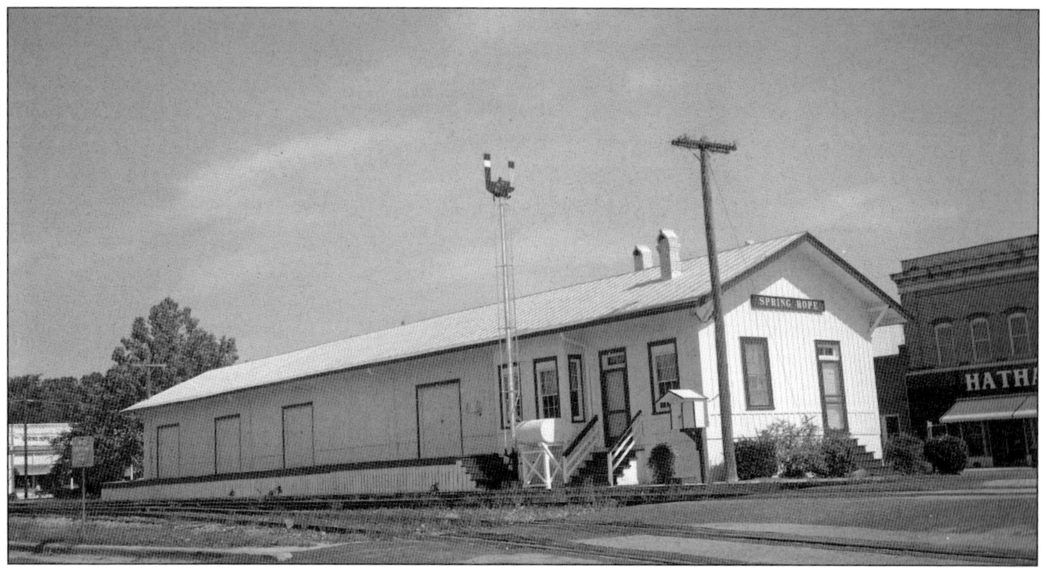

Spring Hope was incorporated in 1889, just a few years after the rail line was completed. The town was named due to the local springs in the area, used by farmers and travelers alike. The depot looks just as good today as it did in July 1967. (Photograph by Tom King, courtesy of the King-Marsh collection.)

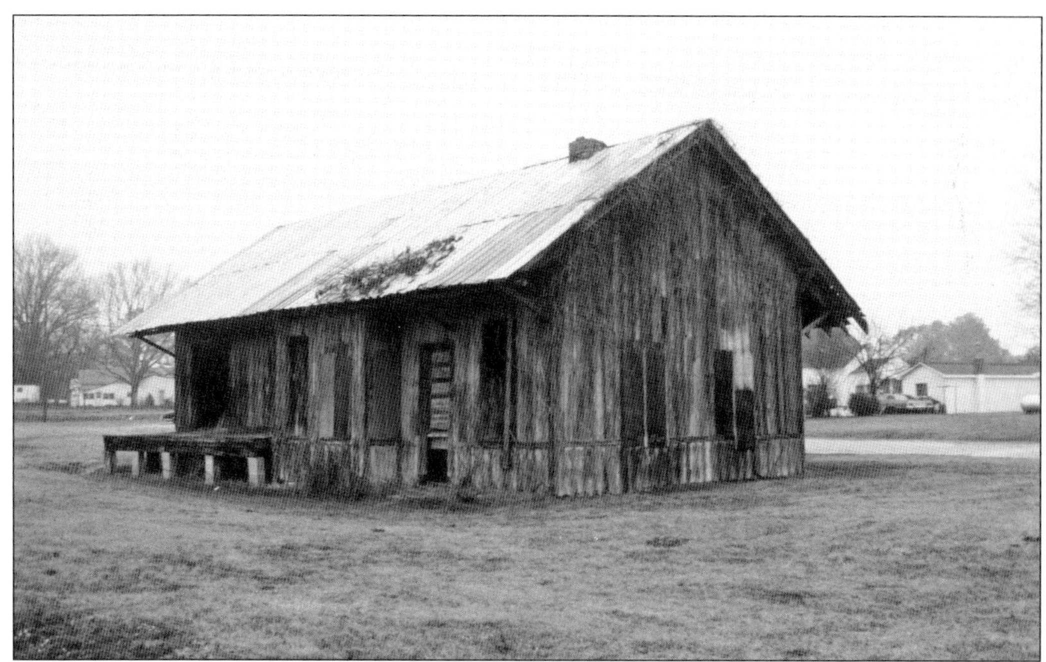

Bunn was named for Green Walker Bunn and was incorporated in 1913. Lumber was a huge industry when the town was formed, which allowed the rail line to be extended east from Spring Hope. The depot was built by the 1910s, and by 1992 it was showing its age but still standing strong. (Author's collection.)

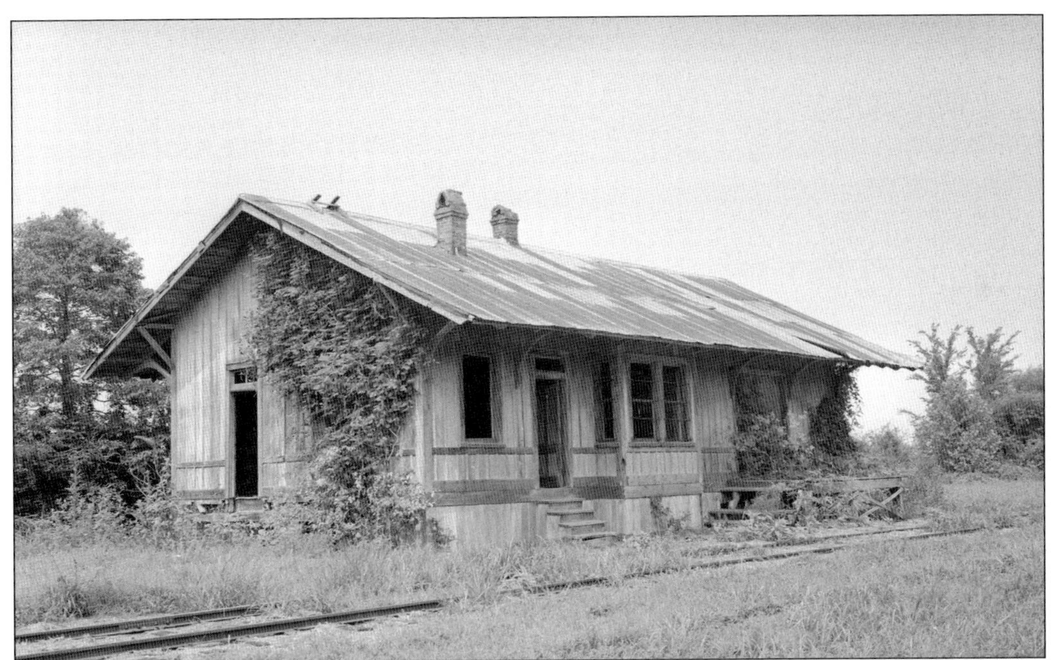

Spring Hill was located on the branch line from Pender to Parmele, and represented one of the routes of the Parmele Circle that reached many small farming communities like spokes on a wagon wheel. The depot sat abandoned in August 1973. (Photograph by Tom King, courtesy of the King-Marsh collection.)

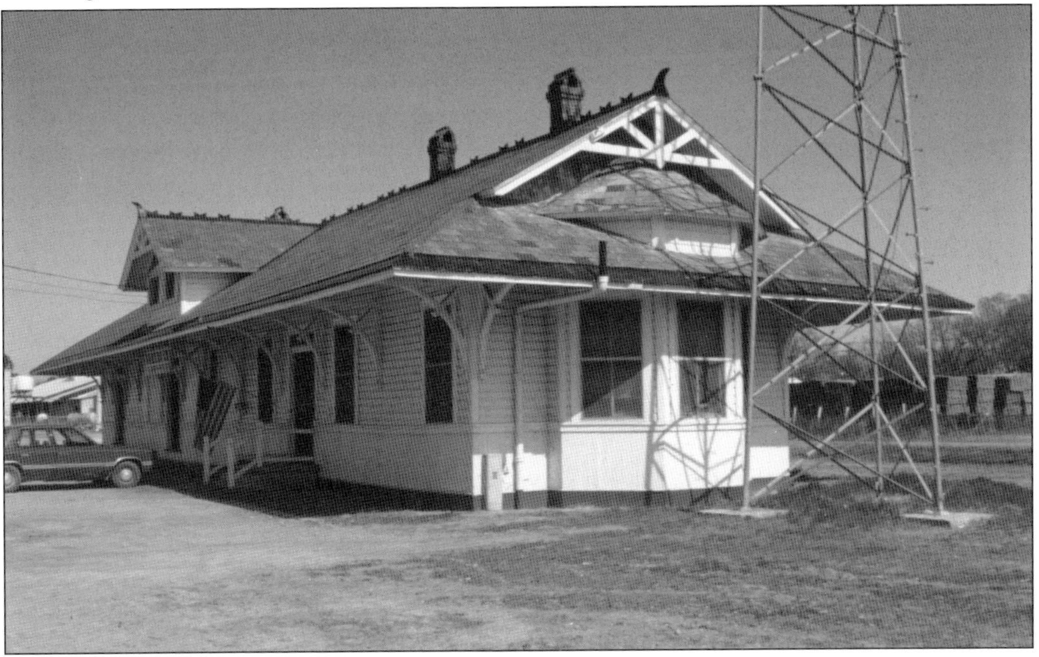

Scotland Neck is named for the Scottish Highlanders that settled in the neck of the Roanoke River in the 1720s. The town was not incorporated until 1867 and received railroad service in 1882. This ornate depot, with the fancy roof trim, dates to 1890 and is similar to the first Chadbourn depot. It still continues to serve Scotland Neck under private ownership. (Author's collection.)

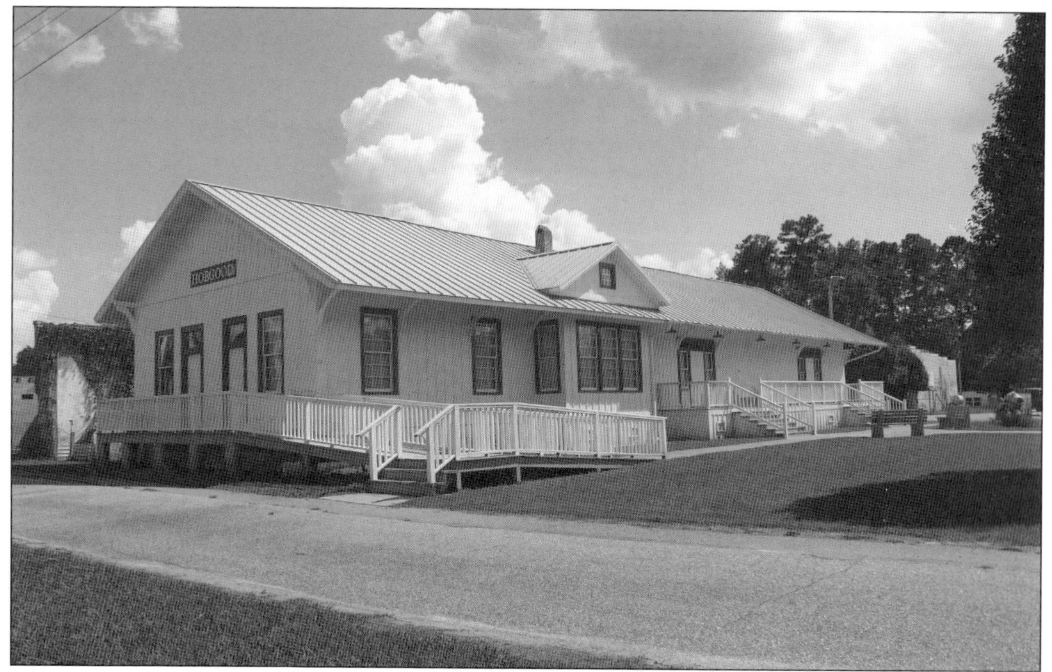

Hobgood was incorporated in 1891; just a short time after the railroad came through town. It was named for a saloon/store in the area. The town recently restored their depot as a community building, repainting the white and purple trim it wore long ago. (Author's collection.)

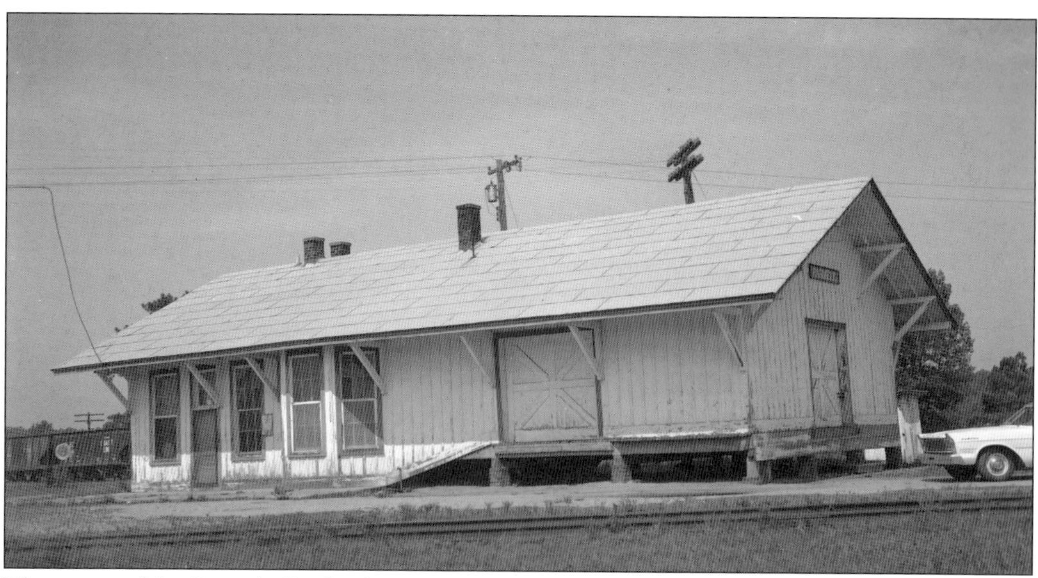
The center of the Parmele Circle, this community had rail lines leading in five directions, showing the prominence of this once thriving lumber area. The town was officially chartered on February 14, 1893. The depot was still looking good in 1966, just a year away from the Seaboard Coast Line merger. (Photograph by Tom King, courtesy of the King-Marsh collection.)

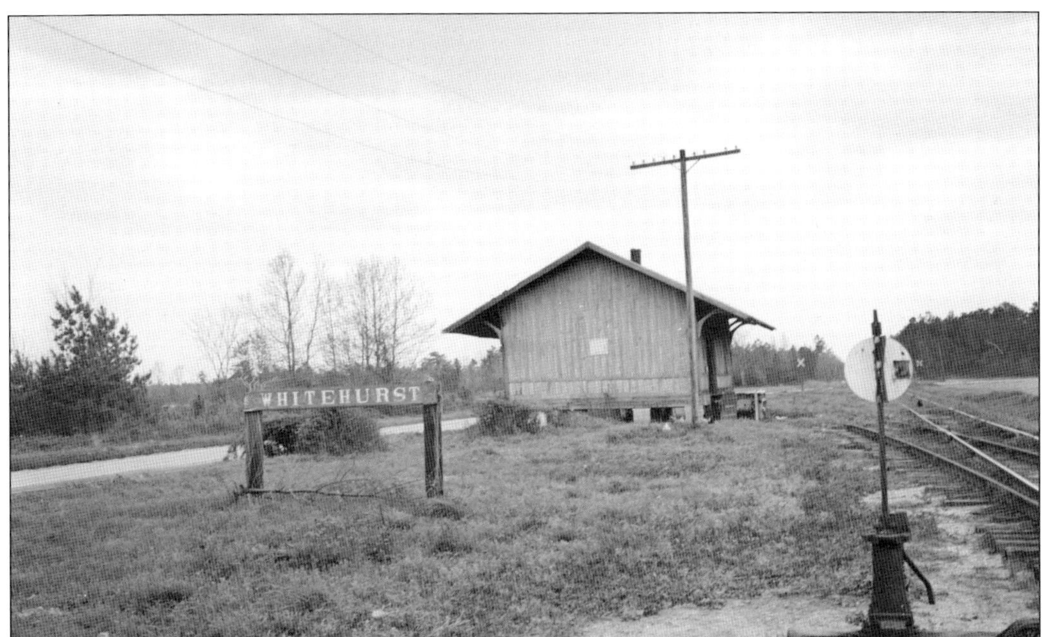

Whitehurst received rail service by 1890, when the ACL extended the line from Parmele to Kinston. The station was small, and when it was closed, the sign board was removed and placed alongside the tracks, which was standard practice on the ACL. The station is shown in 1973, perhaps used by a local farmer for storage. (Photograph by Tom King, courtesy of the King-Marsh collection.)

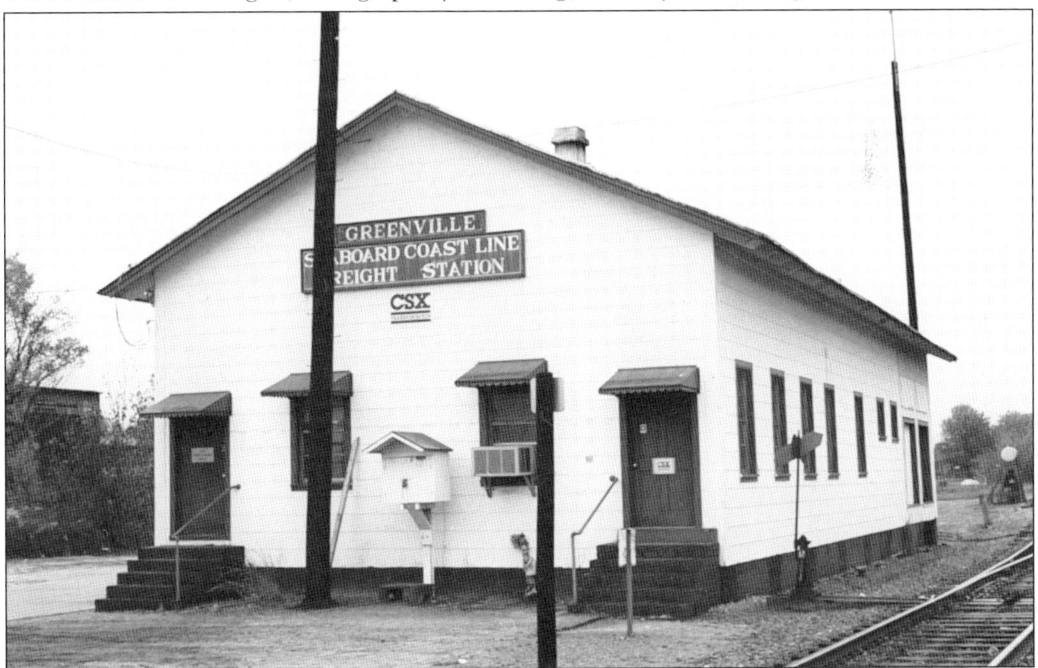

Greenville was founded in 1771 with the name Martinsborough after the royal governor Josiah Martin. The name was later changed in honor of Gen. Nathaniel Greene in 1786. This freight station was apparently converted from the passenger station after the original freight station burned. (Author's collection.)

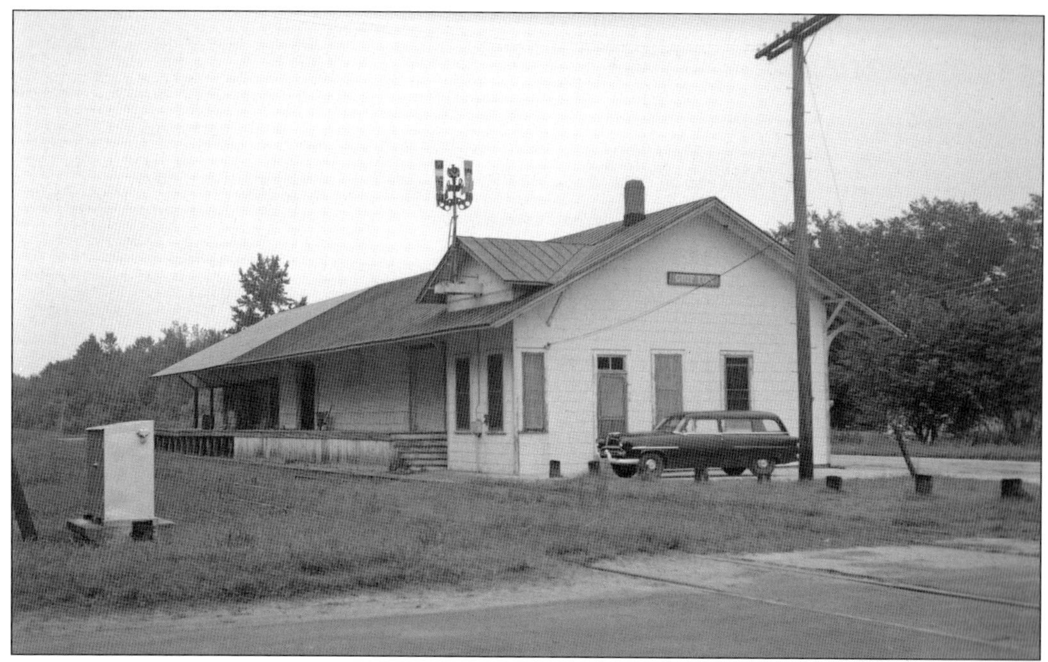

Grifton was named for C.M.A. Grifton when incorporated in 1883. This community is home to the Grifton Shad Festival, the local fish caught in Contentnea Creek. The depot has been preserved for use as a community building. (Photograph by Tom King, courtesy of the King-Marsh collection.)

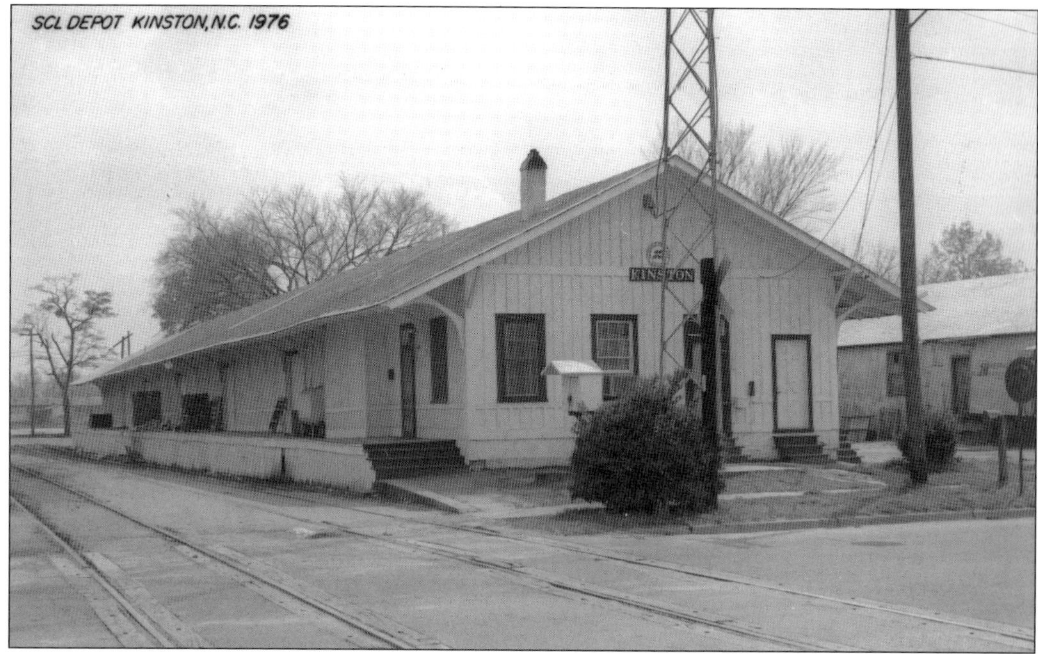

Kinston was the southern terminus of the branch from Pender, completed in 1890. The line connected with the Atlantic & North Carolina Railroad, providing freight interchange to Goldsboro or Morehead City. The depot no longer exists today. Kinston dates to 1791 and was involved in battles in or around the city during the Civil War. (Brian Ezzelle Collection.)

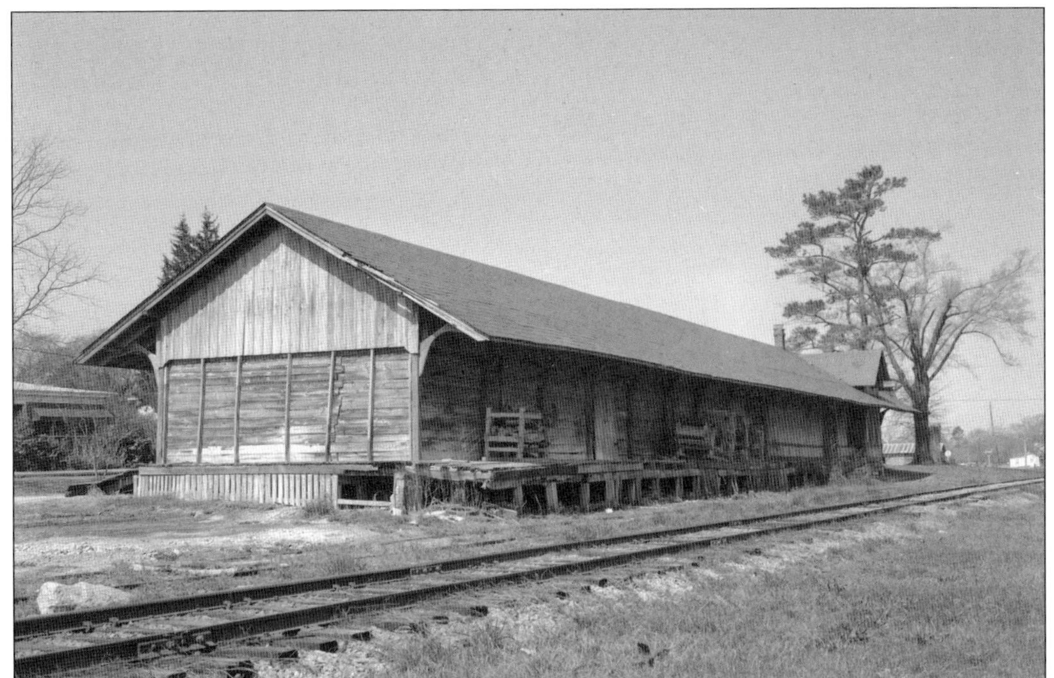

Conetoe is located in Edgecombe County, and located on the rail line from Tarboro to Parmele. No longer used by the railroad when this image was made in March 1972, the building is evidently used for storage since the open-air section has been boarded up. (Photograph by Tom King, courtesy of the King-Marsh collection.)

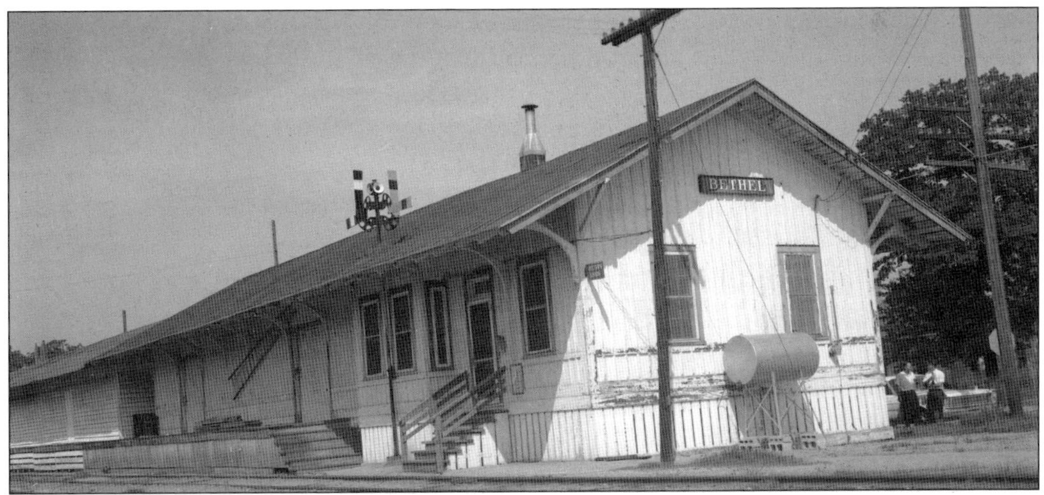

Bethel is a popular name in North Carolina, with no less than four communities using that name. This one, located in Pitt County, was incorporated on December 18, 1873. The railroad came through in 1882, increasing the prominence of the town. The depot has been preserved by the town and still looks very similar to this view from 1966. (Photograph by Tom King, courtesy of the King-Marsh collection.)

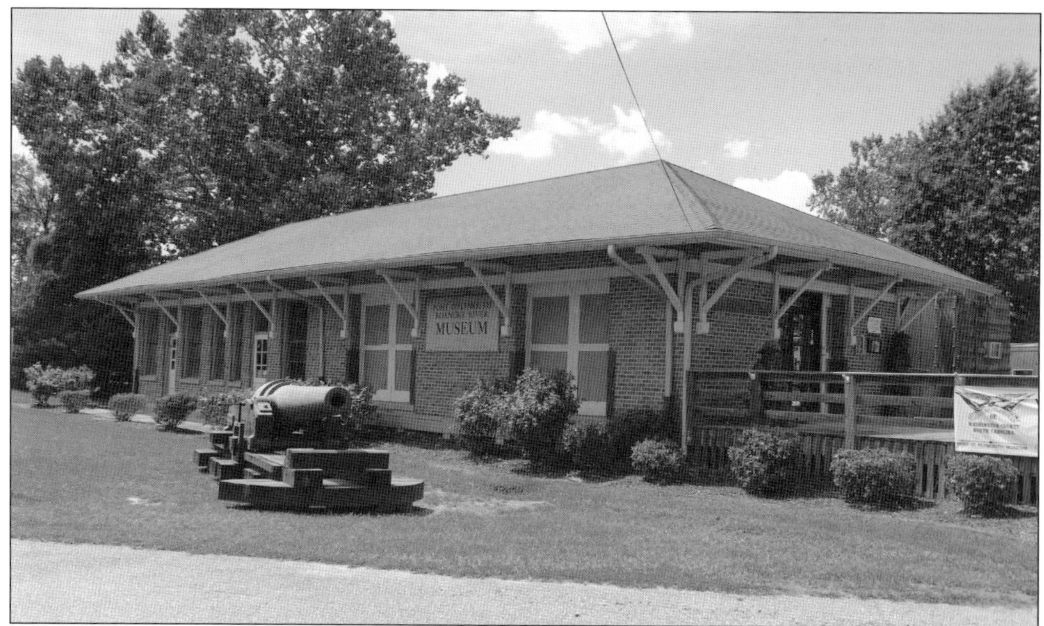

The terminus of the rail line from Tarboro was Plymouth, completed by the ACL in 1889. The town was established in 1787 by Arthur Rhodes, whose land was used for the town. The depot preserved today dates to the 1920s and houses the Port O' Plymouth Roanoke River Museum. The Battle of Plymouth occurred in 1864 and was the last Confederate victory in North Carolina. (Author's collection.)

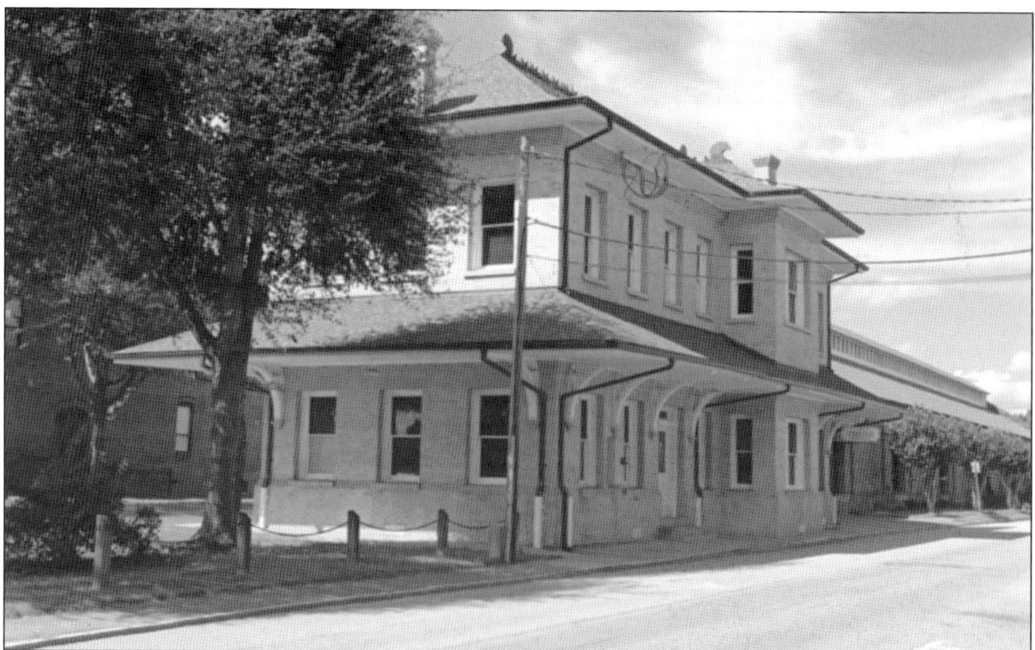
Washington was the terminus of the rail line from Parmele and connected with the Washington & Vandemere Railroad, controlled by the ACL. The town was settled in the 1770s and named Washington in 1776, predating Washington, DC. The depot was built in 1904 and has been beautifully preserved along with the large freight station for community use. (Author's collection.)

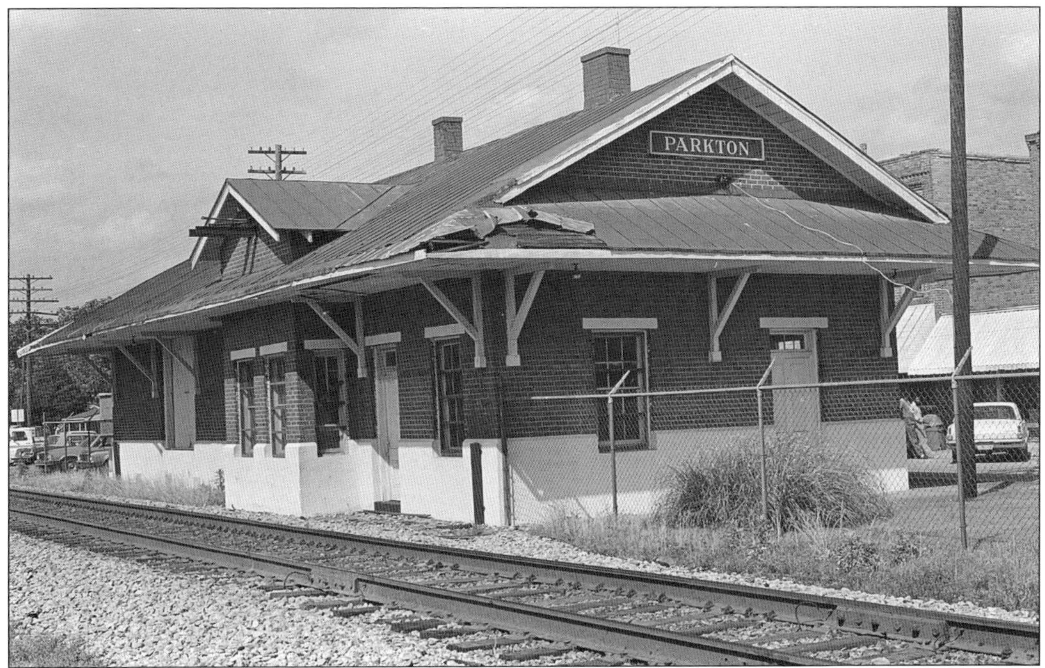

Parkton is located on the rail bypass in Robeson County. From here, an ACL branch headed south through Maxton toward Bennettsville, South Carolina. The depot has been restored by the community and houses a local museum today. (Author's collection.)

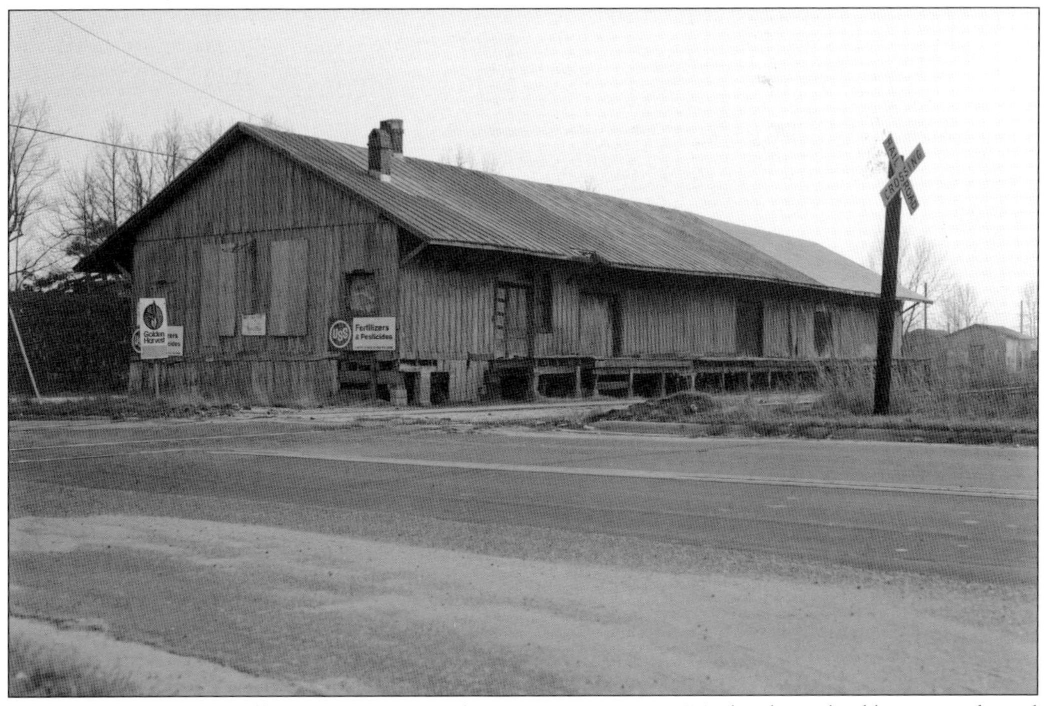

Lumber Bridge is a small community in Robeson County. By 1976, the depot had been purchased and used by a private business. The depot no longer stands today. (Photograph by Tom Sink, courtesy of the King-Marsh collection.)

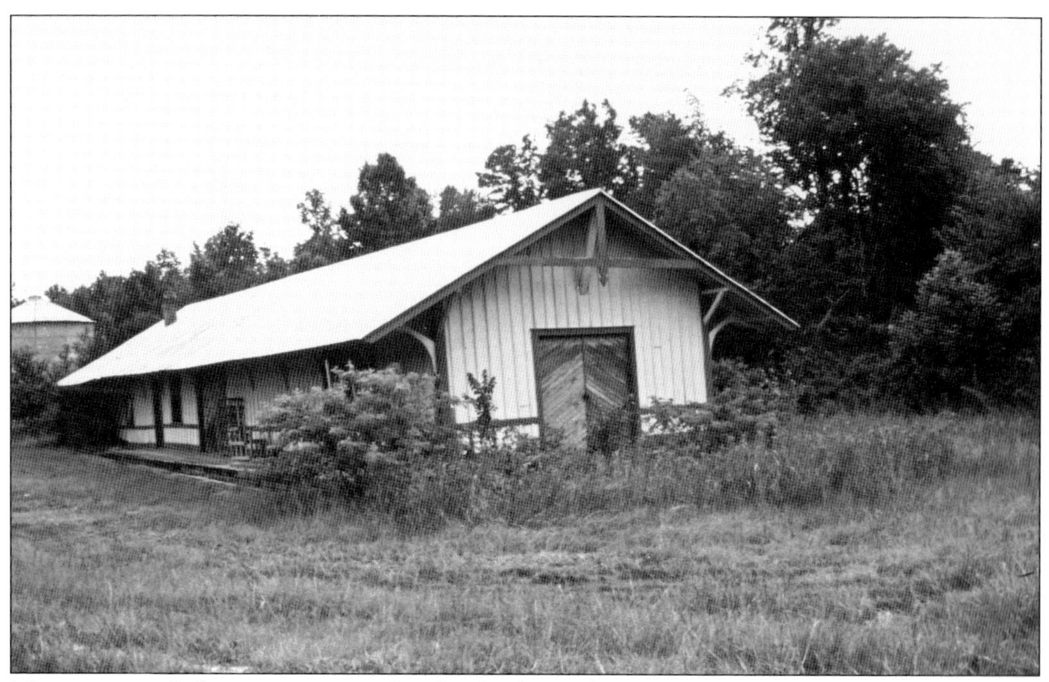

Morven, named after a mountain in Scotland, is located in Anson County. This depot was located on the rail line from Wadesboro to Florence, South Carolina. The depot has been preserved and converted into a hunting lodge. (Author's collection.)

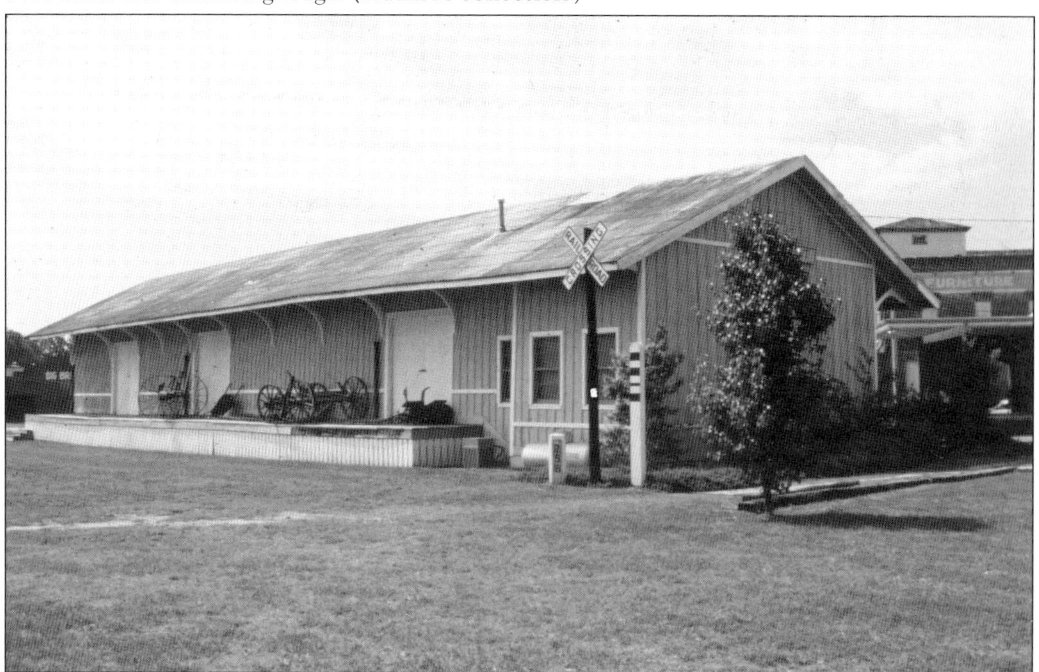

Fairmont was located on an ACL branch line from Elrod on the main line to Chadbourn and onto Myrtle Beach, South Carolina. In later years, the line was abandoned from Fairmont to Chadbourn, and the remainder operated as the Fairmont & Western Railroad. The depot still looks as good today as this image from 1991. (Author's collection.)

Two

Seaboard Air Line

Seaboard Air Line operations in North Carolina began in 1836 when construction started on the Raleigh & Gaston Railroad, beginning with a connection with the Petersburg Railroad at the Roanoke River. The line progressed through Ridgeway, Henderson, and Franklinton, finally reaching the terminus of Raleigh. The first train steamed into Raleigh on March 21, 1840. Other rail lines that eventually came under SAL control were the Seaboard & Roanoke Railroad between Portsmouth, Virginia, and Weldon, and the Carolina Central Railway, which operated between Wilmington and Rutherfordton. All of these were formally merged into the Seaboard Air Line in 1900. Monroe became the junction of the line to Rutherfordton and the main line to Atlanta. Branch lines were later constructed to Durham, Pittsboro, and Lewiston.

The Seaboard main line bisected North Carolina, giving the railroad one of the shortest routes through the state. The term "air line" referred to a relatively flat and straight route between larger cities. The Seaboard line from New York to Tampa was advertised as "straight as a plumb line." The December 1924 public timetable lists 169 stations, though some were flag stops only.

The Seaboard Air Line did have a national railroad distinction of its east-west route through the state. The section starting at East Arcadia (near Wilmington) and ending at Old Hundred (near Hamlet) is 79 miles in length and is still the longest straight tangent of railroad track in the United States.

As passenger trains ended in the 1950s–1960s, the Seaboard Air Line began a process of replacing larger stations with smaller buildings more suited for freight traffic. Several stations in North Carolina received this treatment, and some still remain today.

The Seaboard Air Line helped connect the eastern and western parts of the state, with its western terminus in the foothills of the mountains. Due to these routes, the line from Hamlet to Rutherfordton is included to show the entire railroad in this volume.

The SAL depots are arranged first by the main line, then the Wilmington line, and finally, the branch routes.

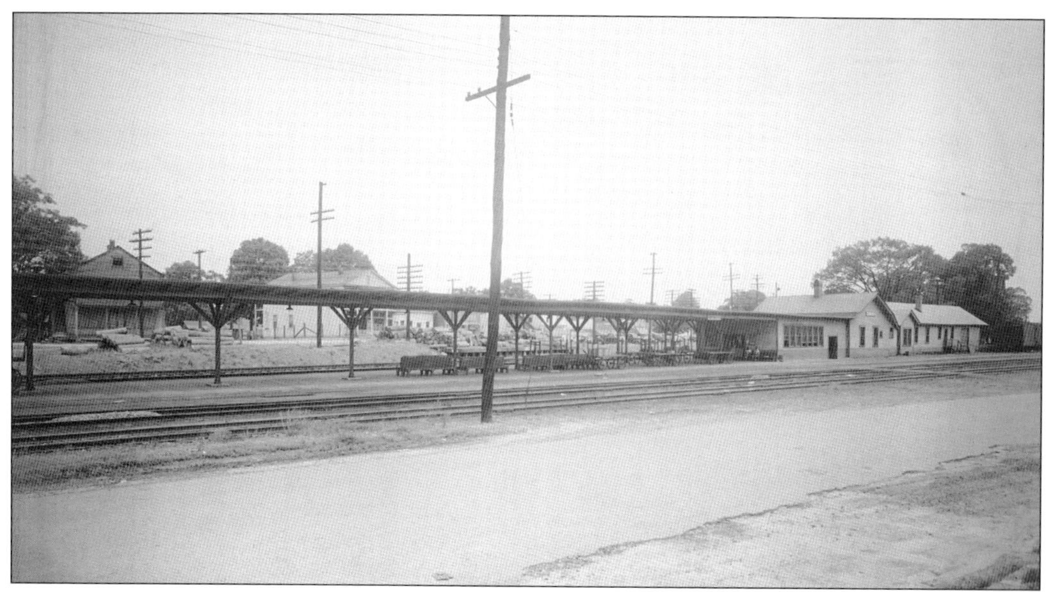

Norlina was the junction between the main line and the secondary line to Portsmouth, Virginia. The area was originally called Woodyard and, later, "the Junction," once the railroad came through. The name changed to Norlina in 1913 and is a combination of the state name. These views show the Norlina depot as it looked in 1947. Note the large and ornate train order board on the back wall. Unfortunately, this station was torn down several years ago. (Both, courtesy of the State Archives of North Carolina.)

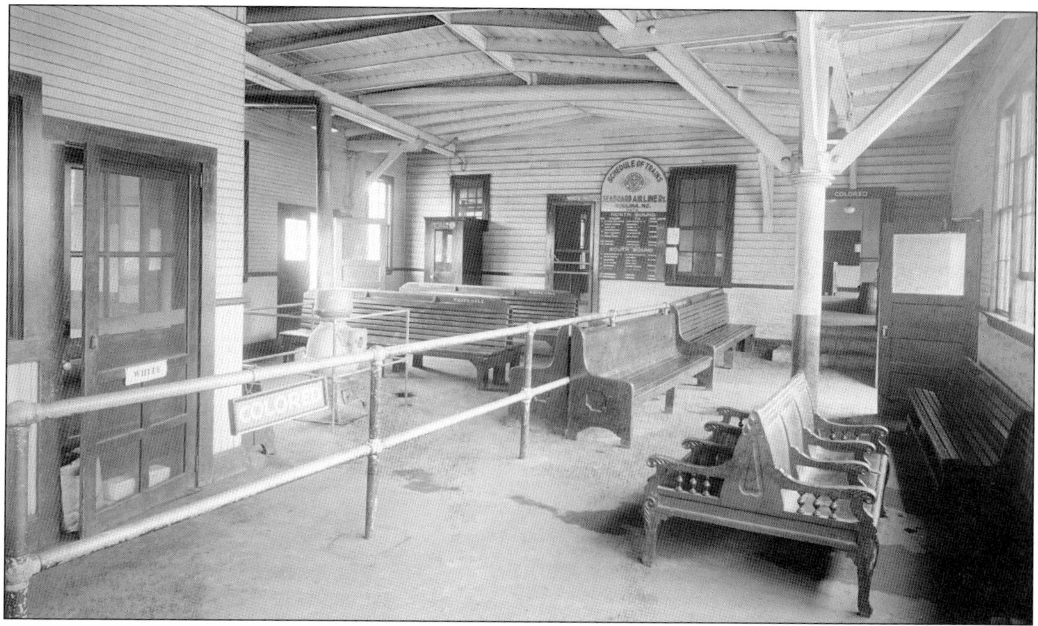

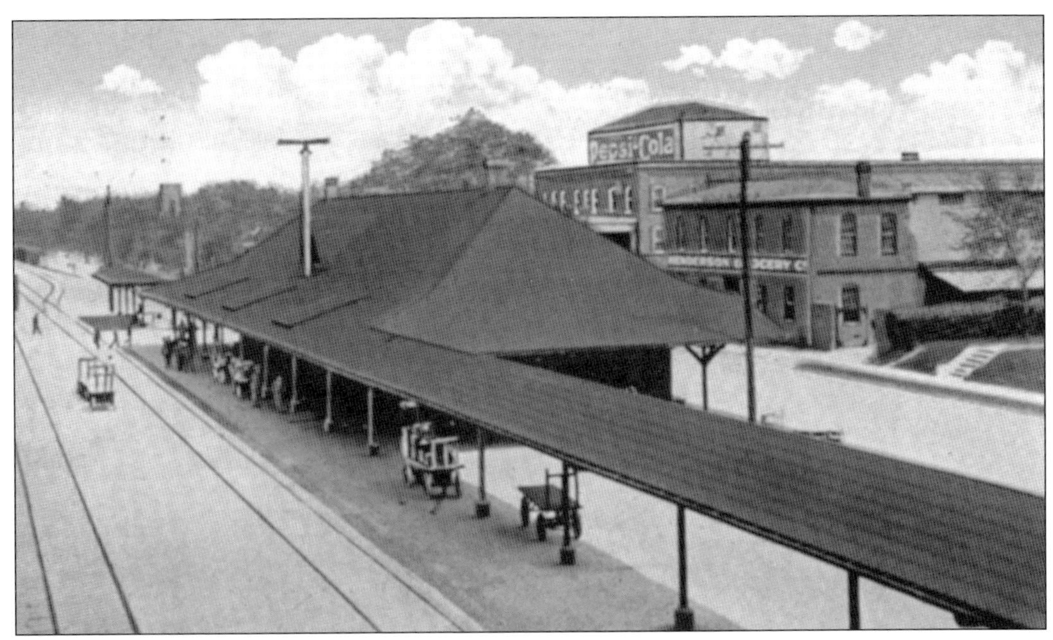

Henderson was named for North Carolina Supreme Court judge Leonard Henderson when it was chartered in 1841, not long after the railroad was completed through the area. Henderson developed as a center for textile, tobacco, and cotton as the county seat of Vance County. The depot no longer exists today. (Above, courtesy of the Larry K. Neal Jr. collection; below, courtesy of the King-Marsh collection.)

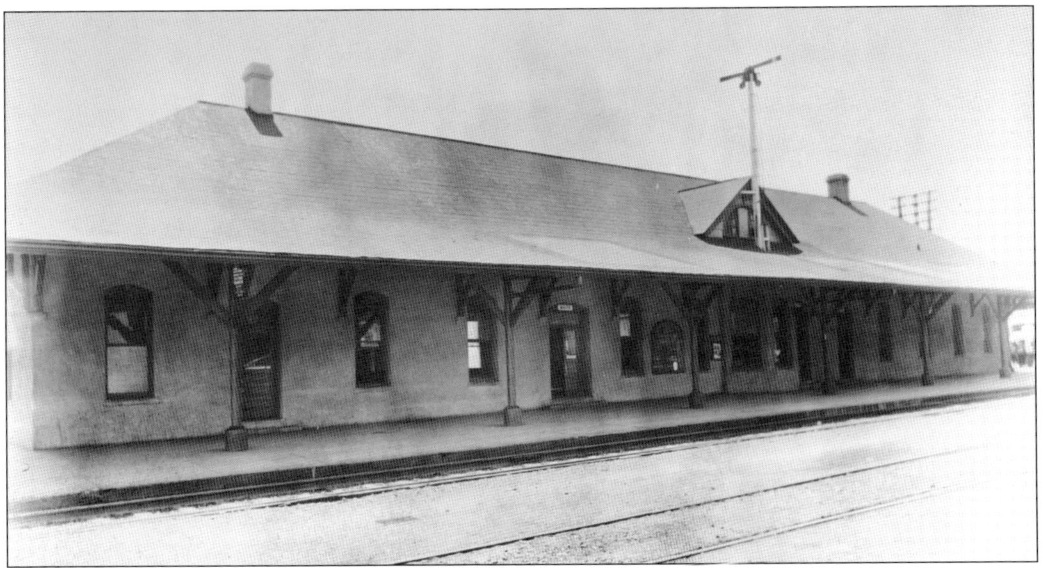

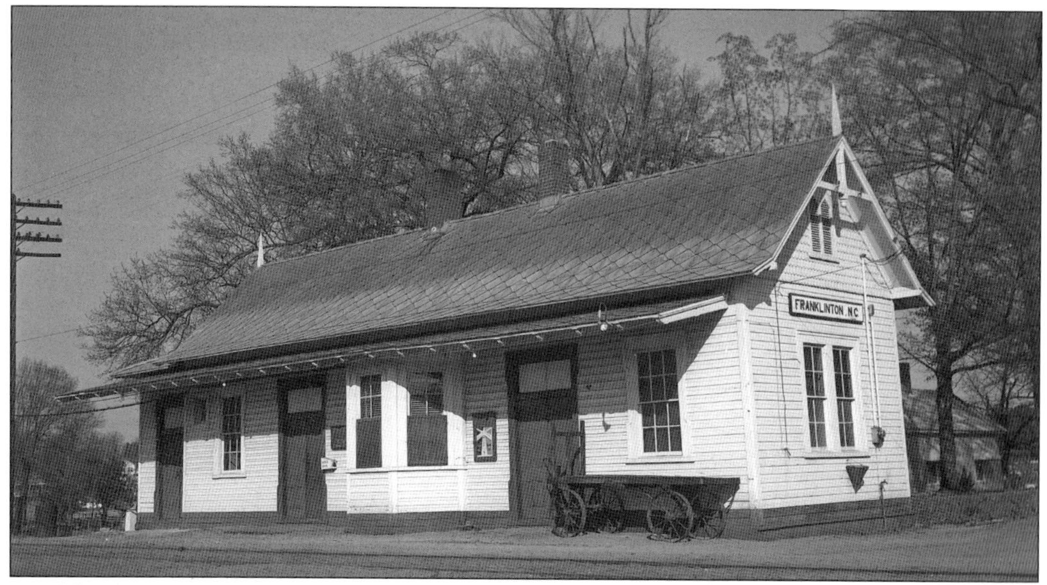

Franklinton was incorporated on December 20, 1842, and named for Benjamin Franklin. The depot was built by the Raleigh & Augusta Air Line in 1890 and has been preserved as a local landmark for the town. (Photograph by Tom King, courtesy of the King-Marsh collection.)

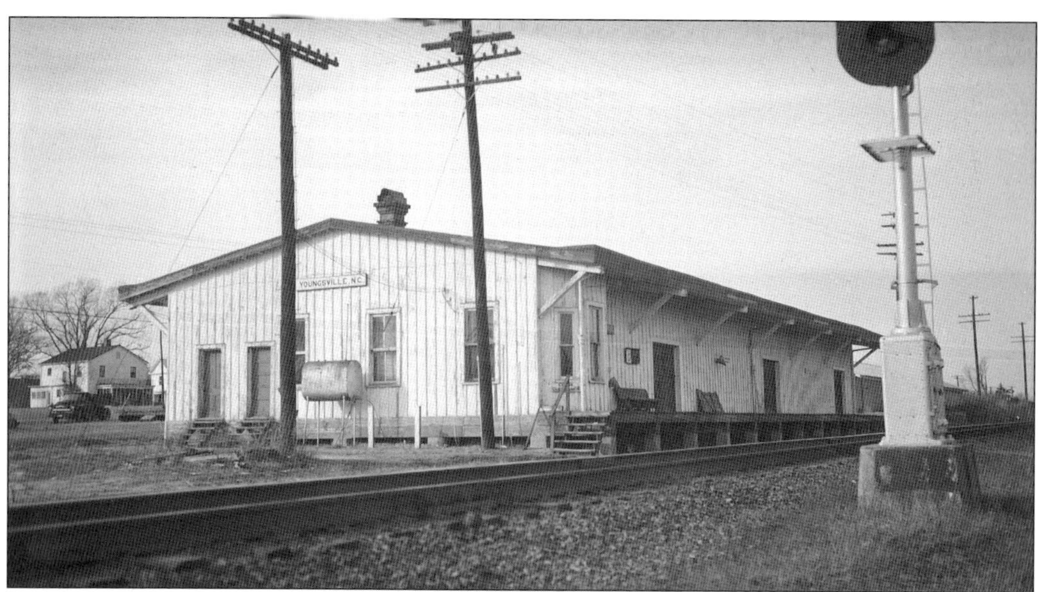

Youngsville, incorporated in 1875, was named for John "Jack" Young when incorporated in 1875. The town prospered by growing cotton and tobacco, becoming one of the largest markets in the state. The depot, photographed in 1967, no longer exists today. (Photograph by Tom King, courtesy of the King-Marsh collection.)

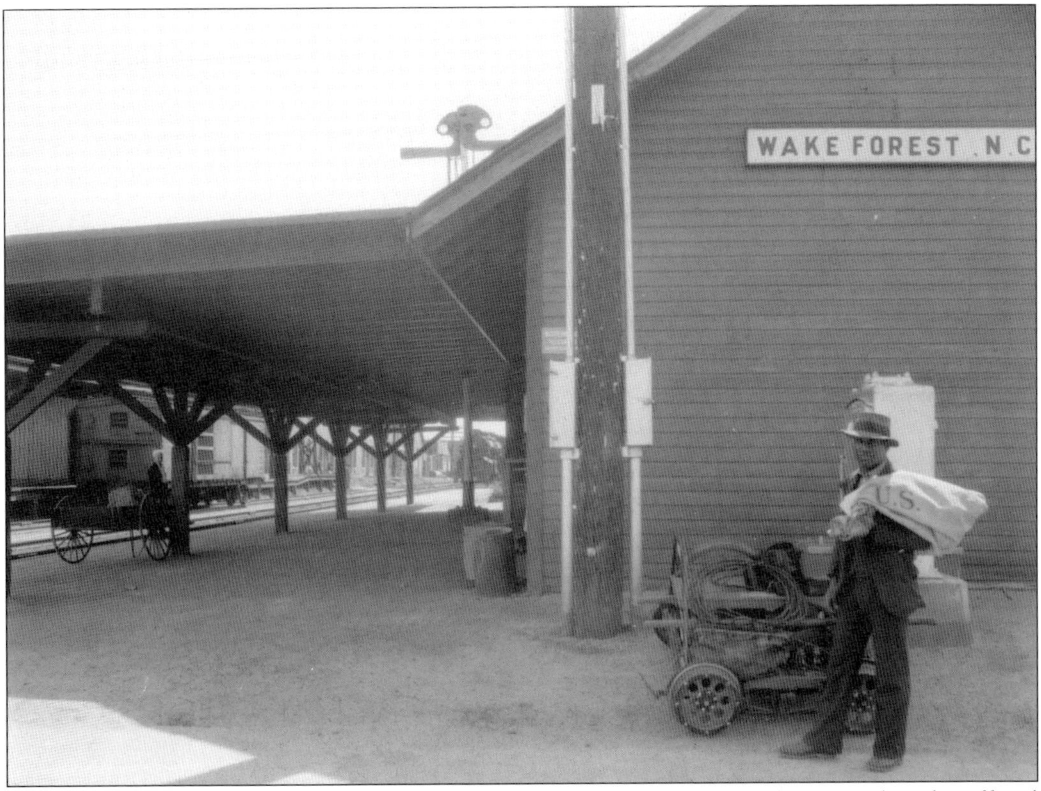

Wake Forest dates back to 1834, when the Wake Forest Institute opened in 1834, but the official current charter dates to 1909. Wake Forest College later moved to Winston-Salem in 1956. The gentleman, photographed in 1932, appears to be waiting on the next train, ready to load the mail bag onto the RPO. The long train shed offered some nice shade on hot summer days. (Courtesy of the State Archives of North Carolina.)

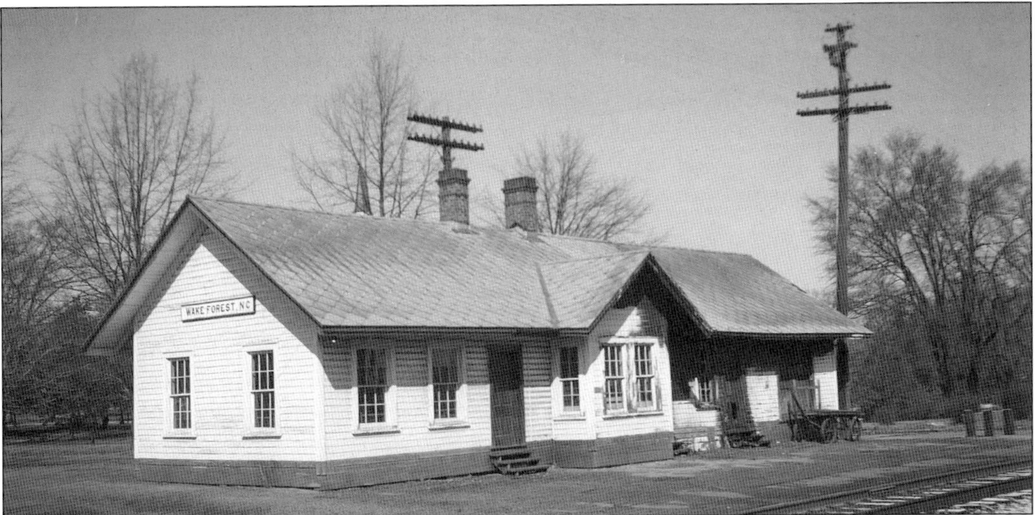

The wooden depot had lost the train shed by the time of this image from 1964. This building was later replaced by a new brick depot, which still remains as a community building in town. (Photograph by Tom King, courtesy of the King-Marsh collection.)

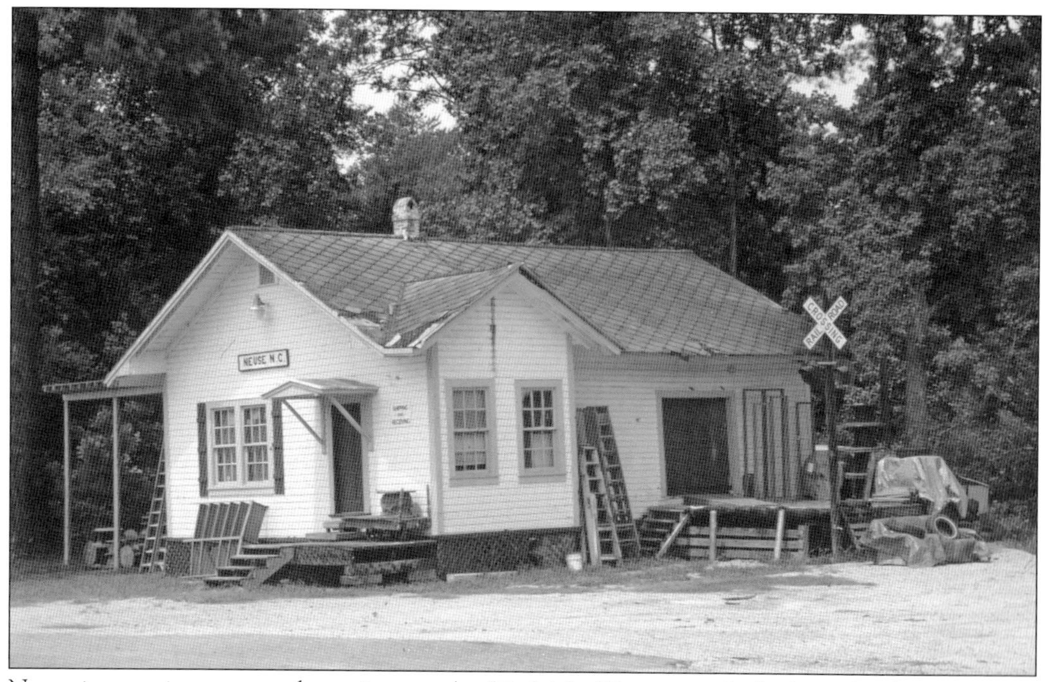

Neuse is an unincorporated area just north of Raleigh. The quaint little depot has been restored and remains today as a local business. (Author's collection.)

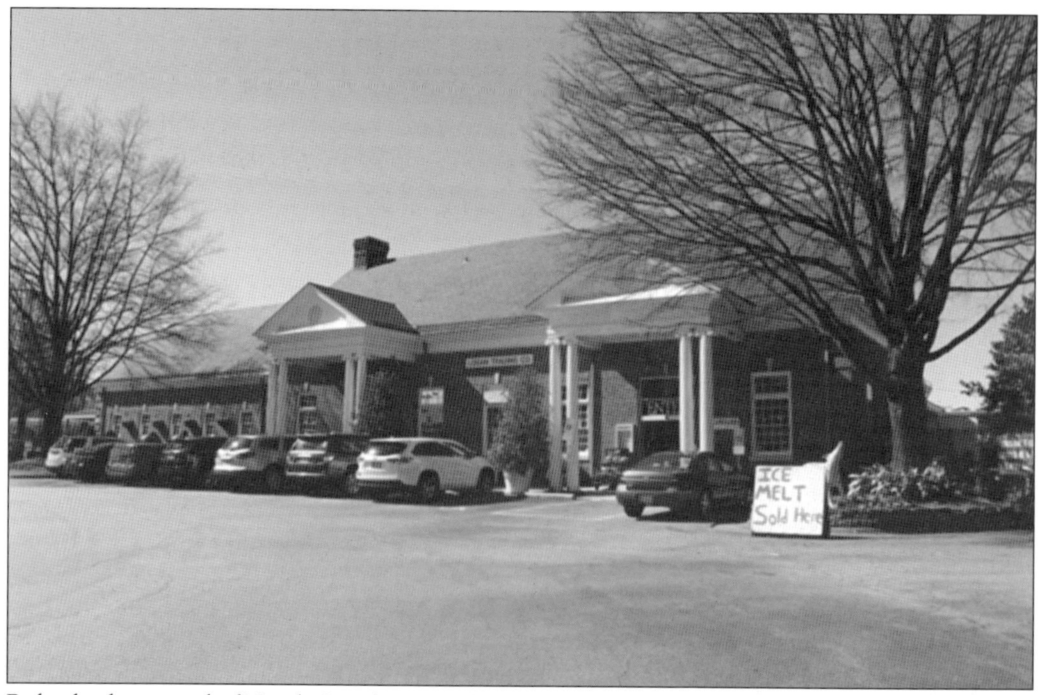

Raleigh, the capital of North Carolina, was laid out in 1788 and incorporated in 1792. The depot was constructed in 1942 when Seaboard Air Line left Union Station. Amtrak used this depot during the 1970s, and today the building is used as a lawn and garden business. (Author's collection.)

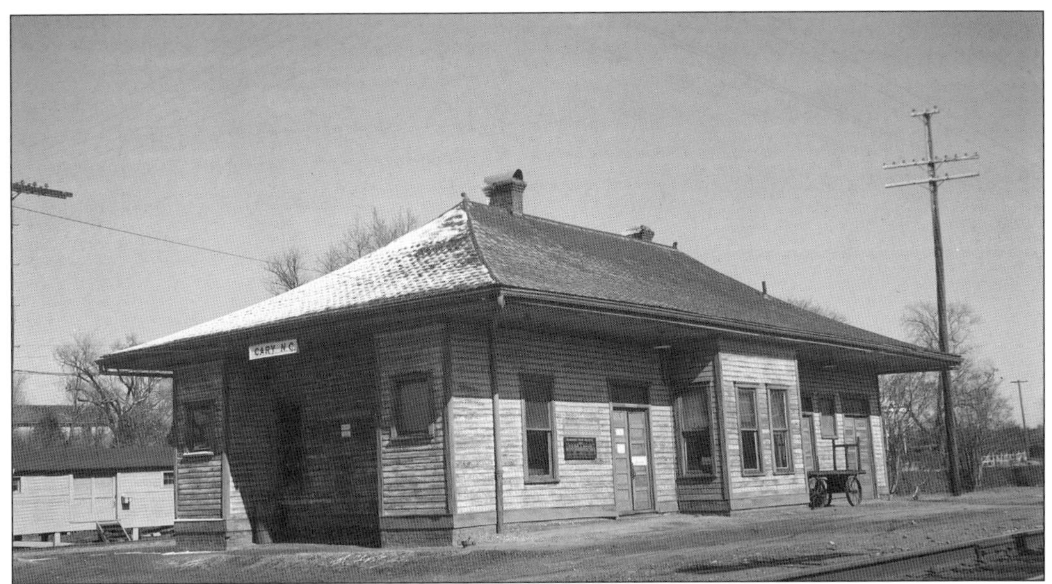

Cary was originally known as Bradford's Ordinary but changed to Cary in 1854 after the railroad came through town. The original depot, shown here from 1964, was later torn down. The North Carolina Department of Transportation built a new station in 1995 to serve rail passengers and as a local DMV office. (Photograph by Tom King, courtesy of the King-Marsh collection.)

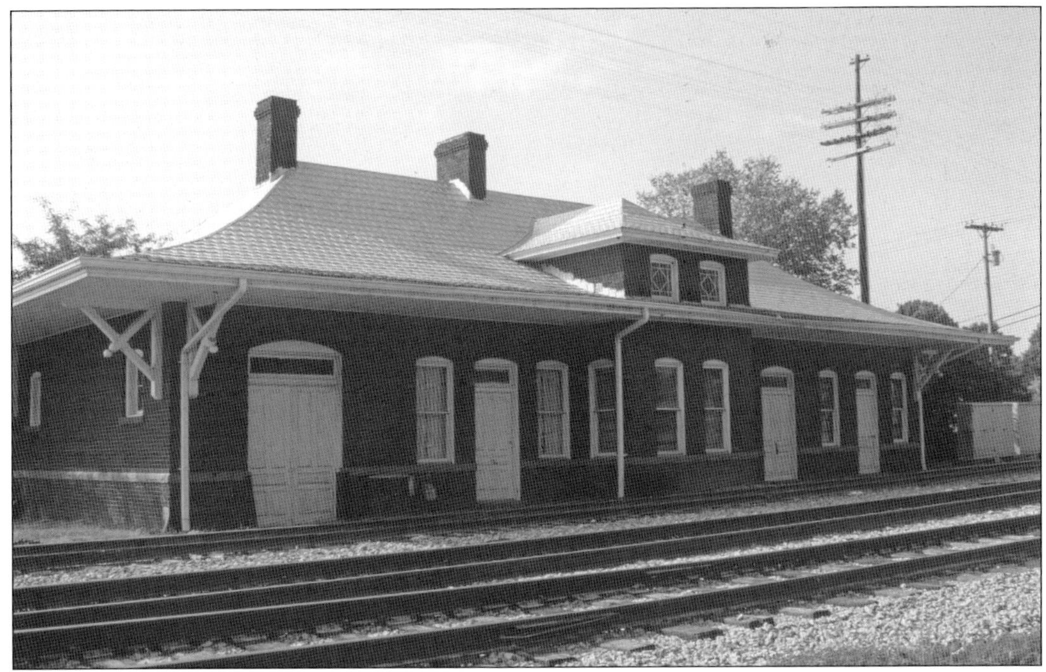
Apex was the highest point on the Chatham Railroad when it was incorporated in 1873. This depot was constructed in 1914 and has been restored, housing the local chamber of commerce. (Author's collection.)

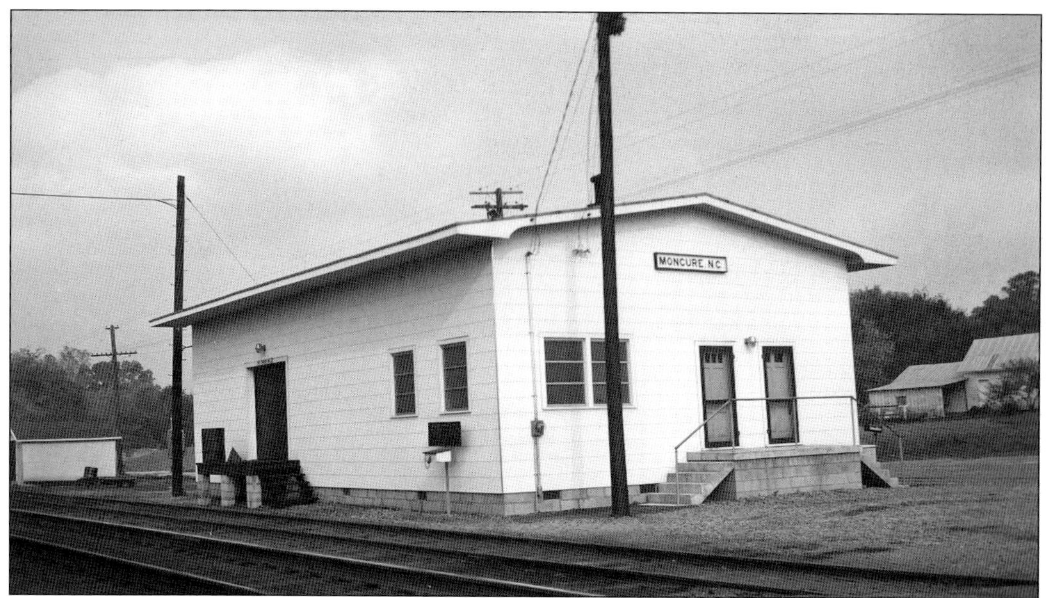

Moncure was the middle name of John Moncure Robinson, who was an engineer and later president of the Seaboard & Roanoke Railroad. The depot, shown in 1965, was modified by the 1960s for freight service. (Photograph by Tom King, courtesy of the King-Marsh collection.)

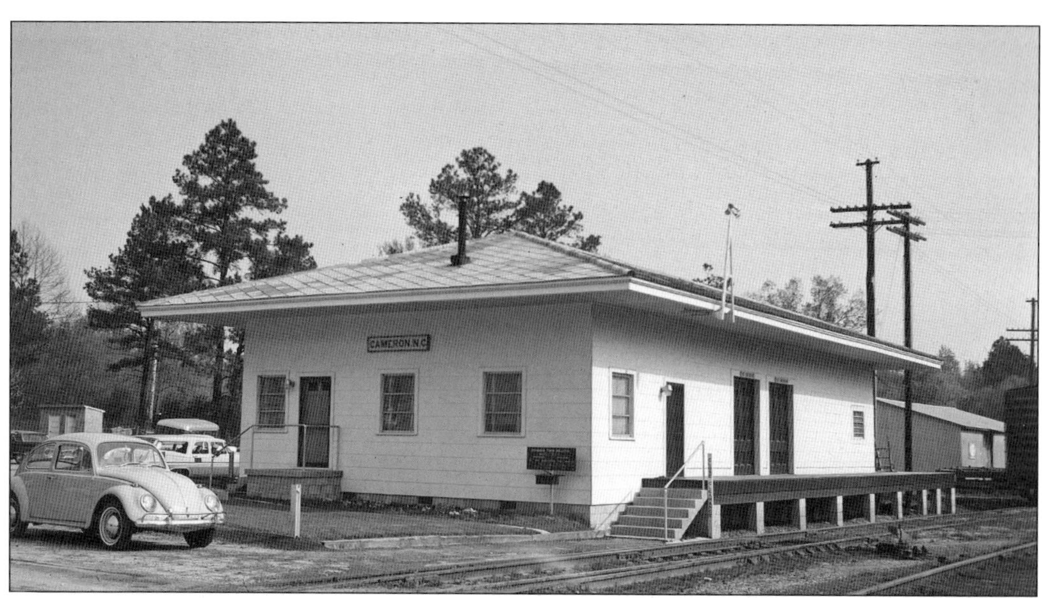

Cameron dates to 1876 and was an important stop on both a plank road and railroad. The depot dates back to the 1870s but was extensively modified by the 1960s. (Author's collection.)

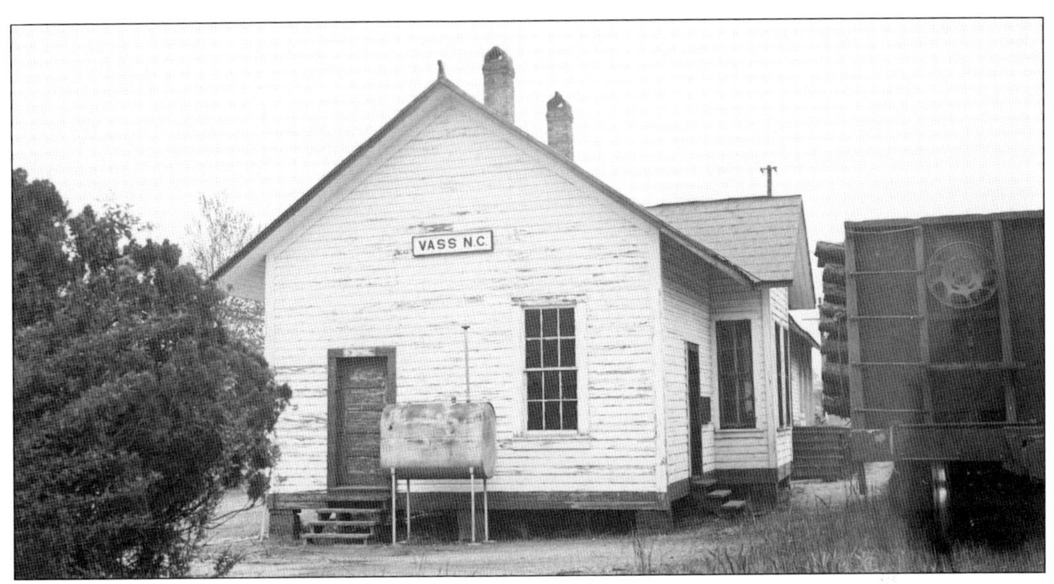

Vass was originally known as Bynum and Winder before it was incorporated in 1892. The two depot images, above from 1965 and below from 1970, illustrate the changes made by the Seaboard Air Line after passenger service ended. (Above, photograph by Tom King, courtesy of the King-Marsh collection; below, photograph by Bill Moneypenny, courtesy of the Brian Ezzelle collection.)

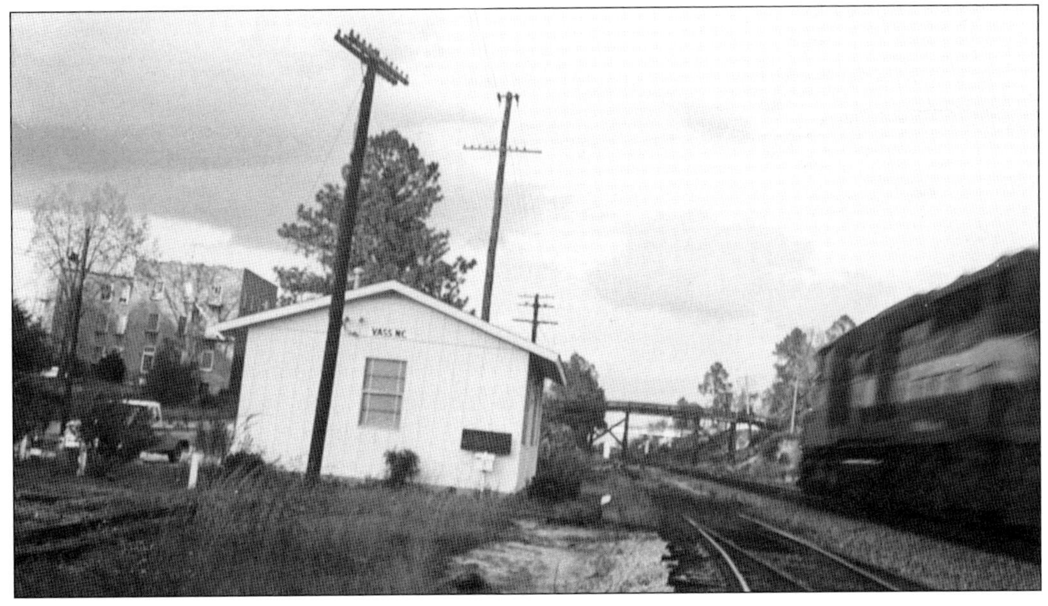

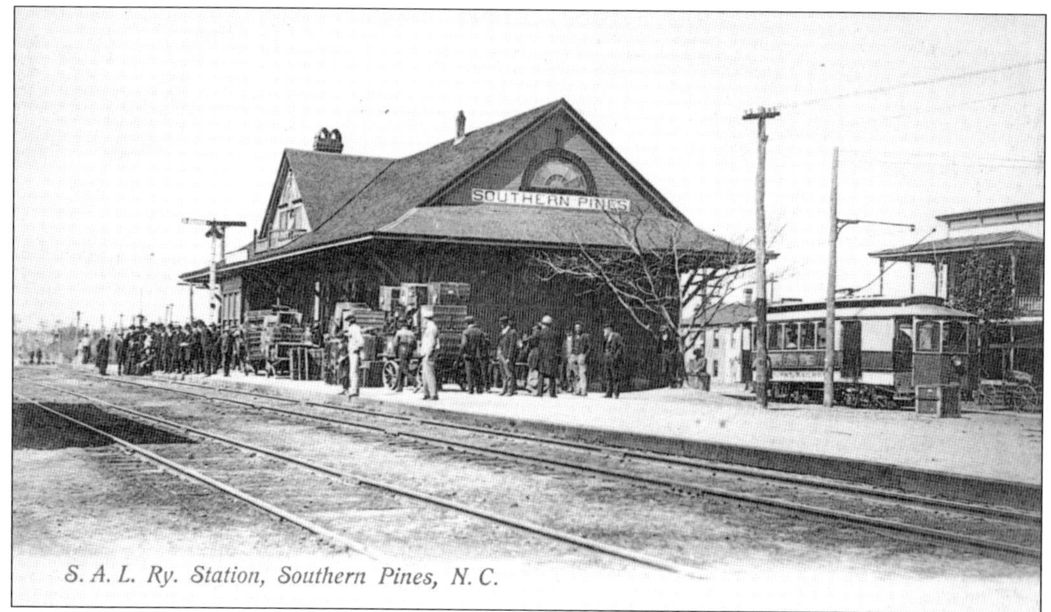

Southern Pines was the depot for travelers wanting to vacation in the sand hills of North Carolina. The area was developed for health reasons due to the climate and, later, for those interested in the golf courses at Pinehurst. This 1910s- or 1920s-era postcard shows a large group of travelers waiting for either the train or the trolley to take them to Pinehurst. (Courtesy of the State Archives of North Carolina.)

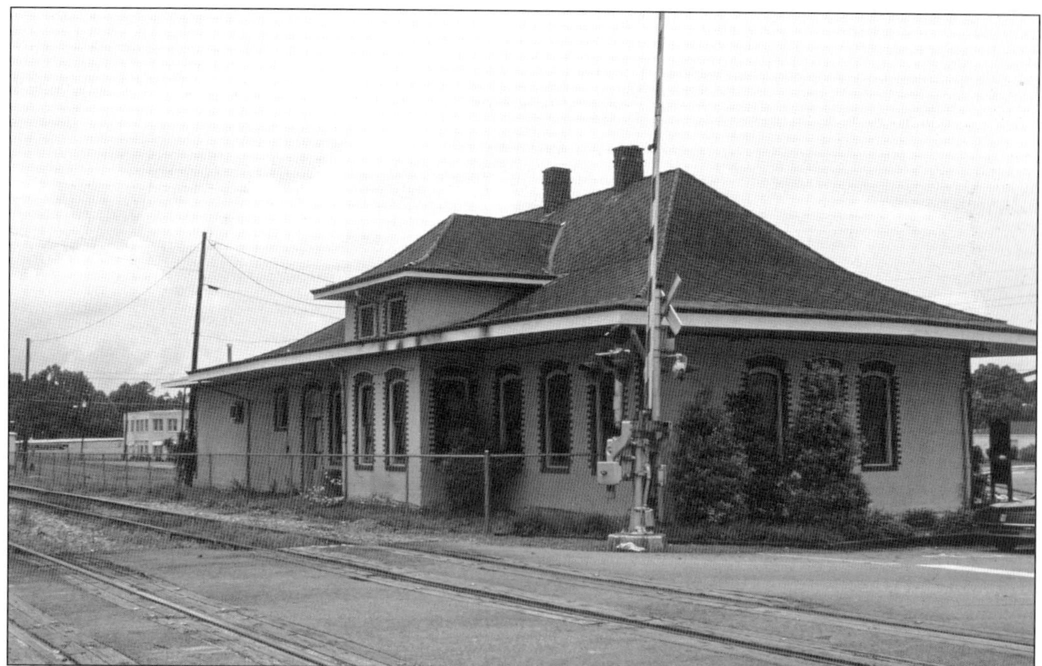

Aberdeen, formally known as Bethesda and Blue's Crossing, was settled by Scottish immigrants during the 1700s. In 1892, John Blue constructed the Aberdeen & Rockfish Railroad, headquartered across from the depot. The line is still owned today by his descendants. The depot has been preserved and is used today by the community. (Author's collection.)

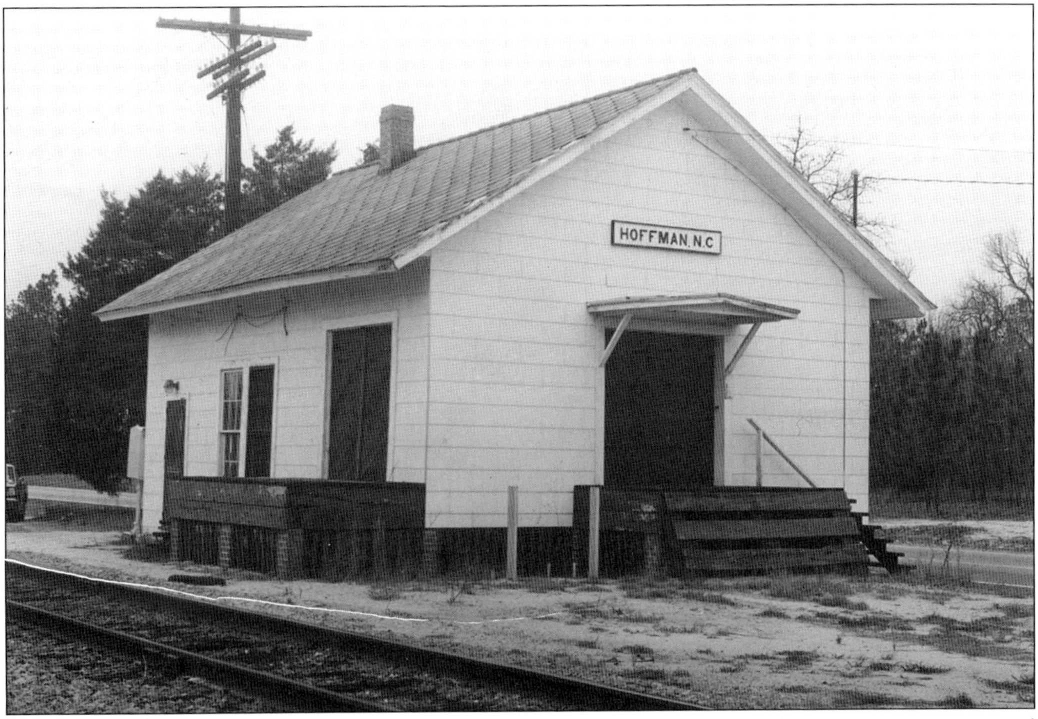

Hoffman is located just north of Hamlet. This depot was later moved onto private property and preserved. (Courtesy of the Brian Ezzelle collection.)

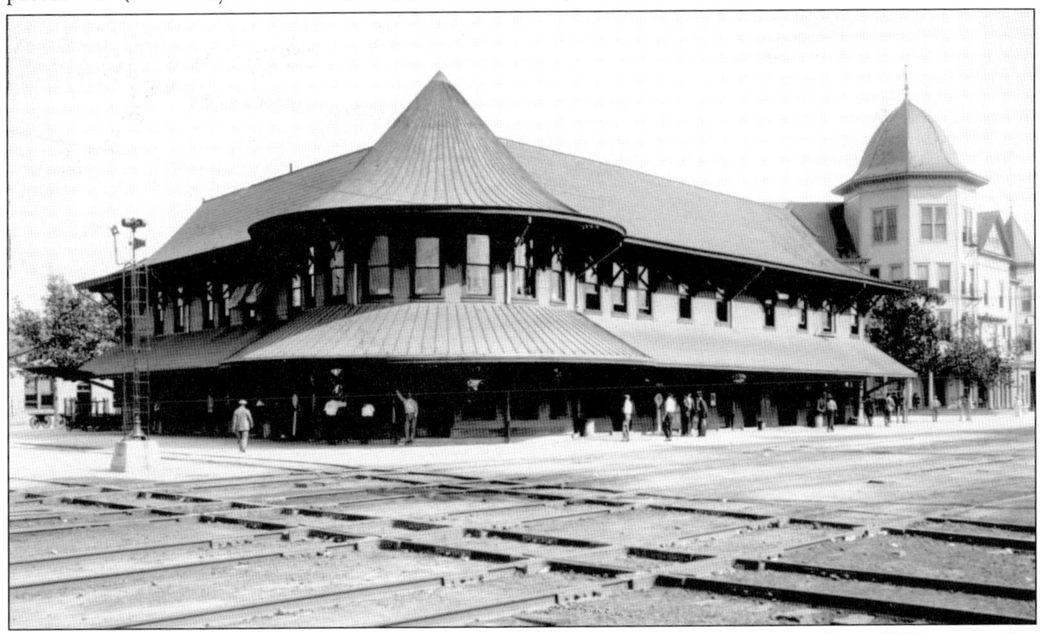

Hamlet, named for an English term for a group of houses, was incorporated in 1877, just a few years after the railroad came through town. The 1895 depot stood over the tracks, linking north, south, east, and west for travelers. A hotel was originally located beside the depot but burned several years after this 1915 image was taken. Jazz musician John Coltrane was born here in 1926. (Courtesy of the State Archives of North Carolina.)

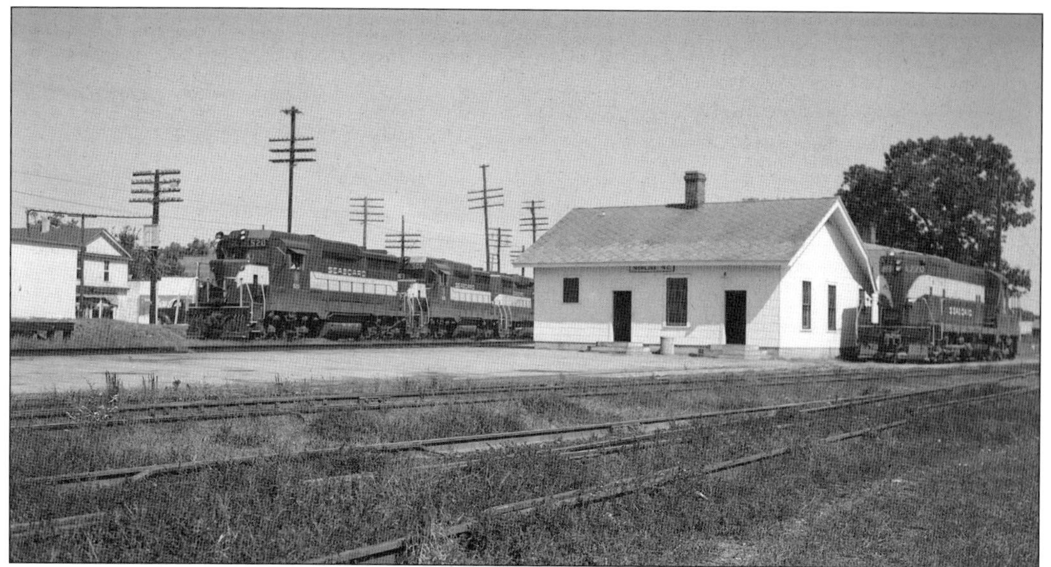

This later view of Norlina from 1966 shows the long train shed has been removed due to the removal of many passenger trains through the town. The locomotive on the right is on the line to Portsmouth. (Photograph by Tom King, courtesy of the King-Marsh collection.)

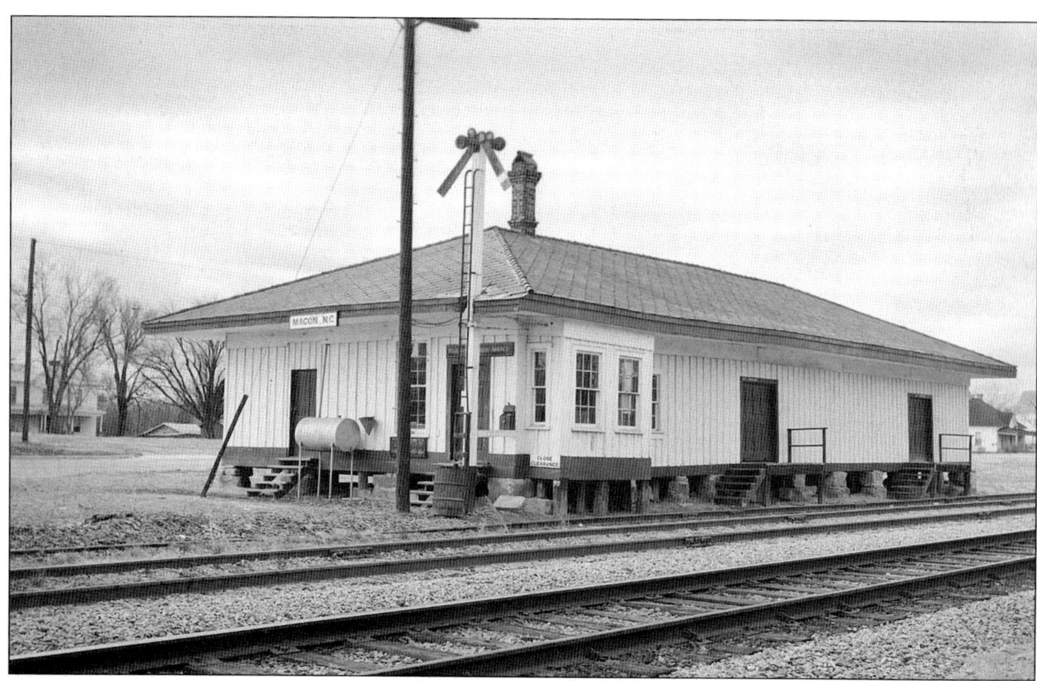

Macon was named for Nathaniel Macon, fifth speaker of the US House of Representatives. The depot, photographed in 1965, was still standing in 2007 on private property. (Photograph by Tom King, courtesy of the King-Marsh collection.)

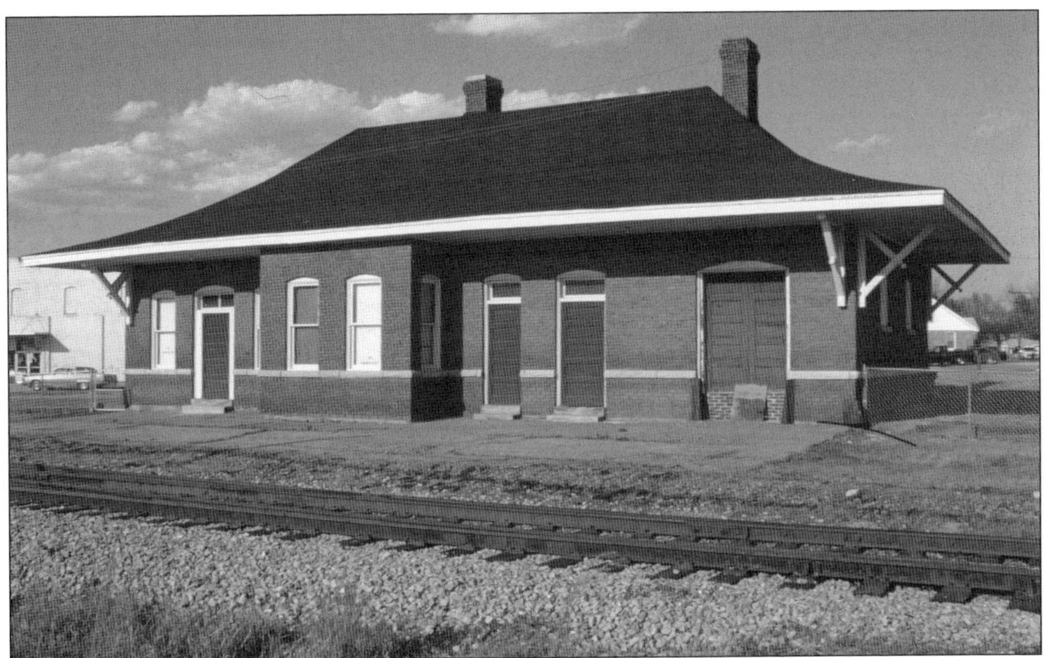

Roanoke Rapids is named after the rapids of the Roanoke River, caused by the fall line where the coastal regions meet at the river. The depot, built in 1920, is still a main feature of this community. (Author's collection.)

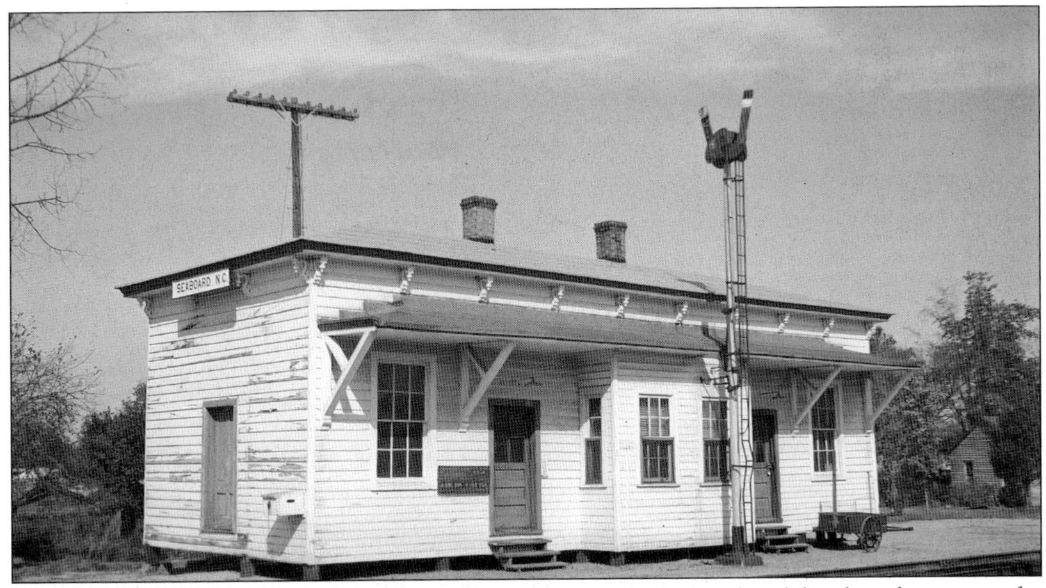

Seaboard Air Line was named by the Seaboard & Roanoke Railroad and developed as a town for employees to live along the line. The small depot appears to have been constructed around 1890, based on the design. Photographed in 1964, the building no longer stands today. (Photograph by Tom King, courtesy of the King-Marsh collection.)

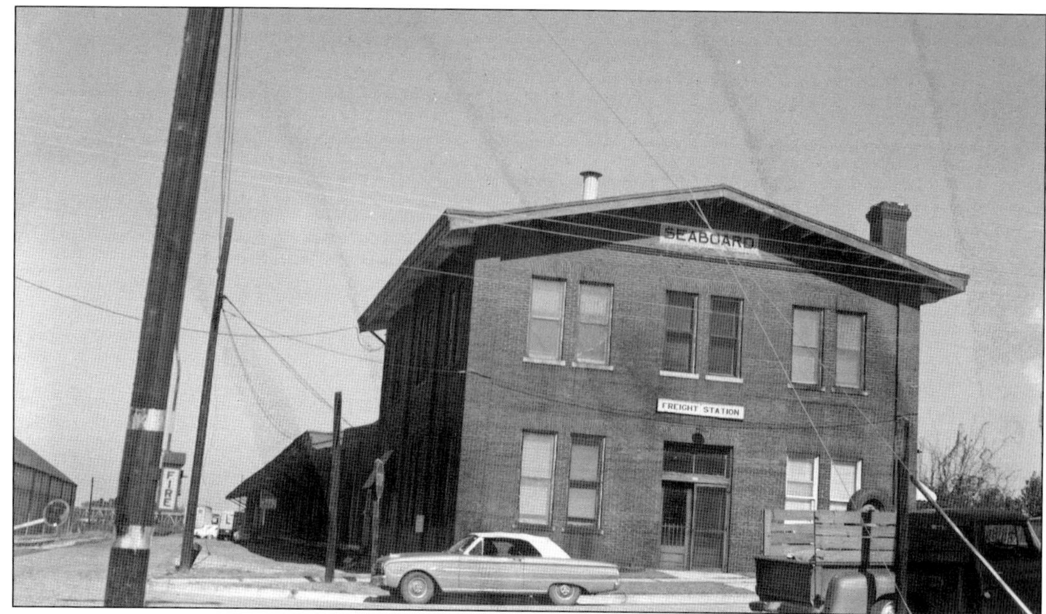

Wilmington is the eastern terminus of the Carolina Central Railroad, which operated through Charlotte to Rutherfordton. Wilmington dates to the 1720s and was incorporated in 1740. The Seaboard Air Line had docks along the river, and a depot and freight yard in Hilton, once known for having the world's largest living Christmas tree. (Photograph by Bill Monypenny, courtesy of the Brian Ezzelle collection.)

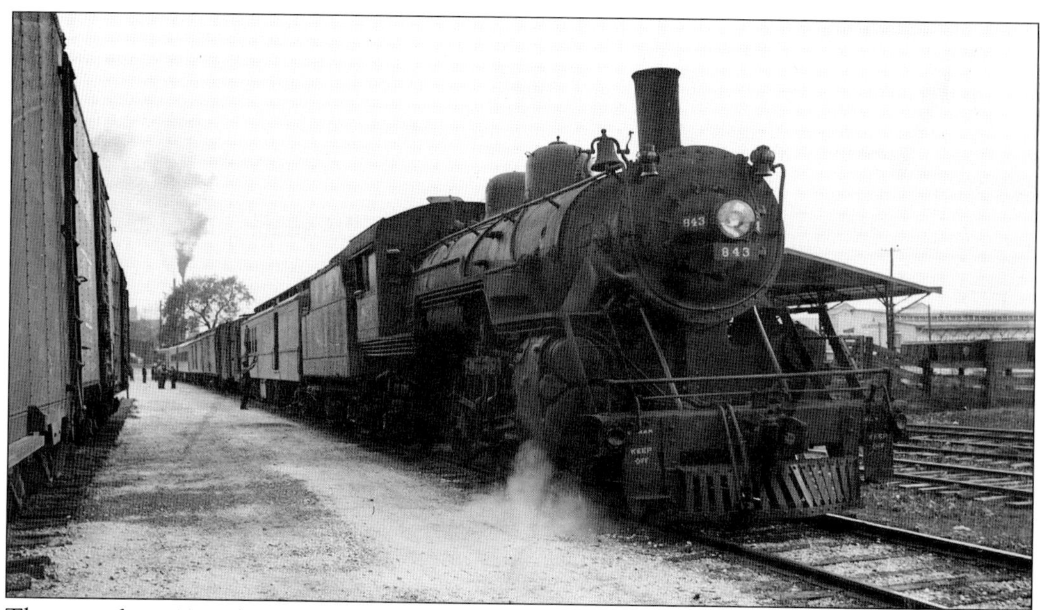

This view from 1943 shows Train 13 preparing to head west to Charlotte. A portion of the docks is visible just to the right of the locomotive. (Author's collection.)

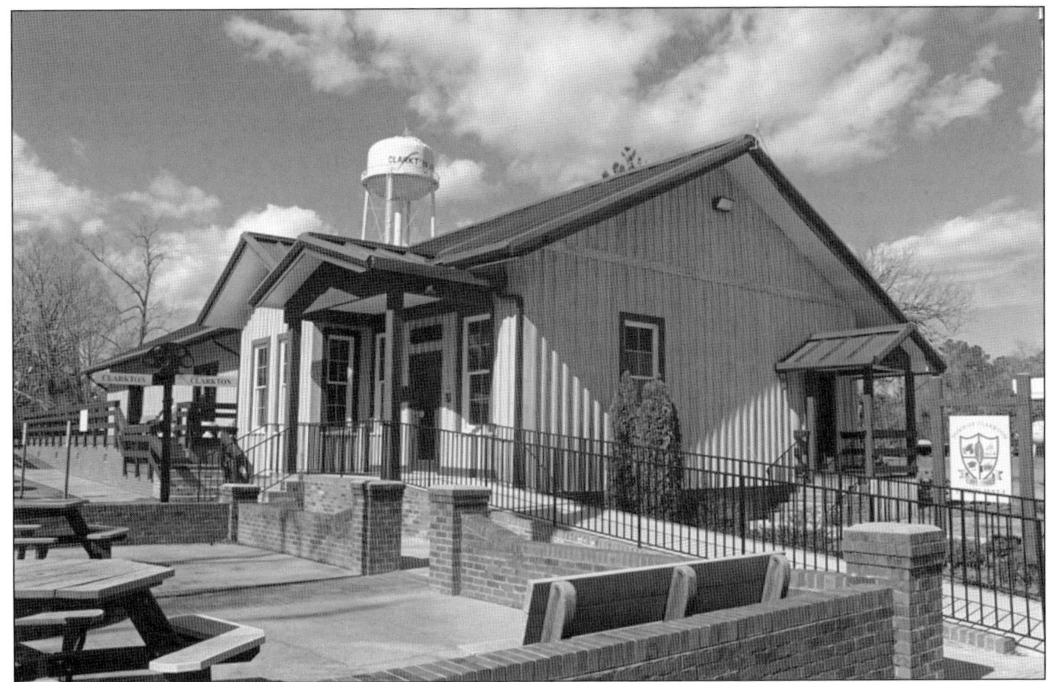

Clarkton depot was built in 1915 and denoted the importance of the town by the size. It was moved to its present location in 1975 and currently serves as the town hall. (Author's collection.)

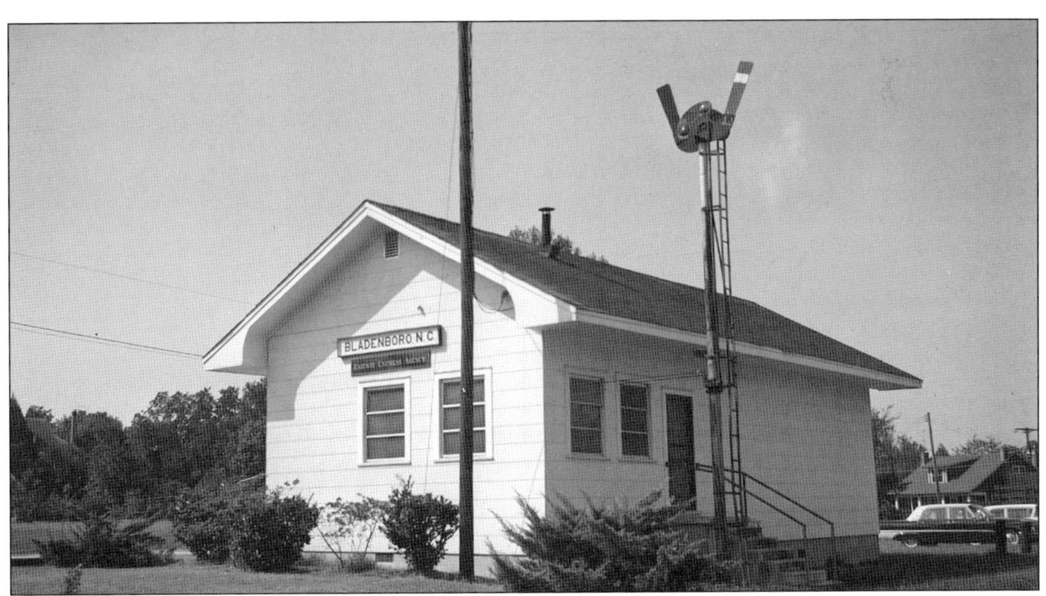

Bladensboro developed as an important source of turpentine and lumber, mainly due to two brothers—R.L. and H.C. Bridger. The depot, built in 1930, shows similar modifications done in the 1960s. At one time, this building served as a magistrate office, but it now is a private business. (Photograph by Tom King, courtesy of the King-Marsh collection.)

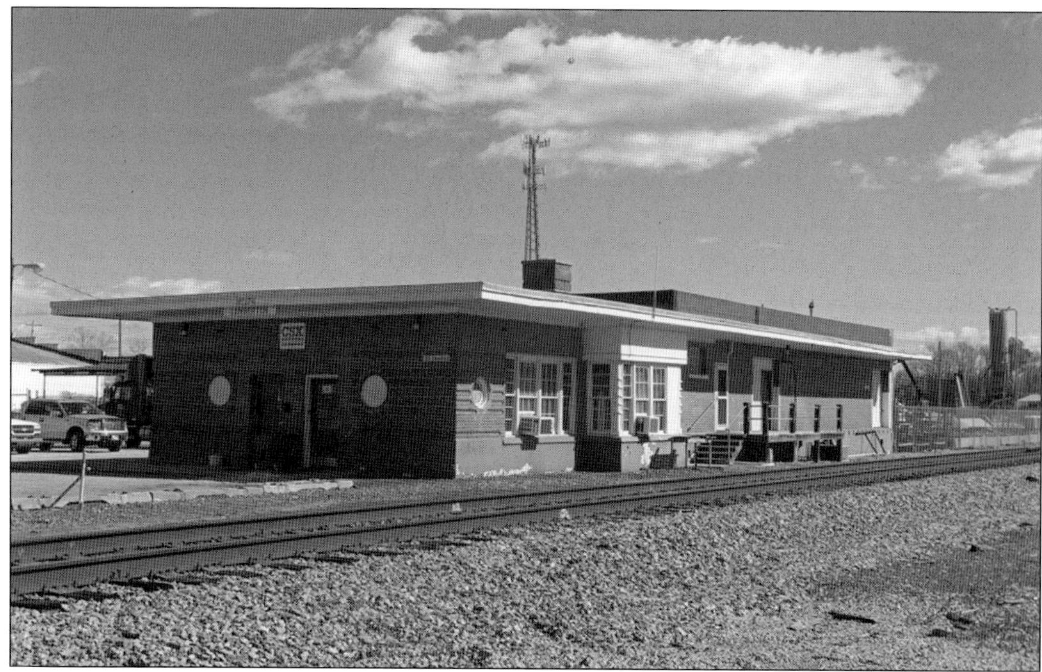

Lumberton dates back to 1787 and is the county seat of Robeson County. The depot dates to the 1950s and shows the importance of freight to the area. The depot still had a large open shed for produce and other freight during the 1990s but has since been removed. (Author's collection.)

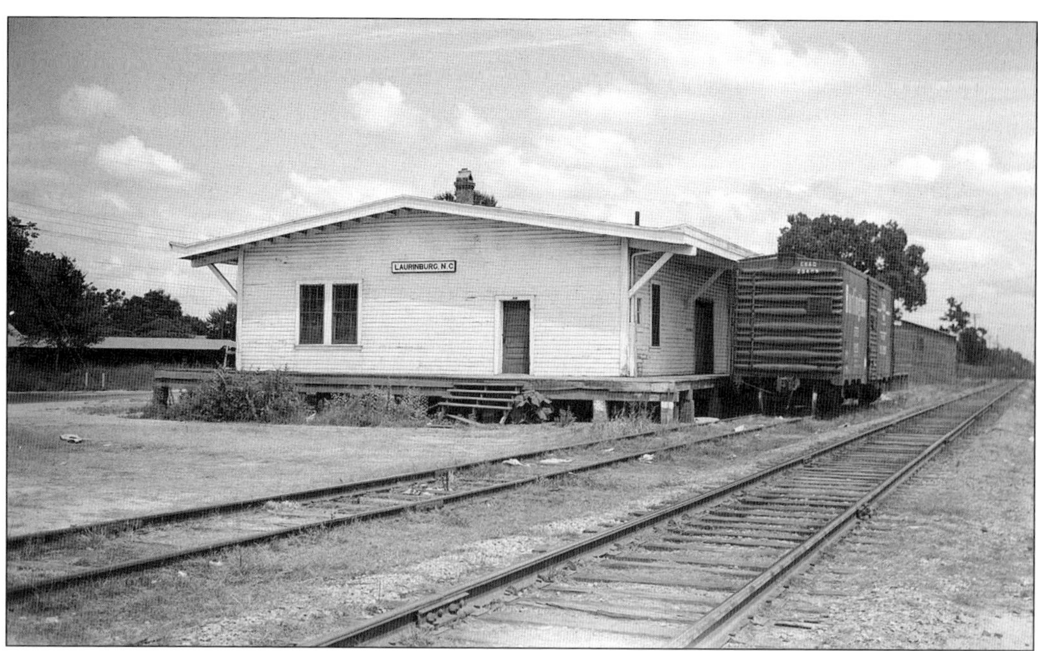

Laurinburg, county seat of Scotland County, was incorporated in 1877. The Seaboard Air Line had one of two depots for the town, with the other used by the Laurinburg & Southern Railroad. Photographed in 1966, this building has since been torn down. (Photograph by Tom King, courtesy of the King-Marsh collection.)

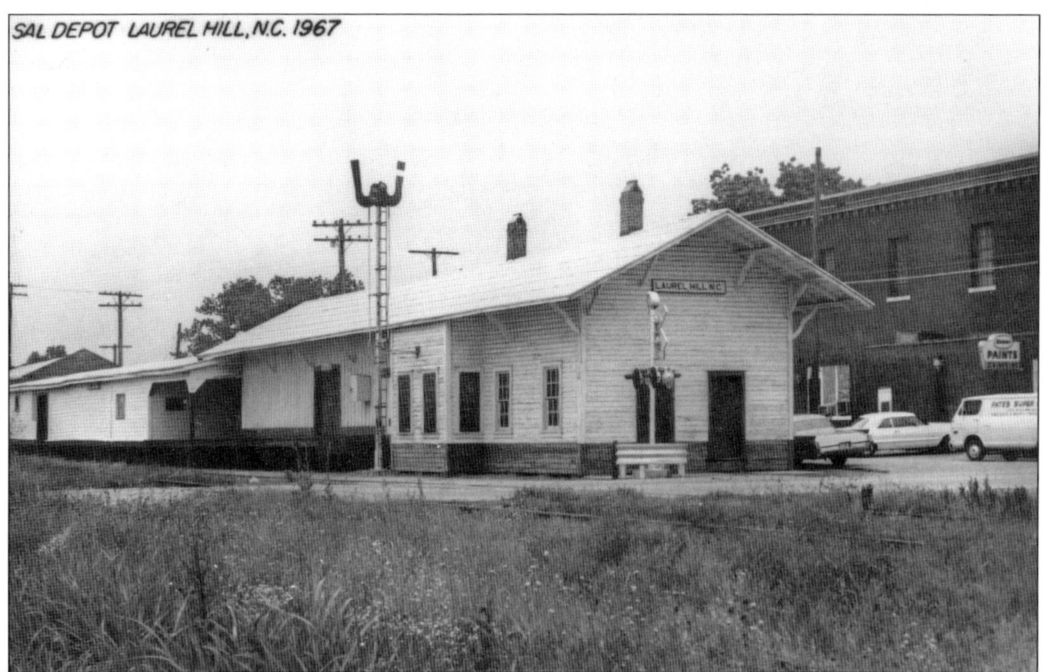

Laurel Hill is an unincorporated community in Scotland County. The depot is no longer standing today. (Courtesy of the Brian Ezzelle collection.)

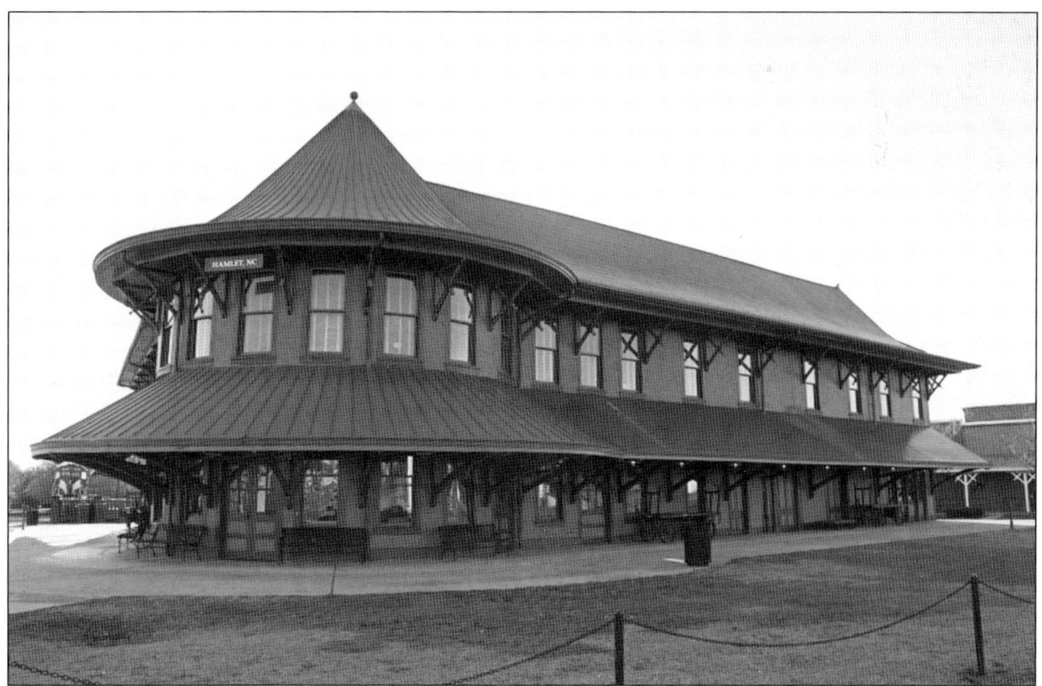

This is a view of the Hamlet depot as it currently looks today. It was moved across the track several years ago and fully restored to its 1920s-era appearance. It still serves and an Amtrak station and houses a local museum. (Author's collection.)

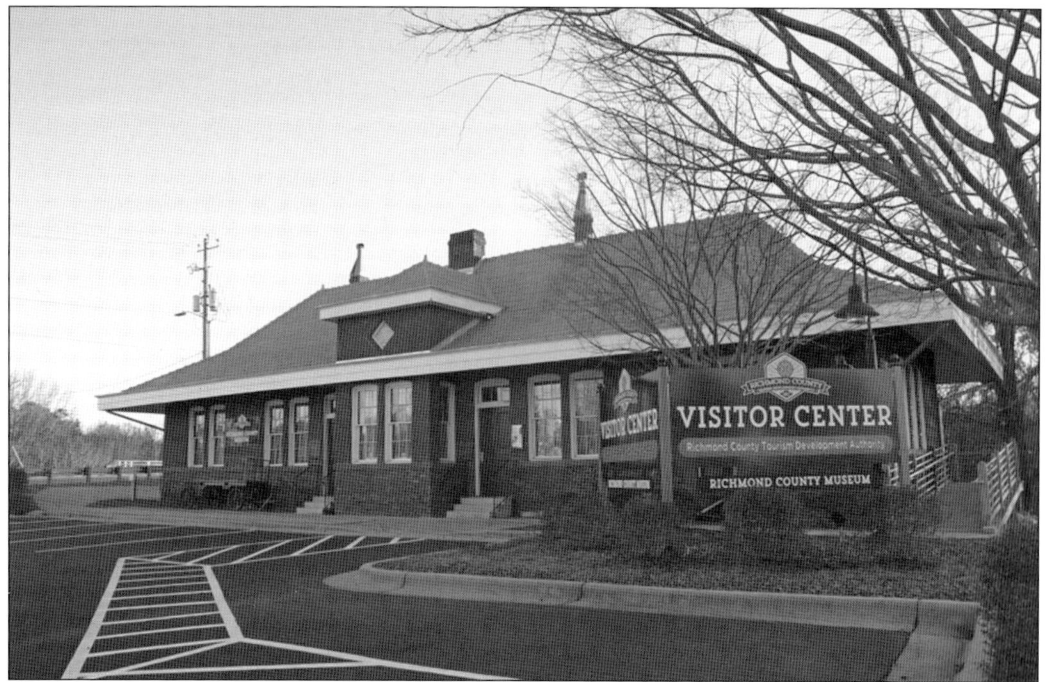

Rockingham is named for Charles Watson-Wentworth, second marque of Rockingham. This town is best known for "the Rock," Rockingham Speedway, used by NASCAR for many years. This depot was moved several years ago to Old Highway 74, and it is used today as a welcome center for the city. (Author's collection.)

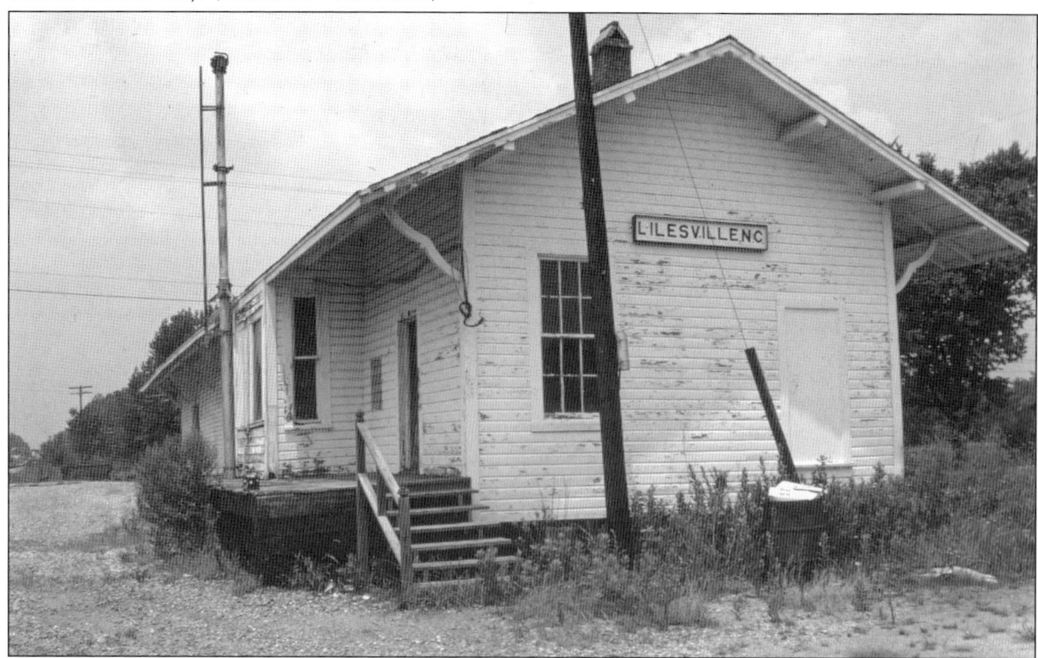

Lilesville has been around since 1827, when a post office was named for a local merchant. The depot was still in decent shape when photographed in 1991, but it was torn down several years later. (Author's collection.)

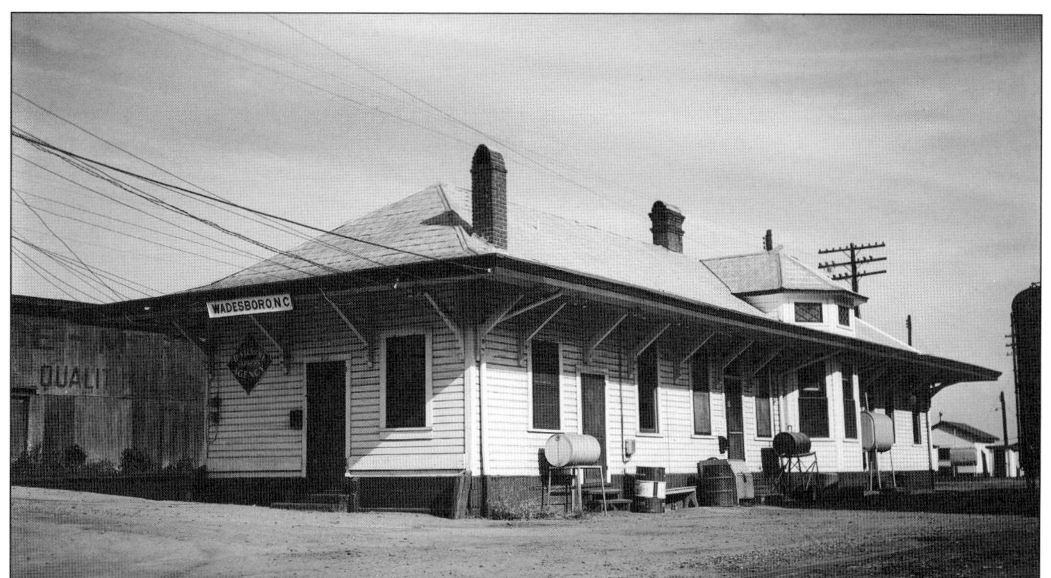

Wadesboro was the junction of three railroads: Seaboard Air Line, Atlantic Coast Line and the Winston-Salem Southbound Railway. The depot was preserved and moved to Blewett Falls Lake but later burned to the ground. (Photograph by Tom King, courtesy of the King-Marsh collection.)

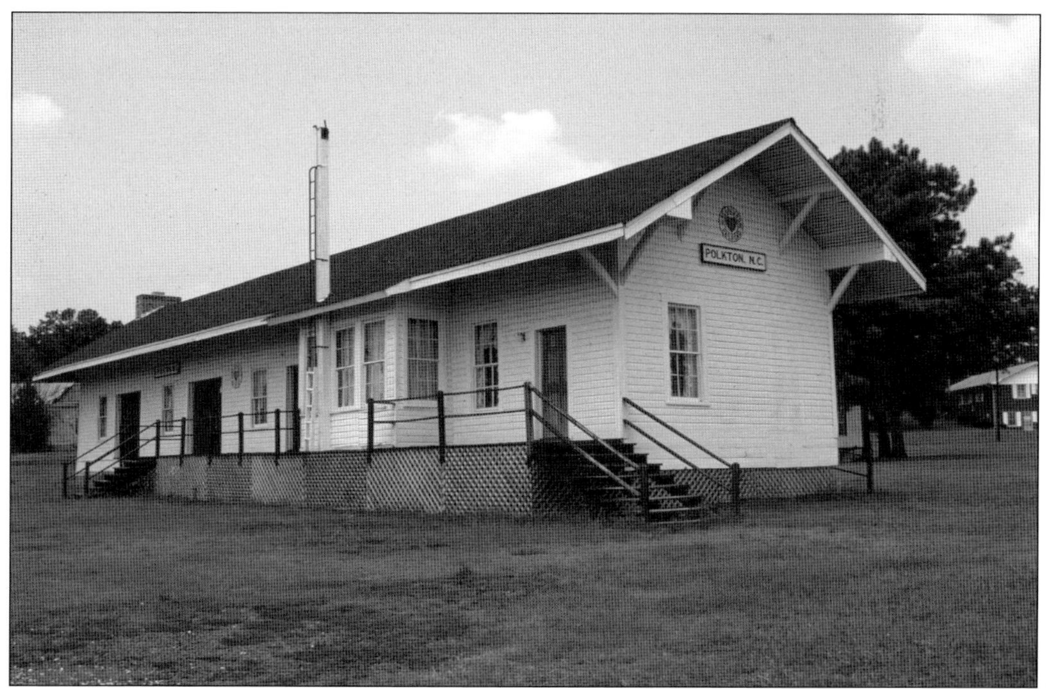

Polkton was founded in 1875 and named for Leonidas Lafayette Polk. The depot, similar in design to Lilesville, was moved and preserved by the town in the 1980s. (Author's collection.)

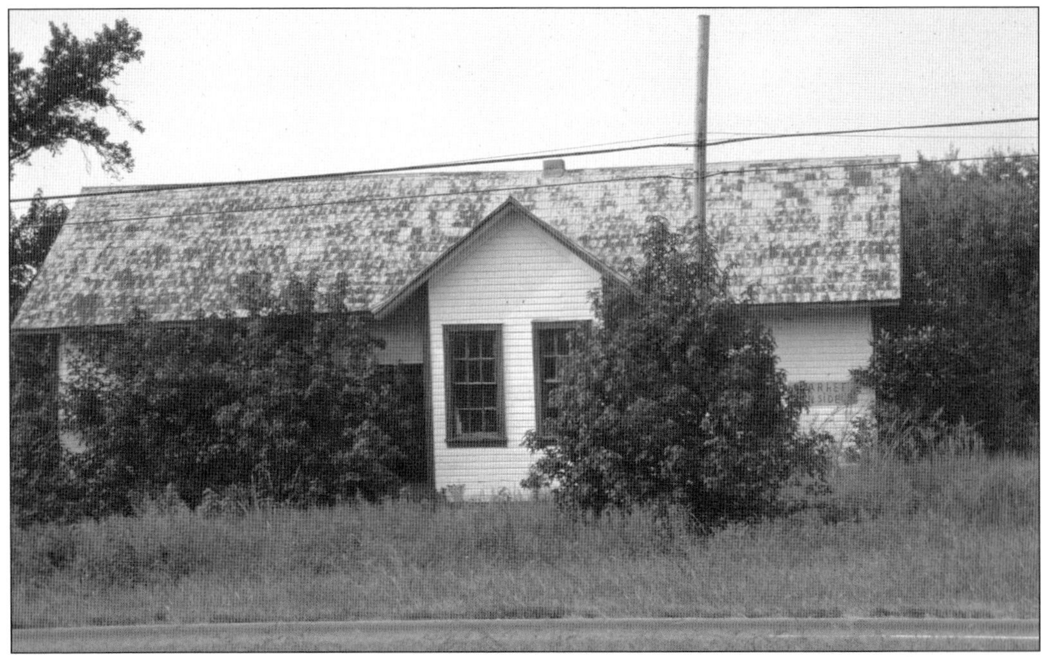

The Peachland depot is seen here as it looked alongside Highway 74 in 1991. The building was apparently torn down before the end of the decade. (Author's collection.)

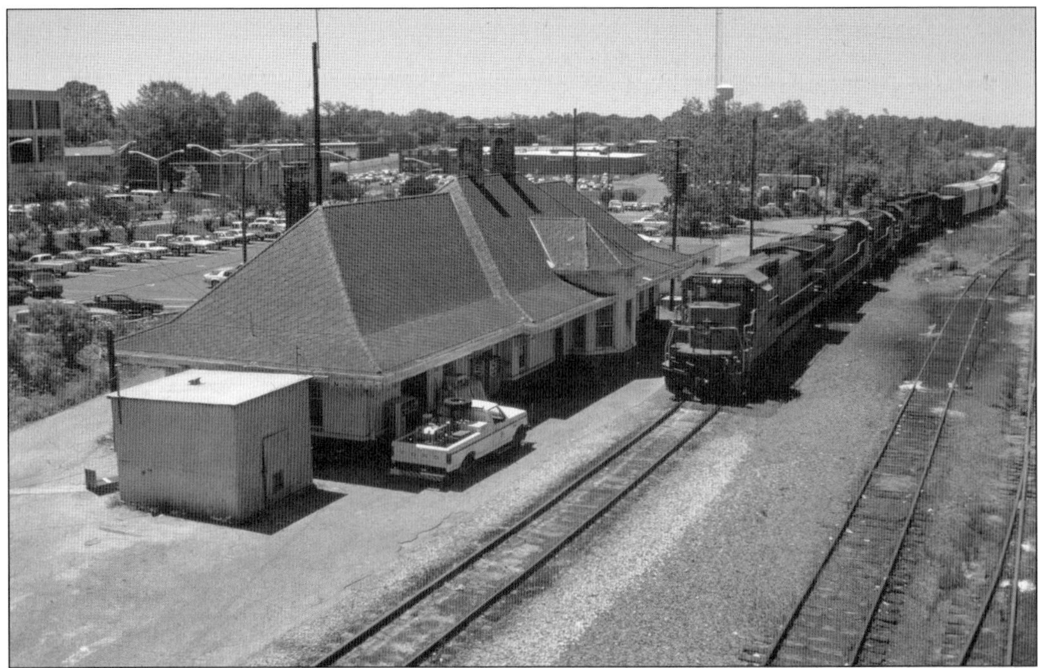

Monroe is the junction of the Carolina Central Railway line to Rutherfordton and the main line toward Atlanta. The town was incorporated in 1843 and named for James Monroe. The depot, dating from the early 1910s, is still used by CSX today for crews working out of the local yard. (Author's collection.)

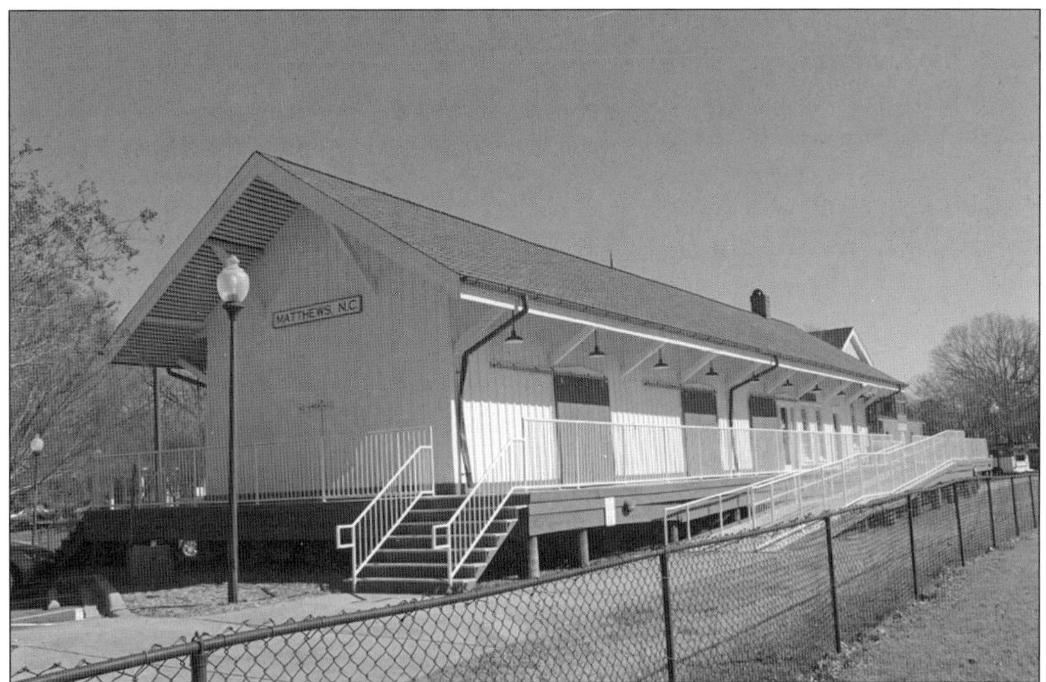

This is a current view of the Matthews depot, preserved for community use. Originally known as Fullwood, the name was changed by the railroad, which named the station after Edward Watson Matthews. (Author's collection.)

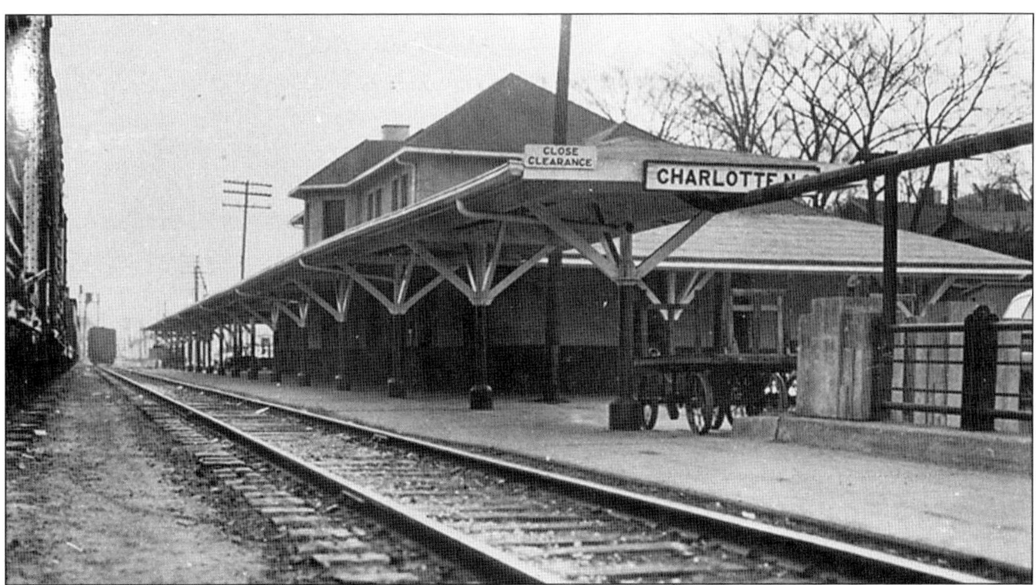

Charlotte became the largest city along the rail line, in part due to the banking center that emerged in the 19th century. Charlotte is named for Charlotte of Mecklenburg-Strelitz and was incorporated in 1768. The depot opened on June 16, 1896, and also contained offices for the railroad. It has been preserved and serves the residents of Mecklenburg County today. (Courtesy of the Robinson-Spangler Carolina Room, Charlotte Mecklenburg Library.)

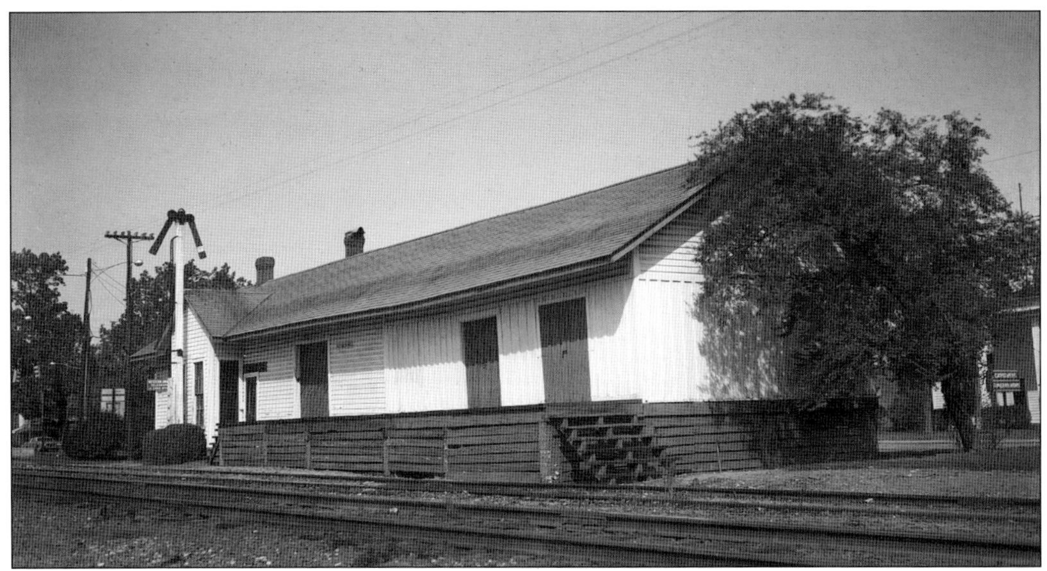

Stanley was originally known as Brevard's Station on the railroad but as Stanley's Creek Community to the locals. The depot no longer stands, but it was still looking sharp on October 29, 1966. (Photograph by Tom King, courtesy of the King-Marsh collection.)

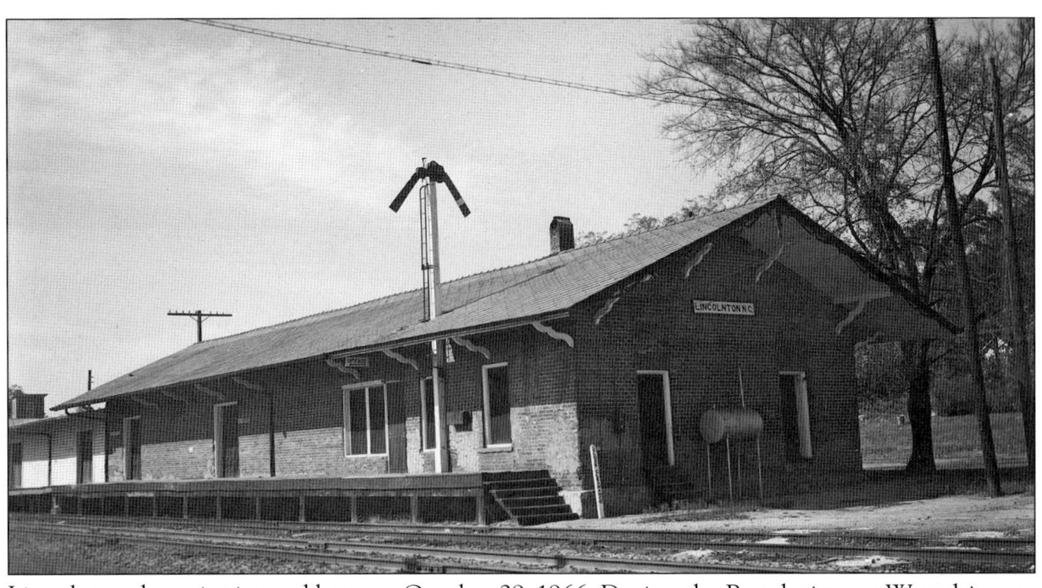

Lincolnton depot is pictured here on October 29, 1966. During the Revolutionary War, this area was the site for the Battle of Ramsour's Mill in June 1780. The depot no longer stands today. (Photograph by Tom King, courtesy of the King-Marsh collection.)

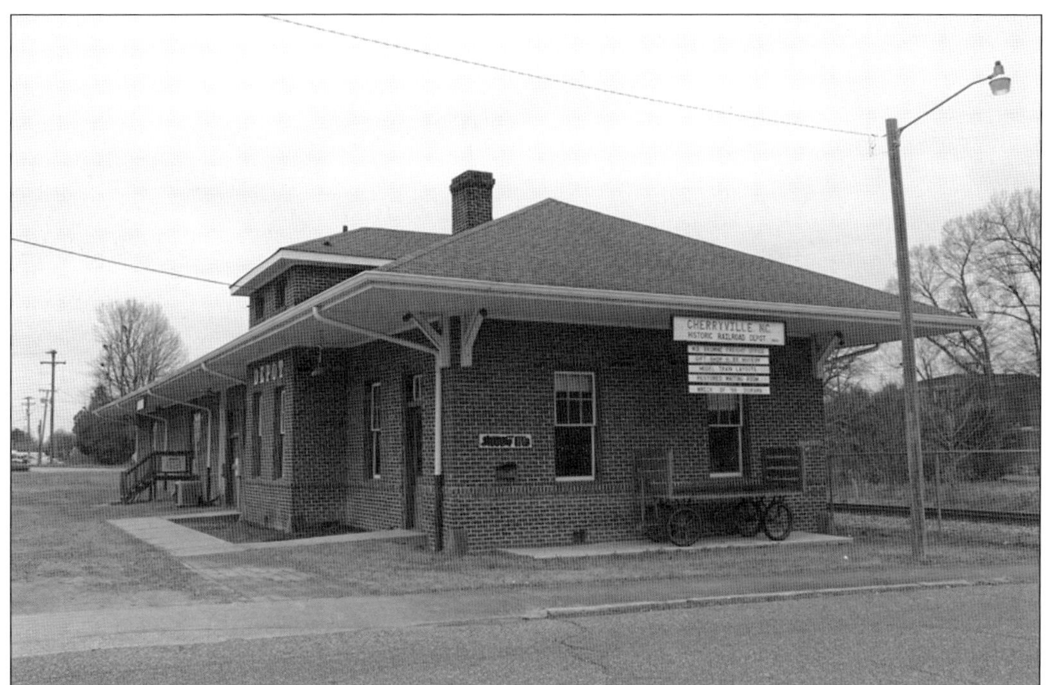

Cherryville was originally known as White Pine when the railroad was built through the area in 1862. This was the western terminus of the railroad until after the Civil War. The name was later changed to Cherryville due to a large grove of cherry trees. The depot has been restored and contains a local museum. (Author's collection.)

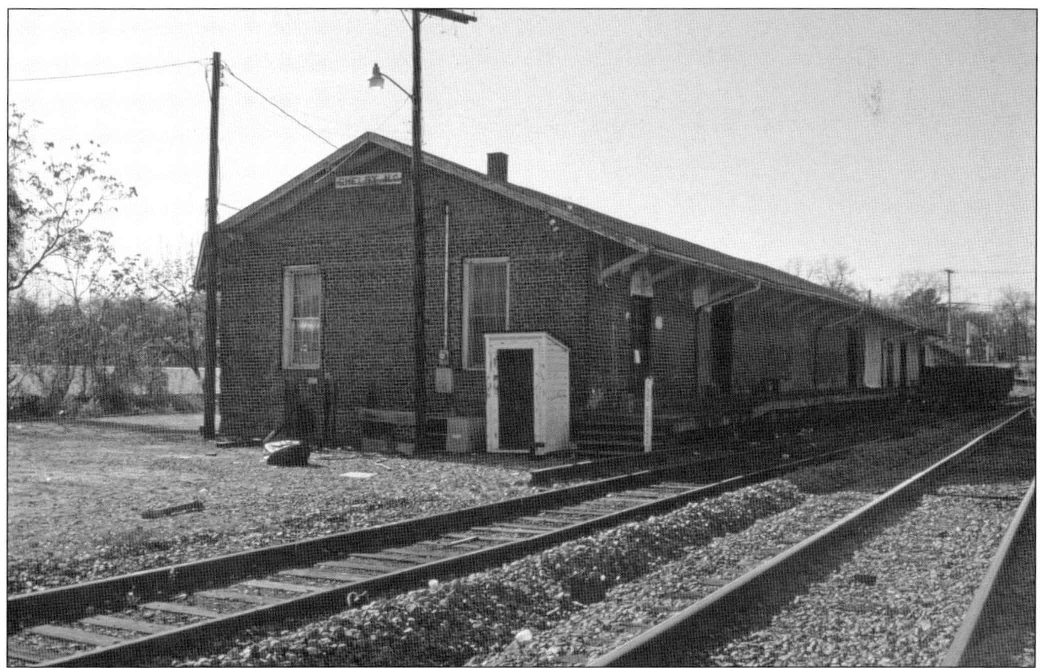

Shelby is the county seat of Cleveland County. The depot still stands today, but it is no longer used by the railroad. (Author's collection.)

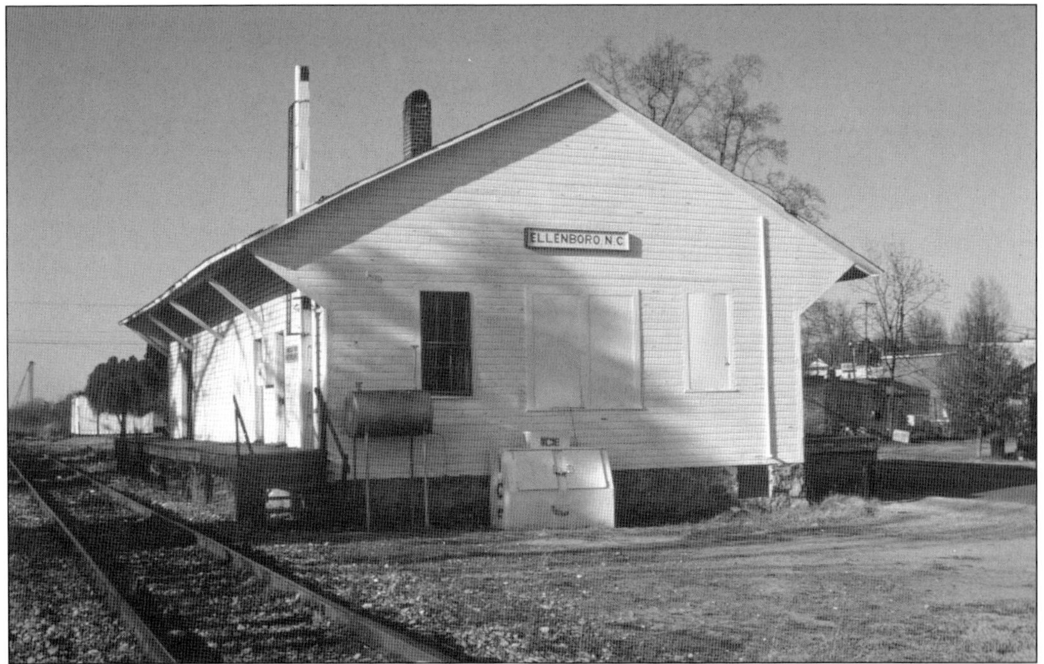

Ellenboro was named for Ellen, daughter of railroad engineer John Robinson, who was dying of fever. This community is the highest point on the line to Rutherfordton and was organized in 1884. A branch line went south from here to Caroleen and connected with the Cliffside Railroad. (Author's collection.)

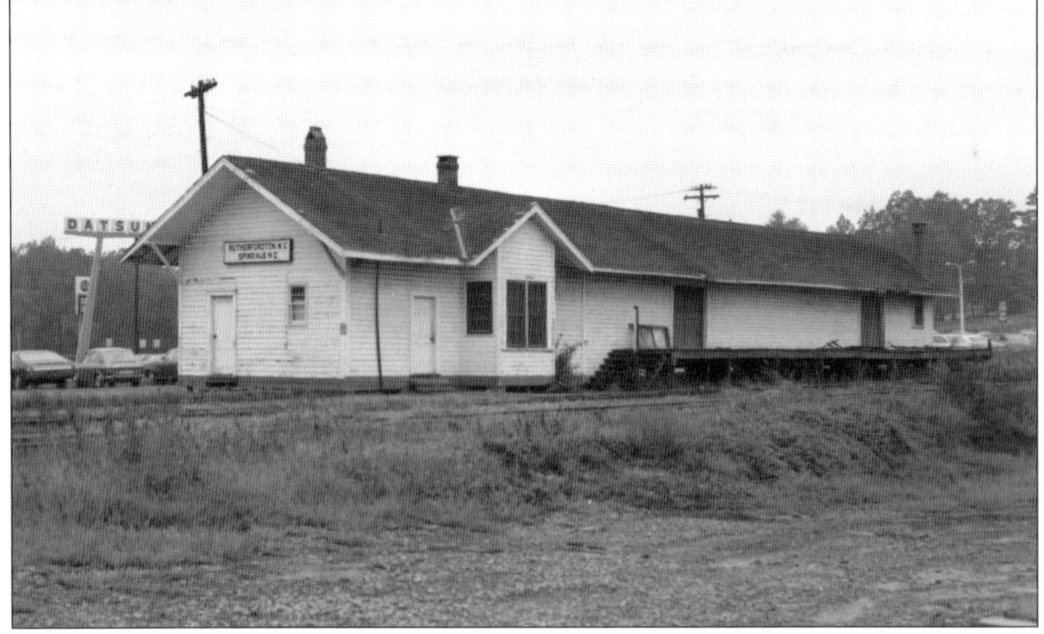

The railroad reached Rutherfordton in 1887, about 100 years after the town was formally chartered as the county seat of Rutherford County. During the 1830s and 1840s, Christopher Bechtler minted gold coins from the mines of North Carolina inside his home, situated three miles from town. The depot no longer stands today. (Courtesy of the Larry Goolsby collection.)

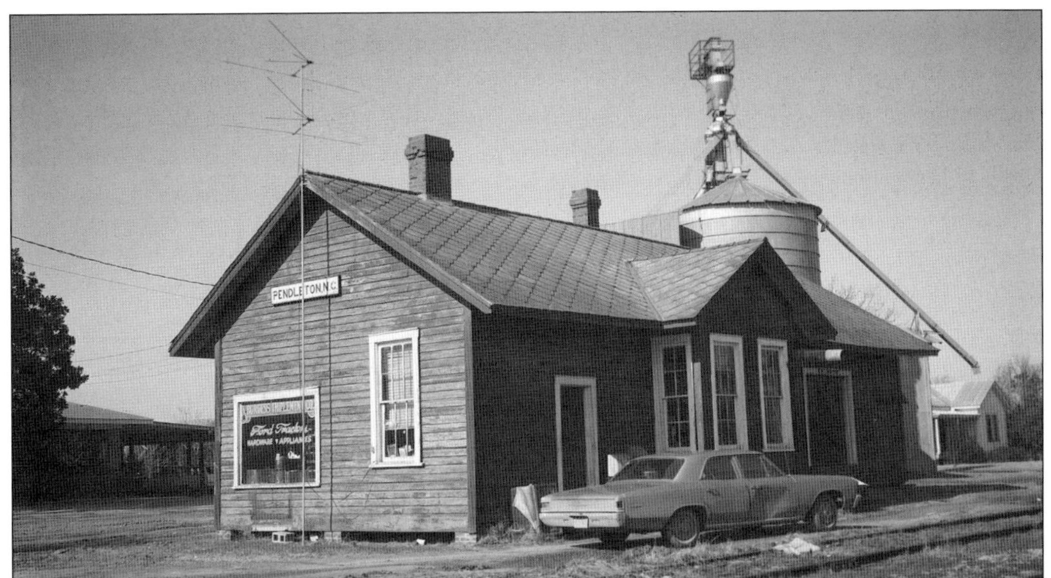

Pendleton is located on the Seaboard Air Line from Boykins, Virginia, to Lewiston, North Carolina. This depot has been preserved by a local resident. (Photograph by Tom King, courtesy of the King-Marsh collection.)

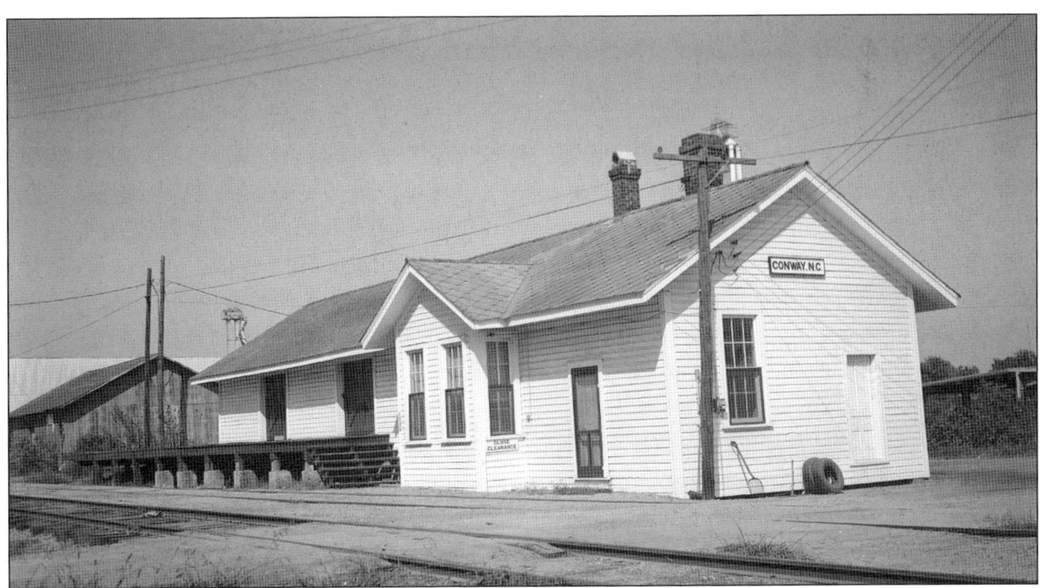

Conway, incorporated in 1913, was originally known as Martin Crossroads but changed to Conway when the railroad came through after a relative of a railroad official. The depot, shown on September 16, 1966, no longer stands today. (Photograph by Tom King, courtesy of the King-Marsh collection.)

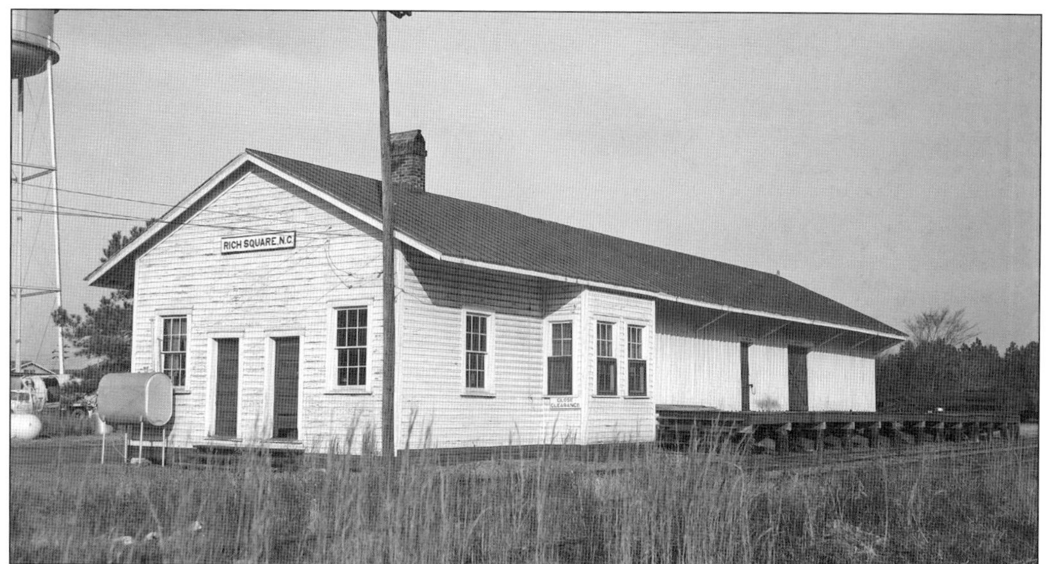

Rich Square depot is pictured on December 8, 1965. The building had both a large waiting room and freight section, denoting the importance of the community. Unfortunately, this depot no longer exists. (Photograph by Tom King, courtesy of the King-Marsh collection.)

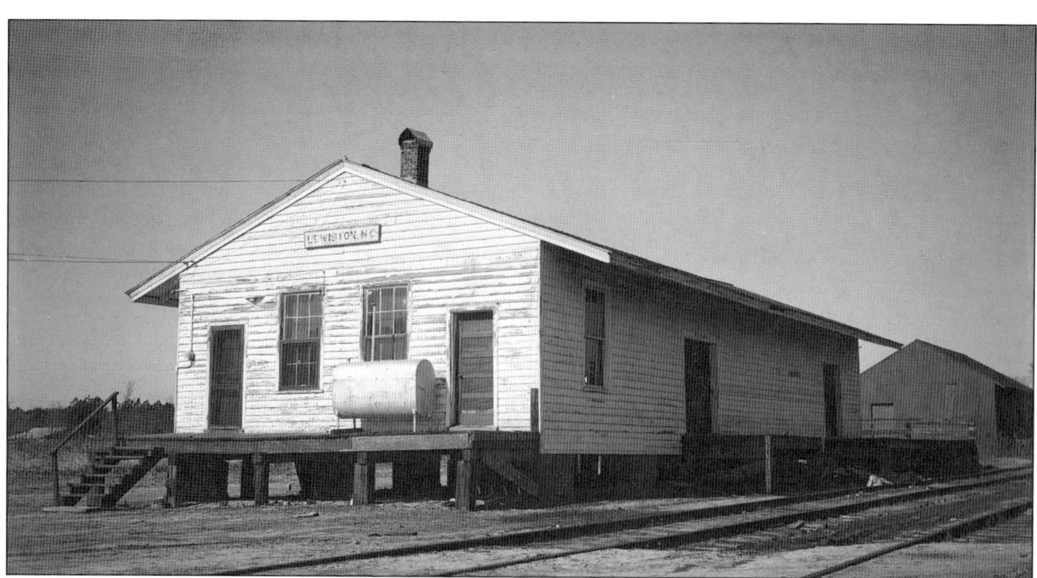

Lewiston depot is seen here on February 3, 1967. The communities of Lewiston and Woodville have combined, and the depot was moved to town property. (Photograph by Tom King, courtesy of the King-Marsh collection.)

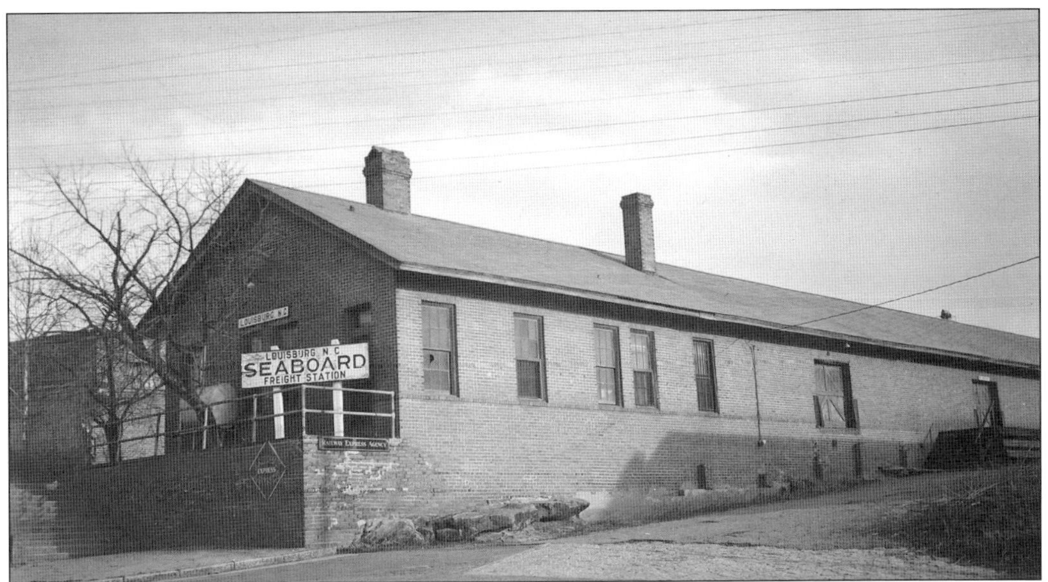

The Louisburg branch operated from Franklinton to Louisburg and was completed in 1885. Part of the depot, shown here in 1967, still stands today but is vacant. Note the Railway Express Agency sign, denoting some shipments were still be made at this late date. (Photograph by Tom King, courtesy of the King-Marsh collection.)

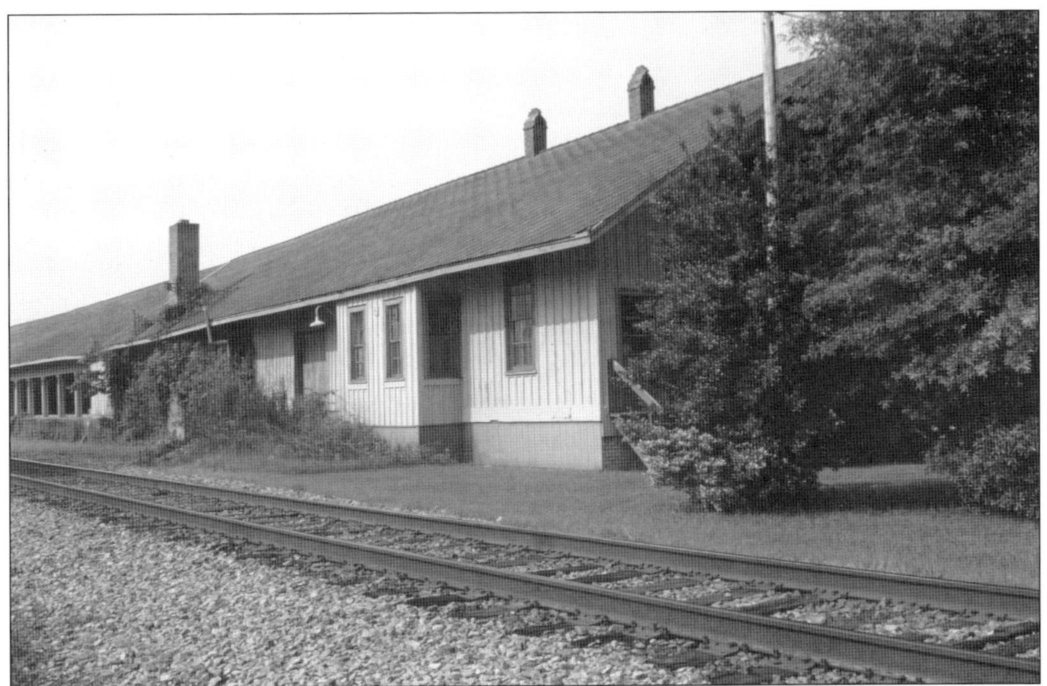

Gibson is located on the line leading south from Hamlet toward Savannah and through Georgetown, South Carolina. This town is located right on the South Carolina line, making it "the crossroads of the Carolinas." The depot still stands today and is used by the town. (Author's collection.)

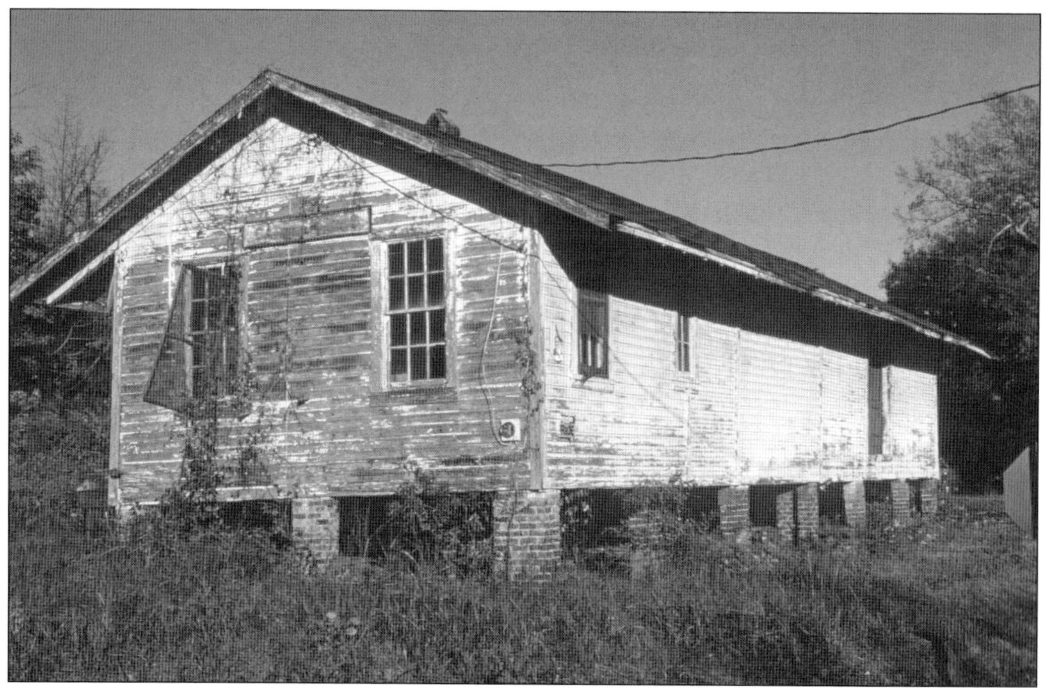

Caroleen is located on the former branch from Ellenboro to a connection with the Cliffside Railroad (now abandoned) at Mill Junction, constructed in 1896. The depot has been preserved and restored back to its former glory. (Author's collection.)

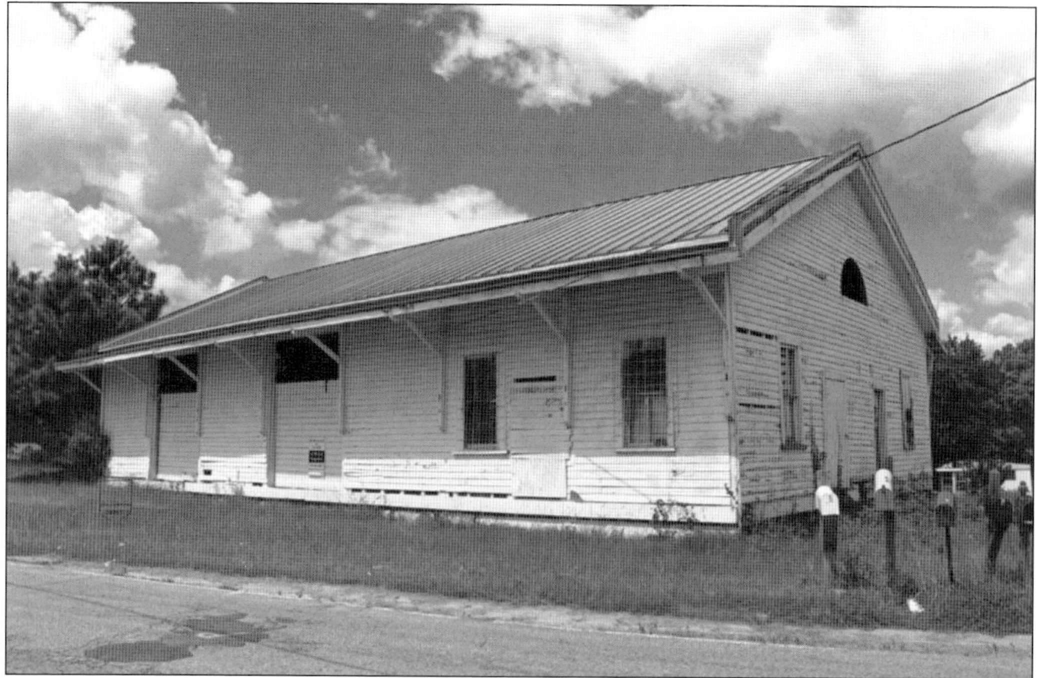

Creedmoor is located on the Durham and Northern Railroad branch, which was completed in 1889. The depot, built during the 1910s, remains today beside the abandoned roadbed. (Author's collection.)

Three

Norfolk and Southern Railway

The Norfolk Southern Railway has an interesting history of consolidating rail lines and periods of receiverships before the 1940s. The first section of this railroad to be constructed was the Elizabeth City & Norfolk Railroad in 1881. Further construction continued the line south to Belhaven by 1892. During the early 1900s, the railroad, under the subsidiary Raleigh & Pamlico Sound, built a line westward toward Raleigh. By 1910, the Norfolk Southern (NS) Railroad, as it was known, had two routes into Virginia, a main line from Norfolk to Raleigh, and a controlling interest in the Atlantic & North Carolina (A&NC) Railroad from Goldsboro to Morehead City. The NS also operated several branch lines to coastal communities. They were not finished with western expansion, though, and finally reached Charlotte by January 1914. They also acquired the Aberdeen & Asheboro Railroad, which connected with their main line at Star.

Due to financial hardships, the railroad went into several receiverships. They went from the Norfolk Southern Railroad in 1883 to the Norfolk & Southern Railway in 1906 and back to the Norfolk Southern Railroad in 1910. They remained under that name until 1942, when the final receivership caused the name to change to Norfolk Southern Railway, which lasted until 1974, when the railroad was merged with the Southern Railway.

The railroad showed 75 station stops between Charlotte and Norfolk by the 1910s and another 77 stations on branch routes, not counting the line from Goldsboro to Morehead City. Through the years, its passenger service was reduced to the main line between Charlotte and Norfolk, which ended on October 31, 1948, but the final runs actually took place on December 12, 1951. Luckily, the railroad chose to keep most of the depots along the line for freight service, allowing many to continue in railroad service through the 1970s.

The main line between Raleigh and Charlotte has been included in this chapter to cover all of the depots used by the Norfolk Southern. The depots are arranged from west to east, since so much of this line was operated in the east. Most depots kept their train order semaphores. The NS ran all trains by scheduled time from their timetable up until the Southern merger in 1974. The A&NC line from Goldsboro to Morehead City will be covered in the following chapter, since it was technically an independent short line.

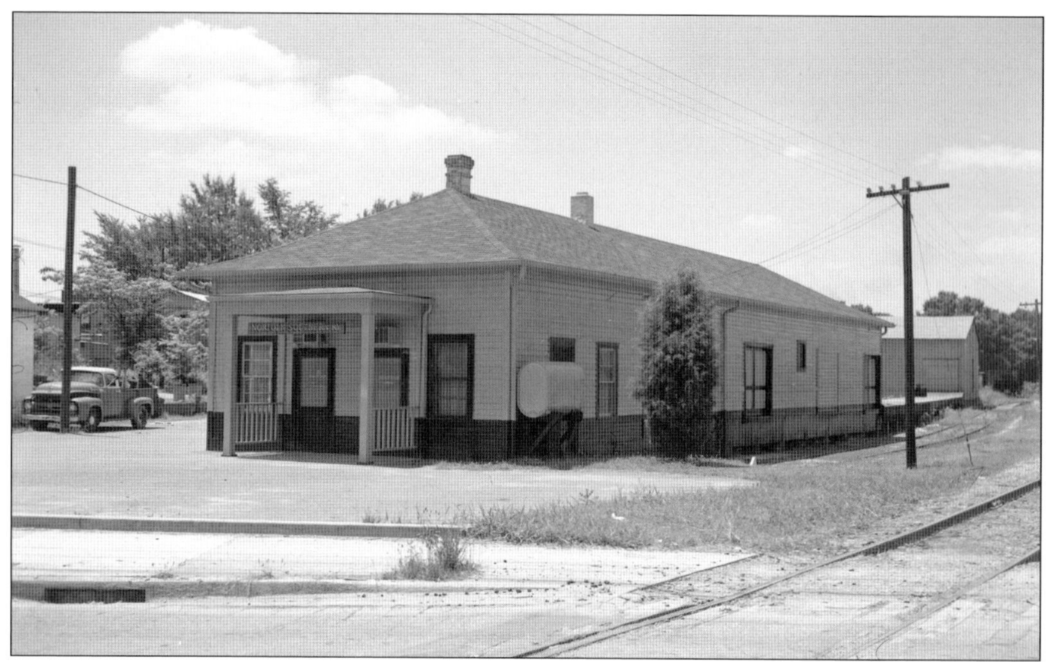

The Norfolk Southern Charlotte yard was located between Brevard Street and the Southern Railway yard in downtown (now Uptown) off Tryon Street. This building, shown on June 15, 1968, housed its local traffic department and freight office. (Photograph by O.W. Kimsey Jr., courtesy of the King-Marsh collection.)

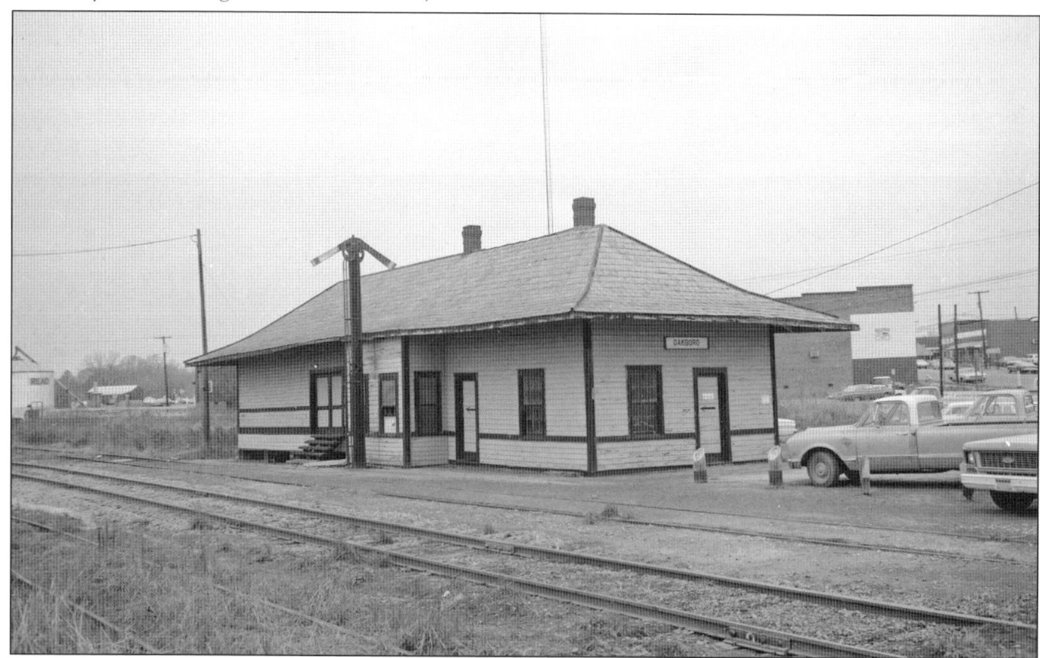

Oakboro was developed because of the railroad, but the location was previously known as Big Lick, due to a large natural salt lick in the area. Originally Furr Town, it changed to Oakboro in 1915. The original depot, viewed in 1973, was later torn down. (Photograph by Tom Sink, courtesy of the King-Marsh collection.)

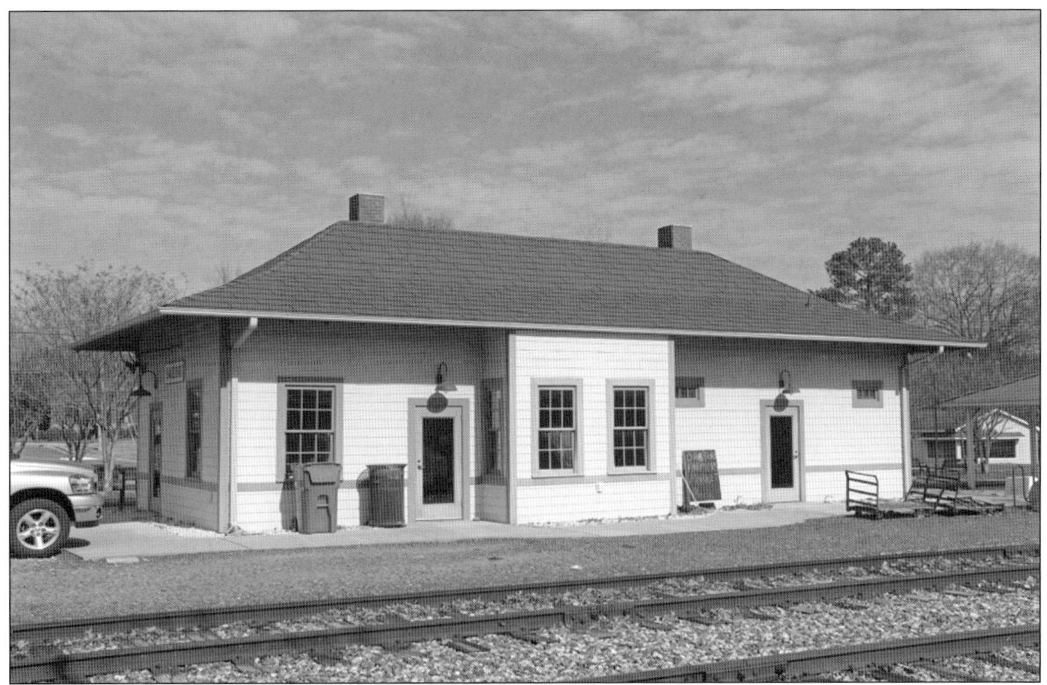

The modern Oakboro depot was constructed in the 2000s on the site of the original depot. It houses a small museum and a covered picnic area for residents and visitors to have a nice lunch. (Author's collection.)

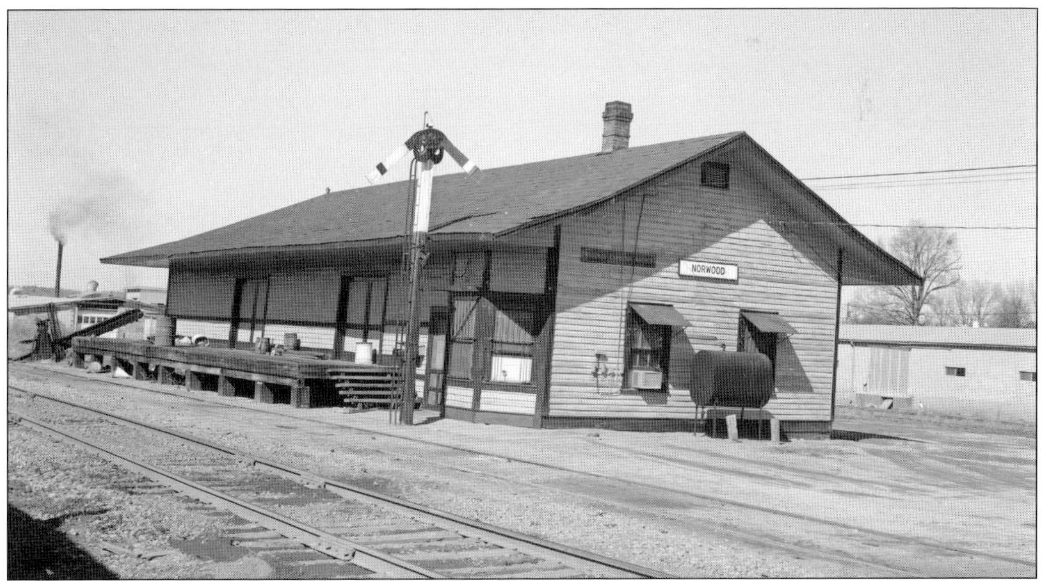

Norwood was a junction town for three different railroads: the Norfolk Southern, the Southern Railway, and the Winston-Salem Southbound. Each railroad constructed its depot, of which none still exists today. Incorporated in 1891, Norwood grew into an important agricultural and trade center by the early 20th century. (Photograph by C.K. Marsh, courtesy of the King-Marsh collection.)

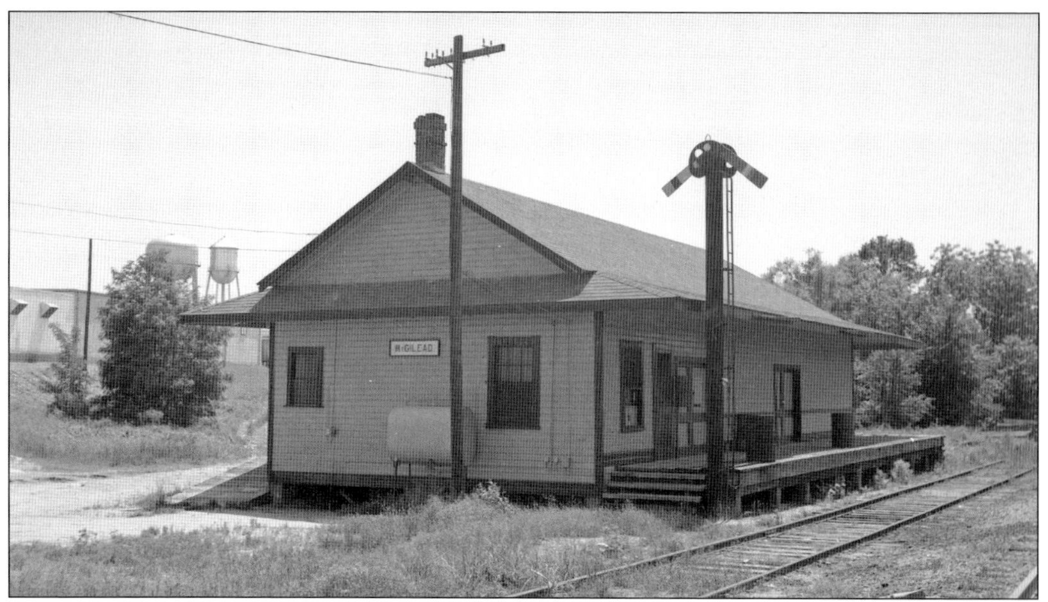

Mt. Gilead, a small town in Montgomery County, was incorporated in 1899. The nearby area houses Native American burial mounds, interpreted at Town Creek Indian Mound. (Photograph by C.K. Marsh, courtesy of the King-Marsh collection.)

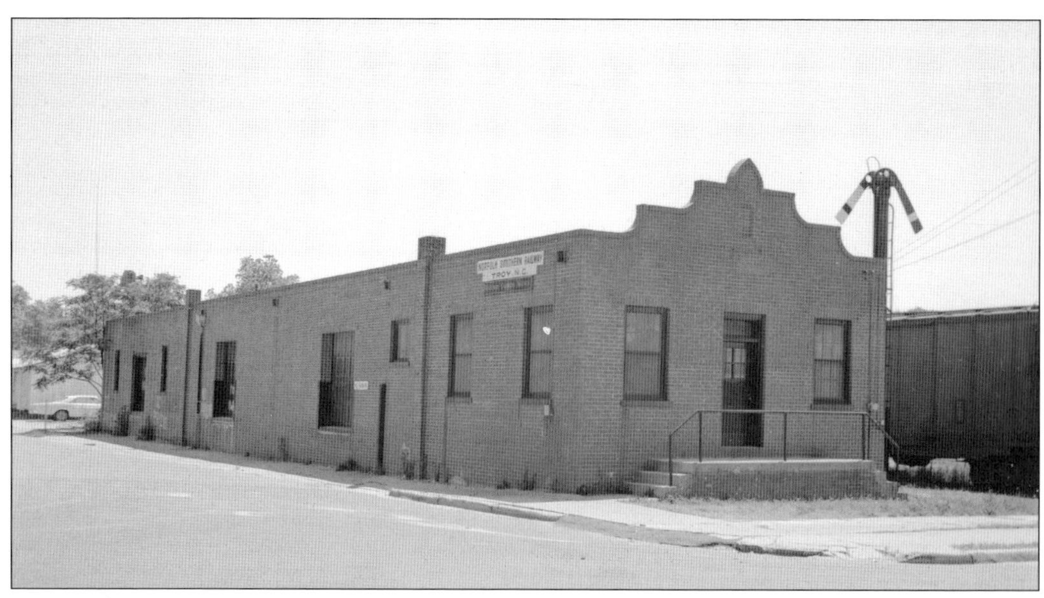

Troy is the county seat of Montgomery County. The depot was somewhat nontraditional for Norfolk Southern, being made of brick rather than wood. Unfortunately, this building no longer stands today. (Photograph by C.K. Marsh, courtesy of the King-Marsh collection.)

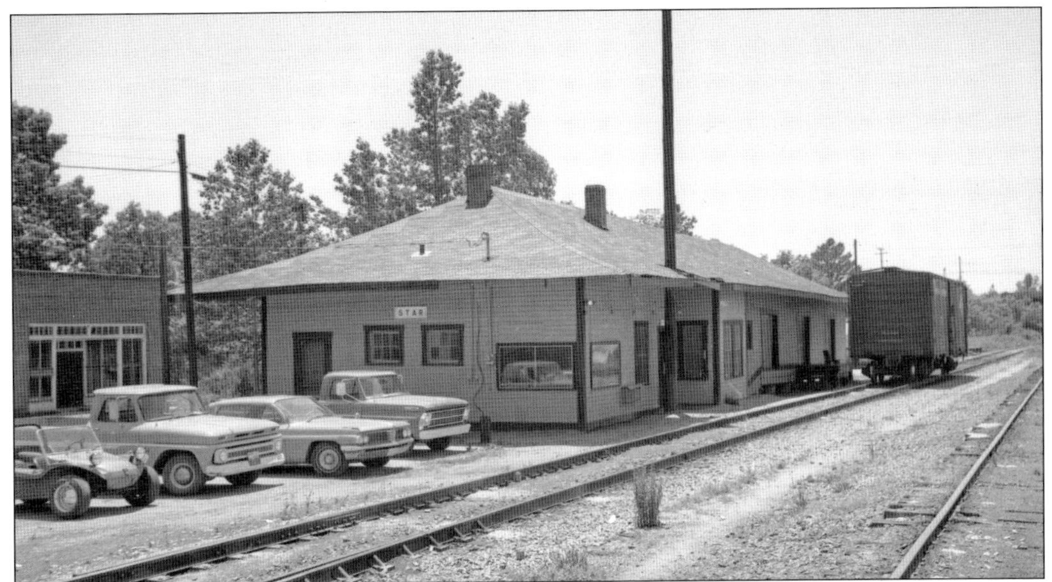

Star was the connection between the Norfolk Southern line to Charlotte and the Aberdeen & Asheboro Railroad, which it controlled. The small yard offered space for interchange and basing locomotives for local service. Seen here in 1971, the depot and yard still remain today, used by the Aberdeen, Carolina & Western Railway. (Photograph by C.K. Marsh, courtesy of the King-Marsh collection.)

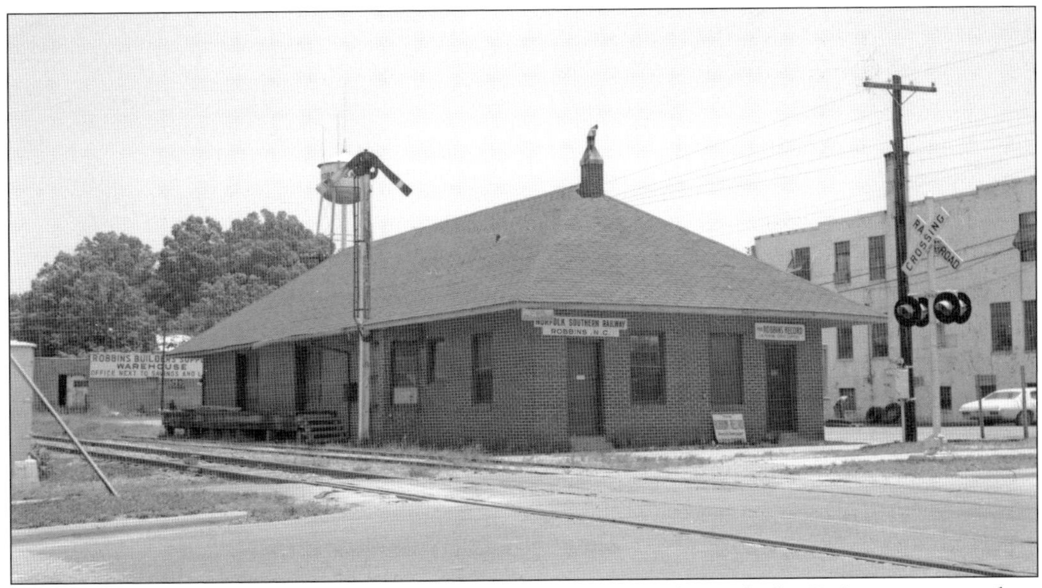

Robbins was incorporated as Elise in 1900, named for the daughter of John B. Lenning, president of the Durham & Charlotte Railroad. The town changed its name to Hemp in 1935 and finally to Robbins, named for Karl Robbins, in 1943. The depot still stands today, looking similar to this image from 1971. (Photograph by C.K. Marsh, courtesy of the King-Marsh collection.)

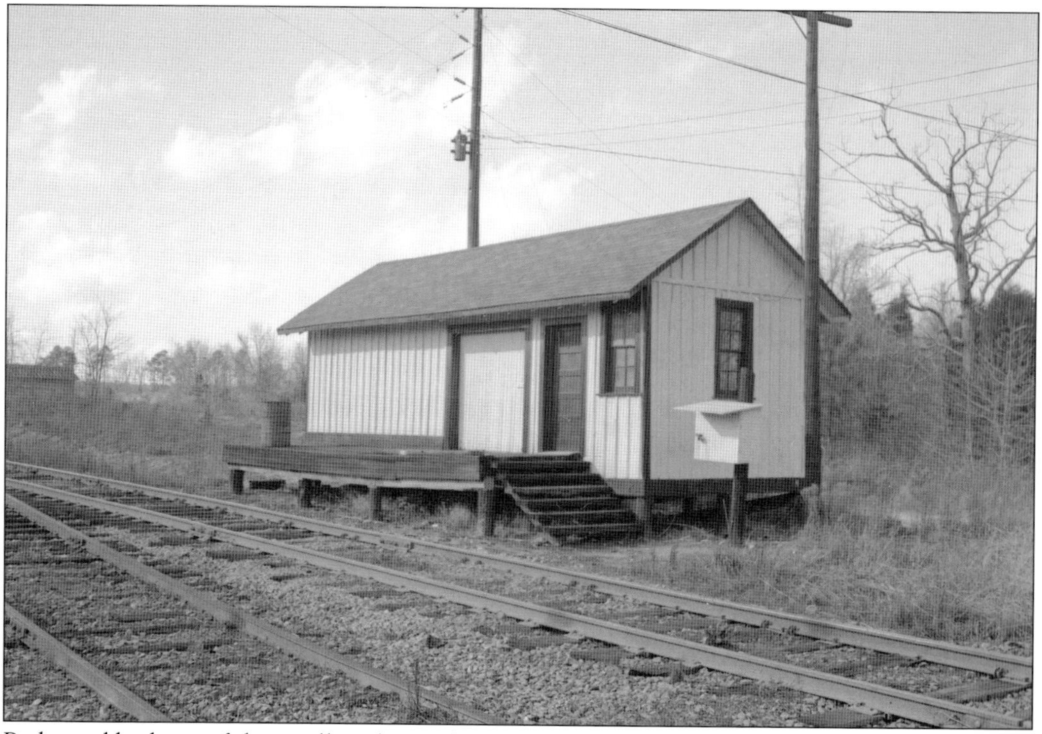

Parkwood had one of the smallest depots (mainly used for freight) on Norfolk Southern. Shown with a fresh coat of paint in 1974, the building no longer stands today. (Photograph by Tom Sink, courtesy of the King-Marsh collection.)

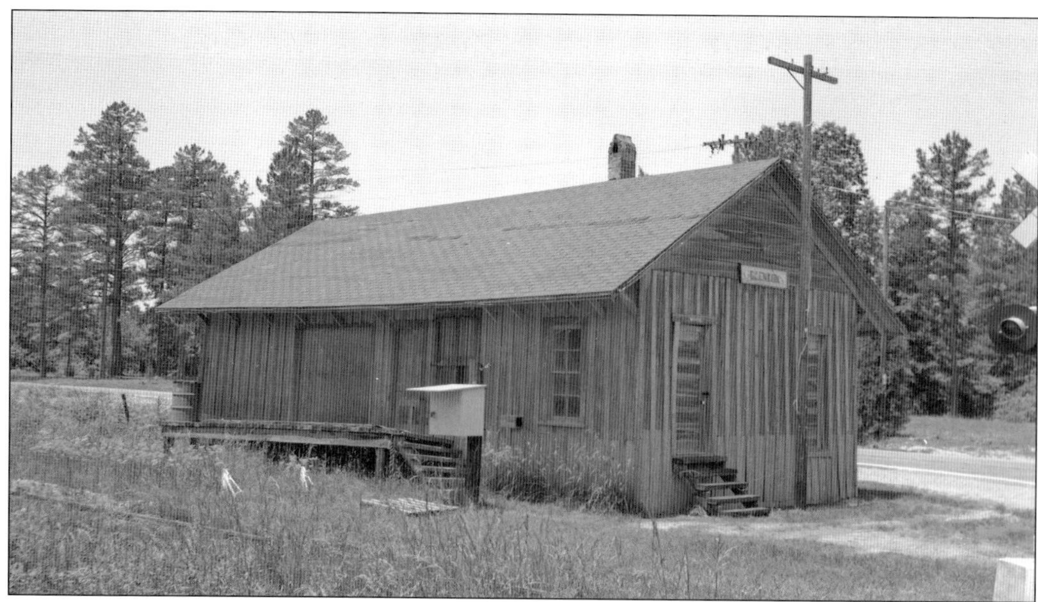

Glendon was named for E.F. Glenn, a local landowner. Photographed in 1971, this depot no longer stands today. (Photograph by C.K. Marsh, courtesy of the King-Marsh collection.)

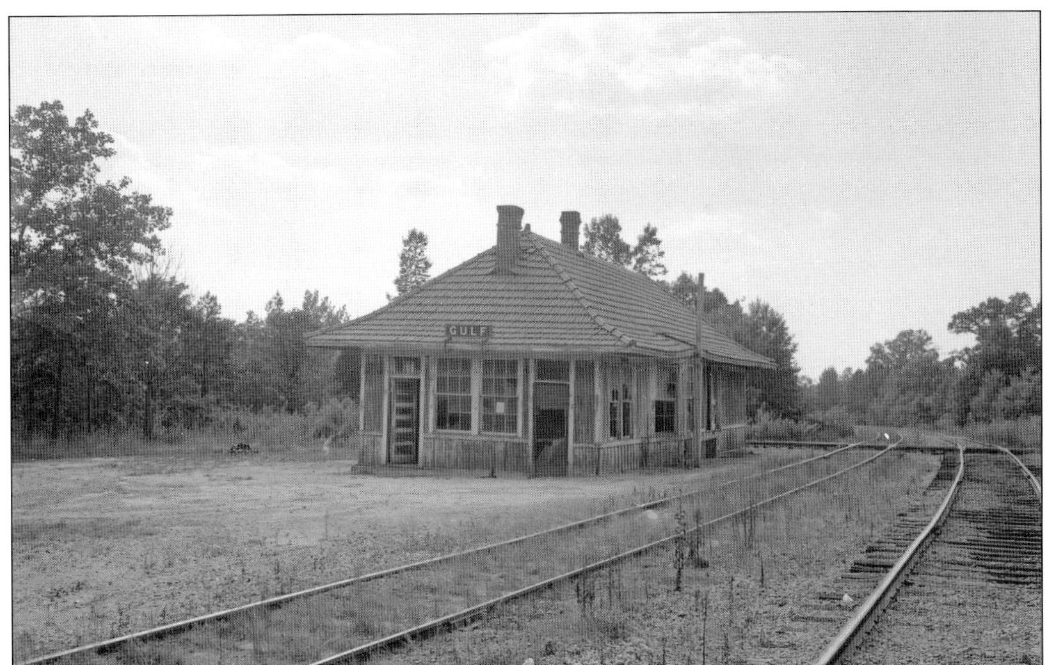

The Gulf depot is looking a little worse for wear in 1974 and probably did not last too many years after this photograph was taken. The Norfolk Southern crossed the tracks of the Atlantic & Yadkin (controlled by Southern Railway since 1899) at Gulf, with this depot serving both railroads. (Photograph by Tom Sink, courtesy of the King-Marsh collection.)

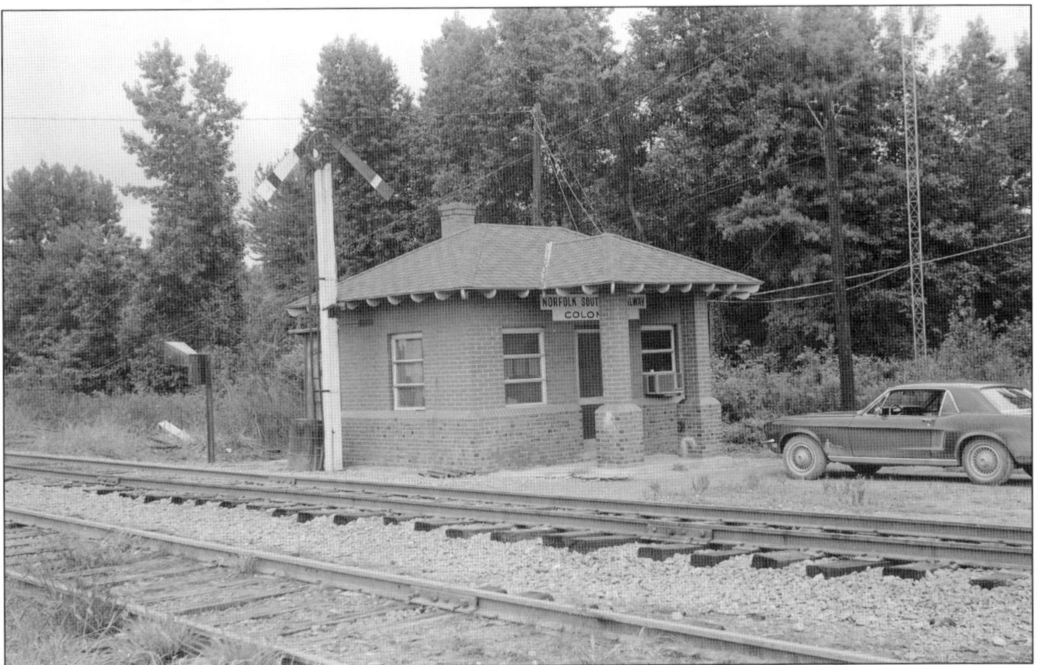

Colon was the location of a brick plant, hence the tiny brick station. An interesting little building that still stands today, it is no longer used by the railroad. (Photograph by Wiley Bryan, courtesy of the King-Marsh collection.)

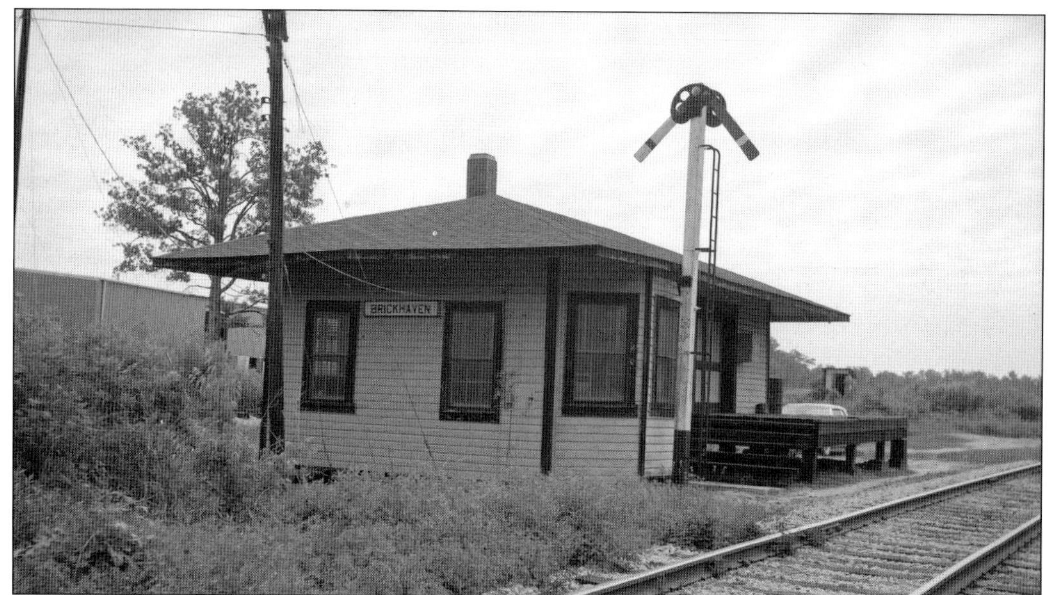

Brickhaven is another community that was tied to brick plants and clay pits. Pictured here in 1971, the depot no longer stands today. (Photograph by C.K. Marsh, courtesy of the King-Marsh collection.)

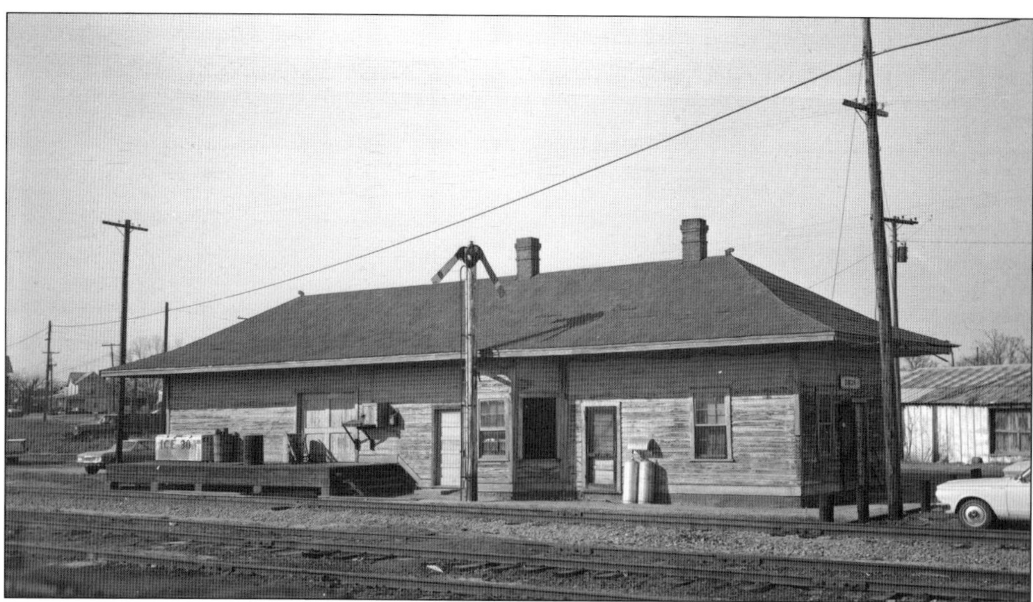

Duncan was the location of the spur to Durham, which had one train each way for many years. The depot now serves as a convenience store off Highway 42. (Photograph by Tom King, courtesy of the King-Marsh collection.)

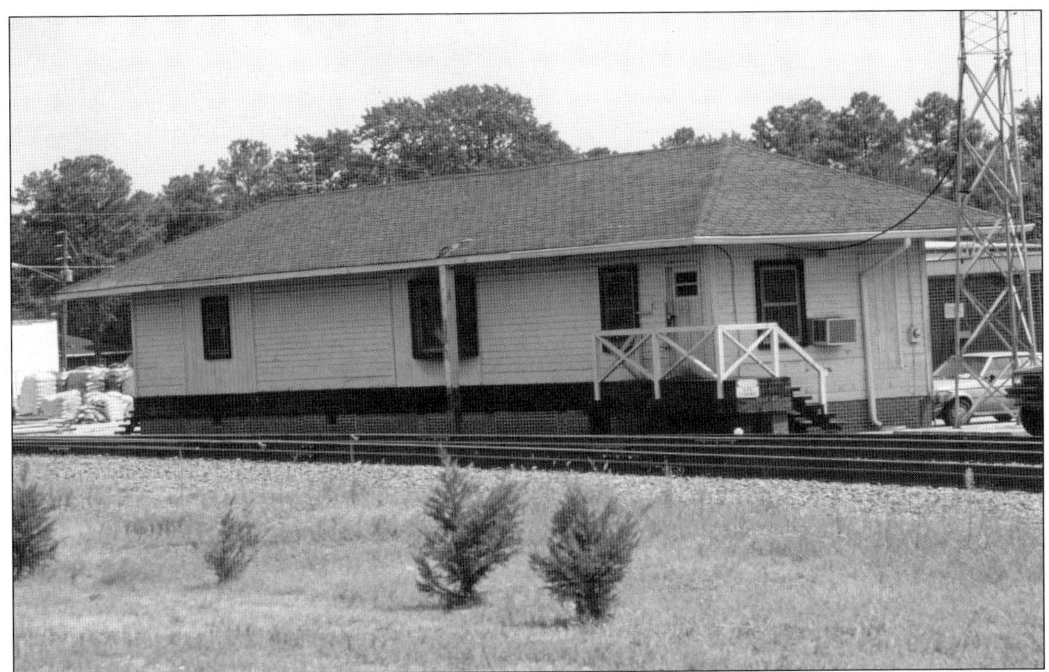

Varina, as it was originally known, was the location of the branch to Fayetteville. Fuquay-Varina was formed from the merger of two separate towns: Fuquay Springs and Varina in 1963. The depot is still used by Norfolk Southern Corporation today. (Author's collection.)

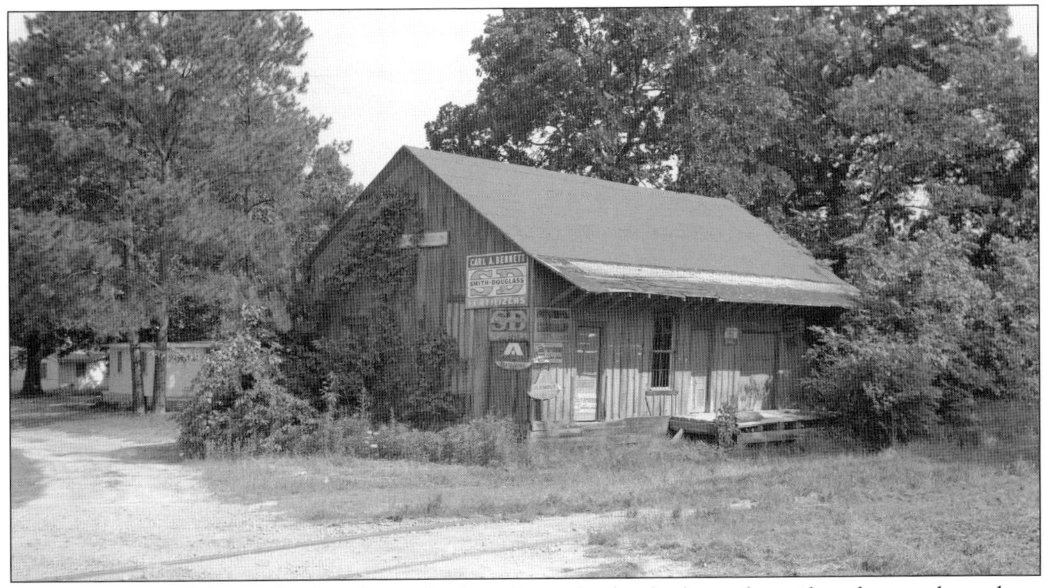

Willow Springs (also spelled without the last s) was located where the railroad turned north to head to Raleigh. The station remained through the 1970s, but obviously under private ownership. (Photograph by C.K. Marsh, courtesy of the King-Marsh collection.)

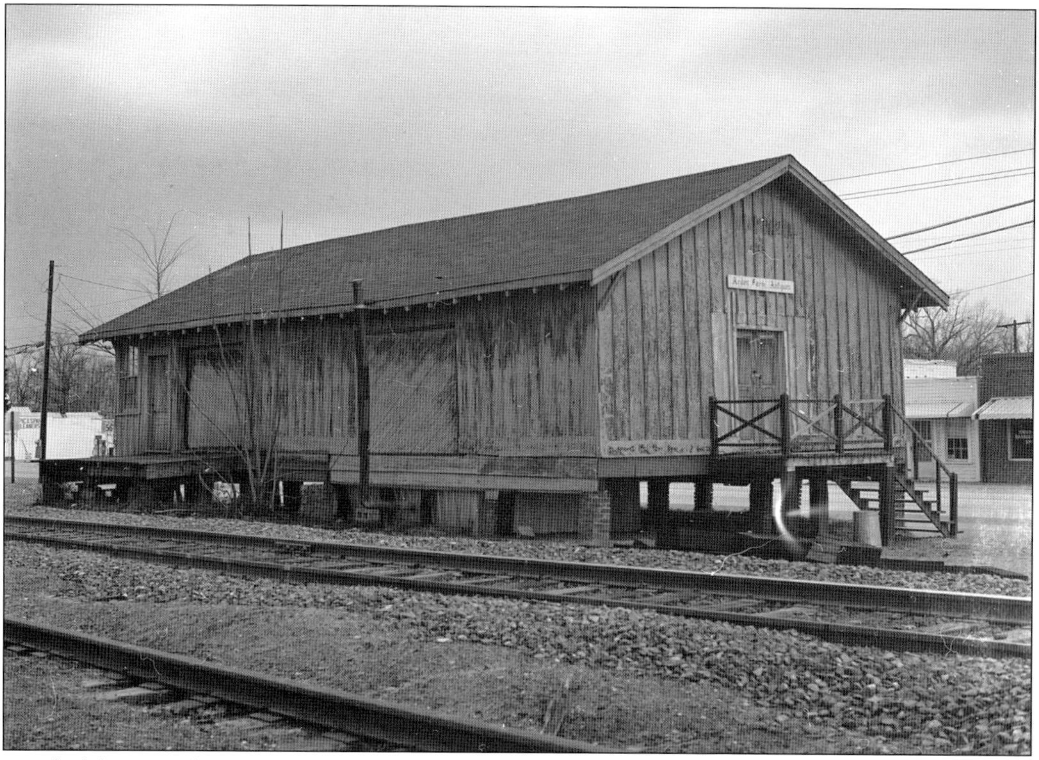

Knightdale, named for Henry Haywood Knight, grew from the construction of the railroad. Although the depot no longer exists, a stationmaster's house still stands along the tracks. (Photograph by Tom King, courtesy of the King-Marsh collection.)

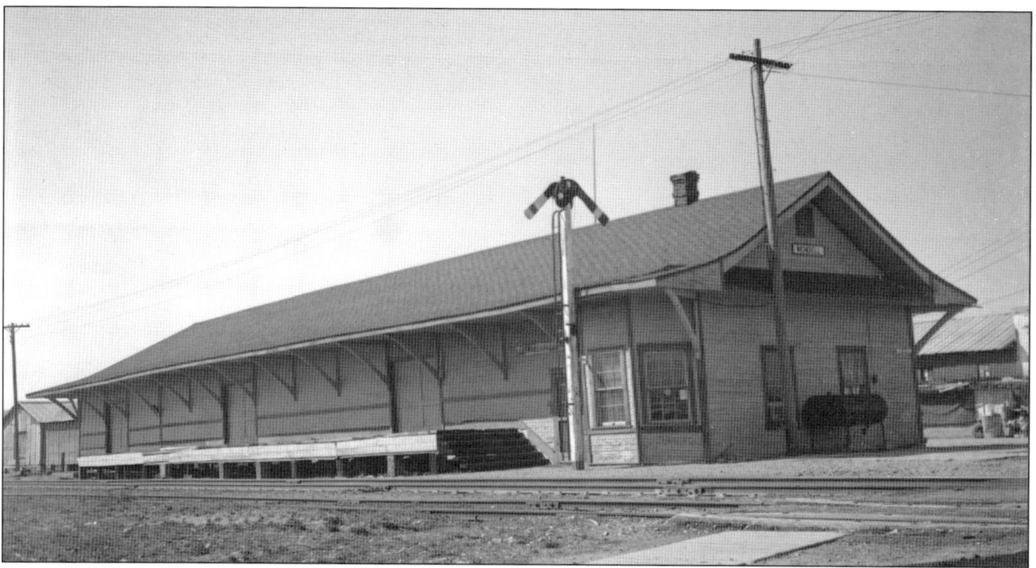

Wendell, named for Oliver Wendell Holmes Jr., was incorporated in 1903, not long before the railroad came through town. The depot was torn down in 1969. (Photograph by Tom King, courtesy of the King-Marsh collection.)

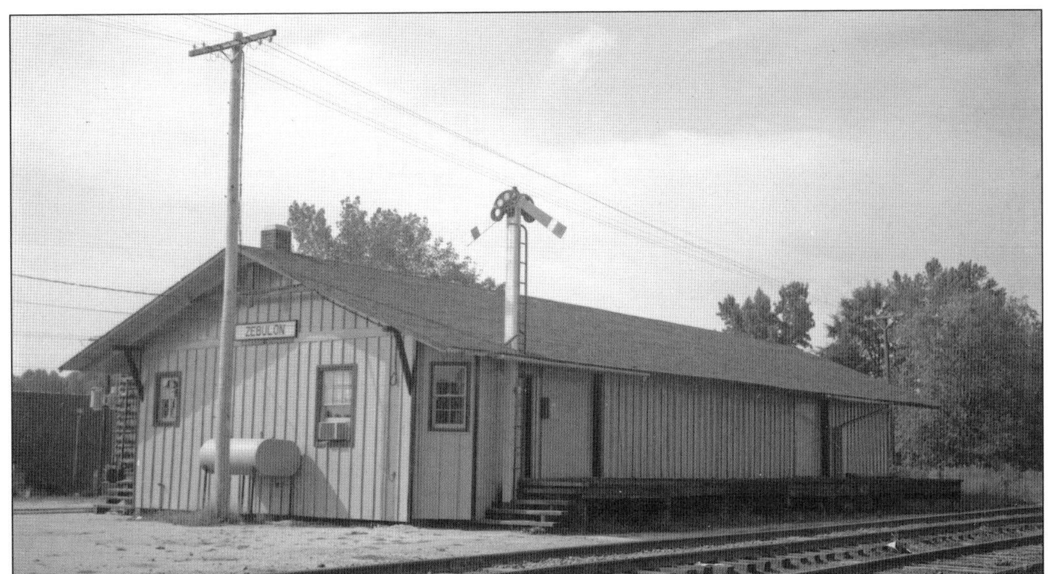

Zebulon, named for Gov. Zebulon B. Vance, was incorporated on February 16, 1907, as a direct result of the new rail line. The Zebulon Company was created by two gentlemen to subdivide and create the town. The depot still stands today and is used as a daycare center. (Photograph by Tom King, courtesy of the King-Marsh collection.)

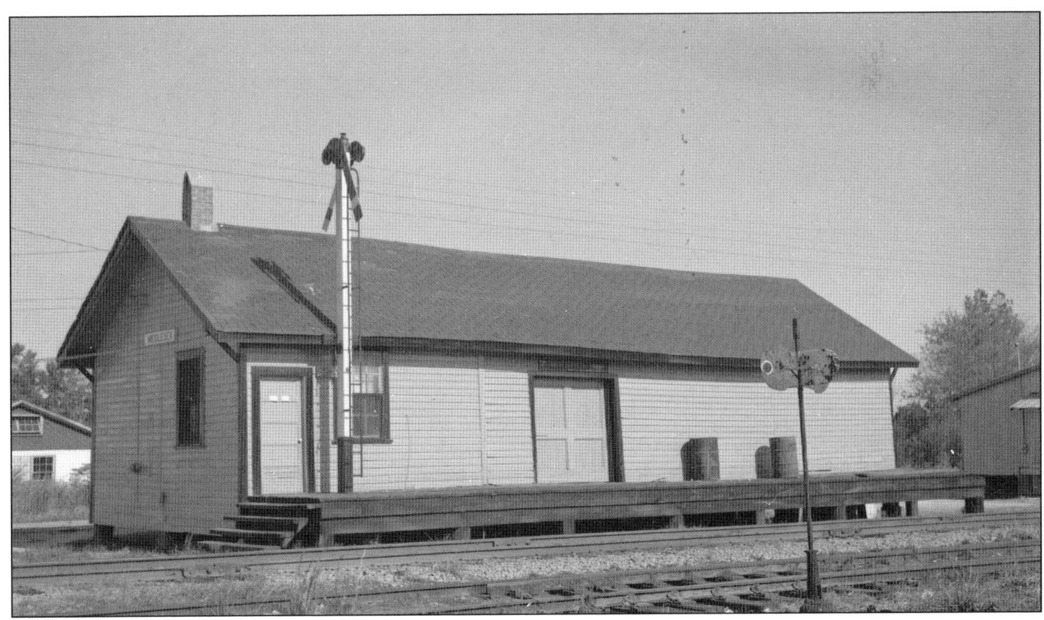

Middlesex depot as it looked on November 6, 1966, having been repainted within the previous two years. Norfolk Southern took great pride in keeping their depots looking good, especially during the late 1960s. (Photograph by Tom King, courtesy of the King-Marsh collection.)

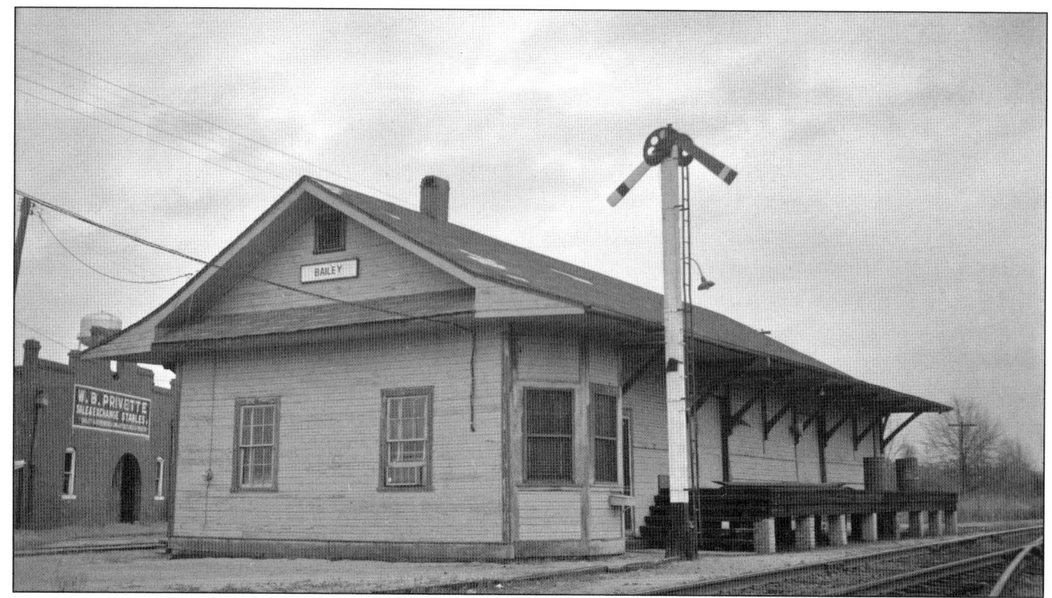

Bailey is home today to the Country Doctor Museum, devoted to the history of rural medical care in North Carolina. The passenger waiting room has been removed from this depot, keeping space for the station agent's office. That was a practice of Norfolk Southern after passenger service ended. This station was closed on March 31, 1970. (Photograph by Tom King, courtesy of the King-Marsh collection.)

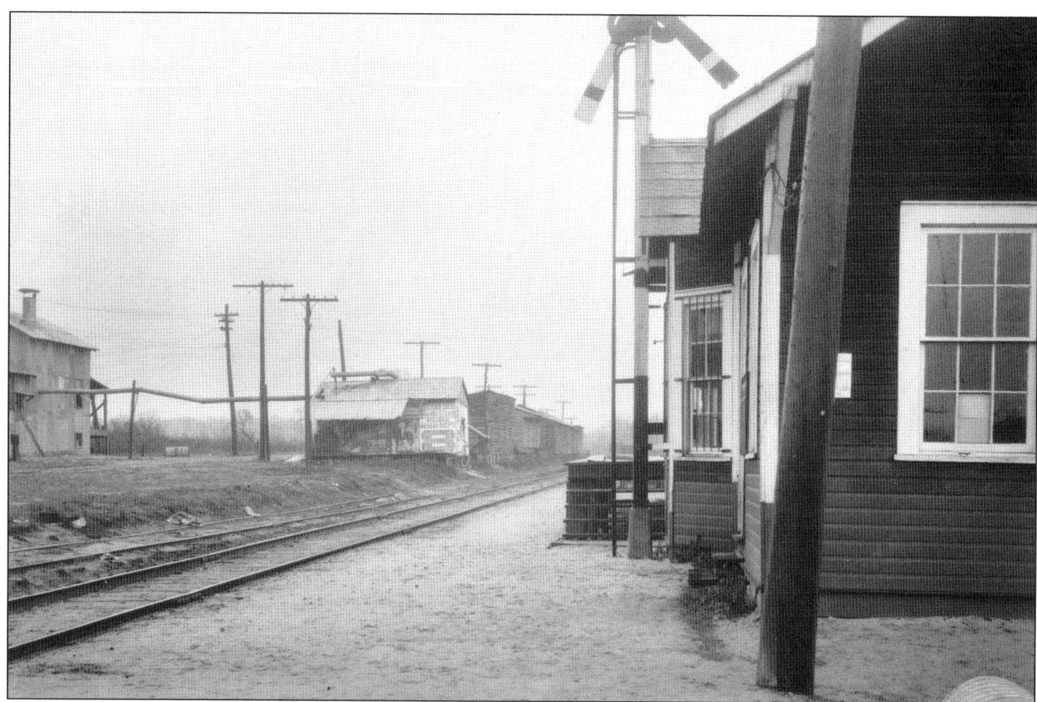

The Sims depot is seen here as it appeared in 1930. The signs on the building in the distance advertise the circus featuring Tony Mix and his Wonder Horse coming to Wilson on September 8, 1930. (Courtesy of the State Archives of North Carolina.)

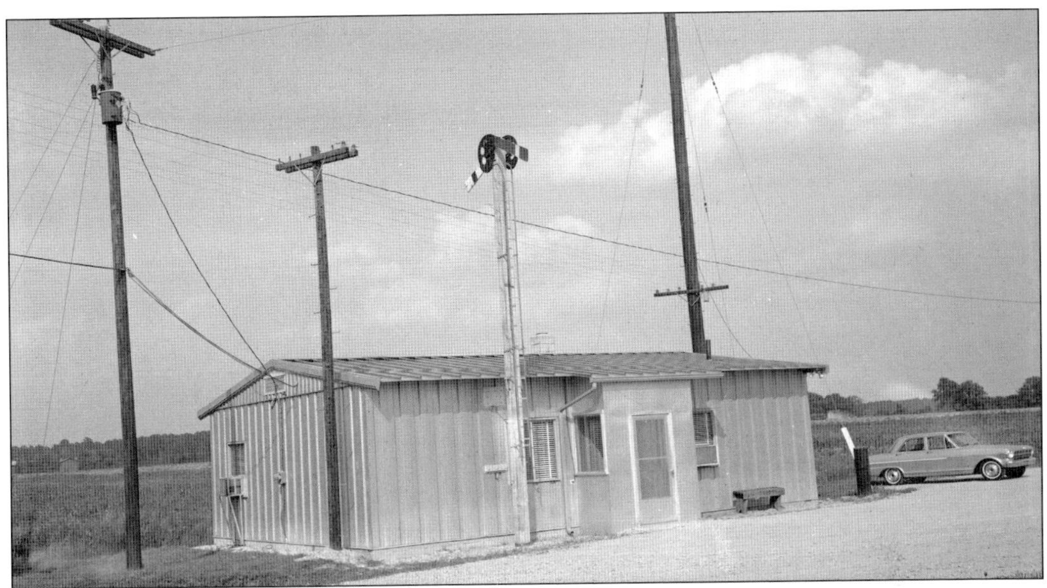

The Wilson, North Carolina, freight station is seen here on June 6, 1966. The railroad even converted a boxcar in Wilson for use as storage, painted the same bright silver as the building. (Photograph by Tom King, courtesy of the King-Marsh collection.)

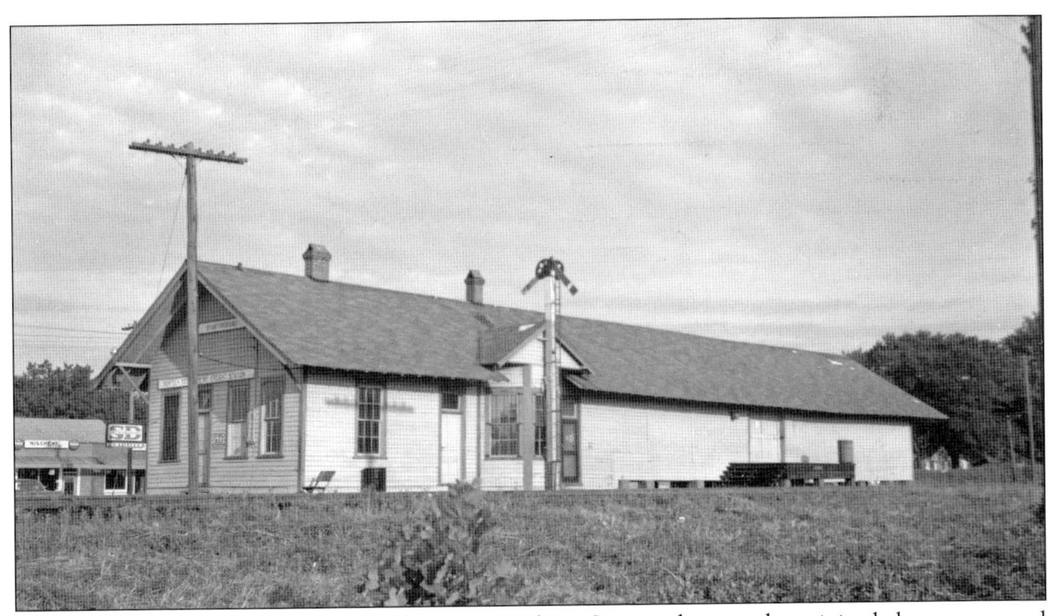

Stantonsburg is the first incorporated town in Wilson County, having the original charter granted on December 20, 1817. The final incorporation date was February 26, 1909. The depot, shown on May 26, 1964, was closed on June 26, 1970. It continued to stand during the 1980s but was later torn down. (Photograph by Tom King, courtesy of the King-Marsh collection.)

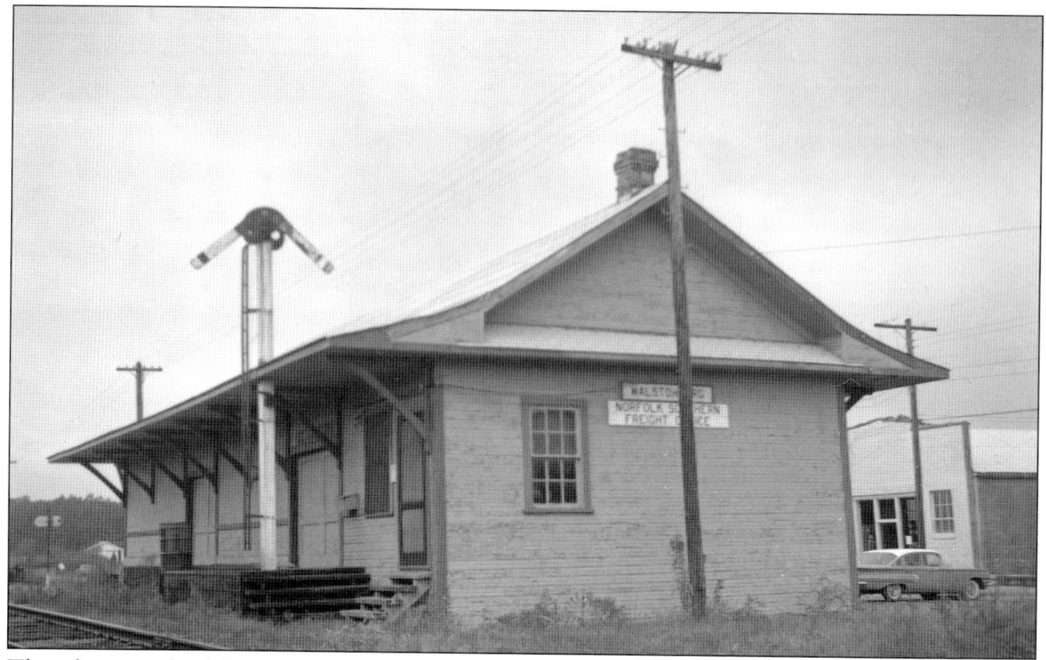

This photograph of the Walstonburg depot shows the modification that was done to many Norfolk Southern depots—removal of the passenger waiting room—during the 1950s. Happily, this station still exists today, painted back to Norfolk Southern–inspired depot colors. (Photograph by Tom King, courtesy of the King-Marsh collection.)

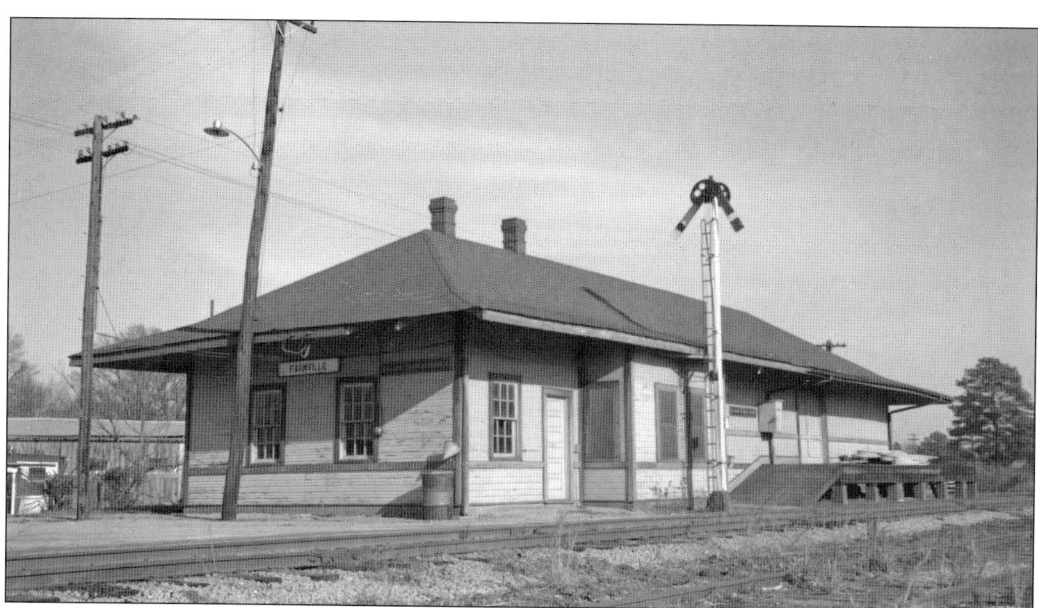

Farmville, originally New Town, was incorporated in 1872. The first depot burned in 1925 and was replaced by this building, photographed on December 22, 1963. The depot no longer stands today. (Photograph by Tom King, courtesy of the King-Marsh collection.)

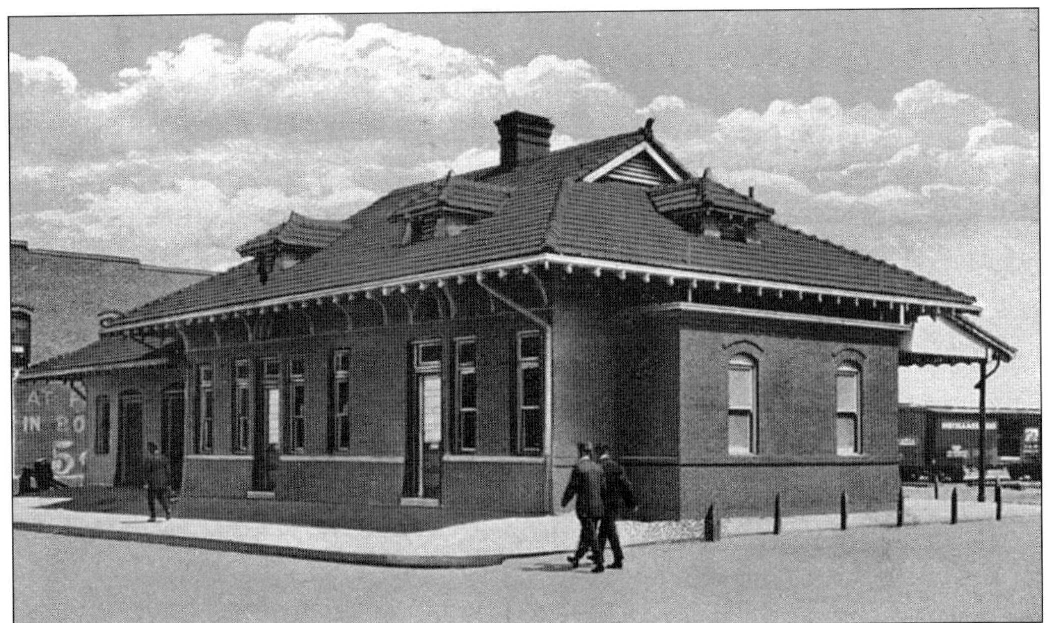

The Greenville passenger station, used by Norfolk Southern, was at the end of a spur track. Trains would back into the neat brick station. The station was torn down after passenger service ended, leaving just the freight station. (Courtesy of the S. David Carriker collection.)

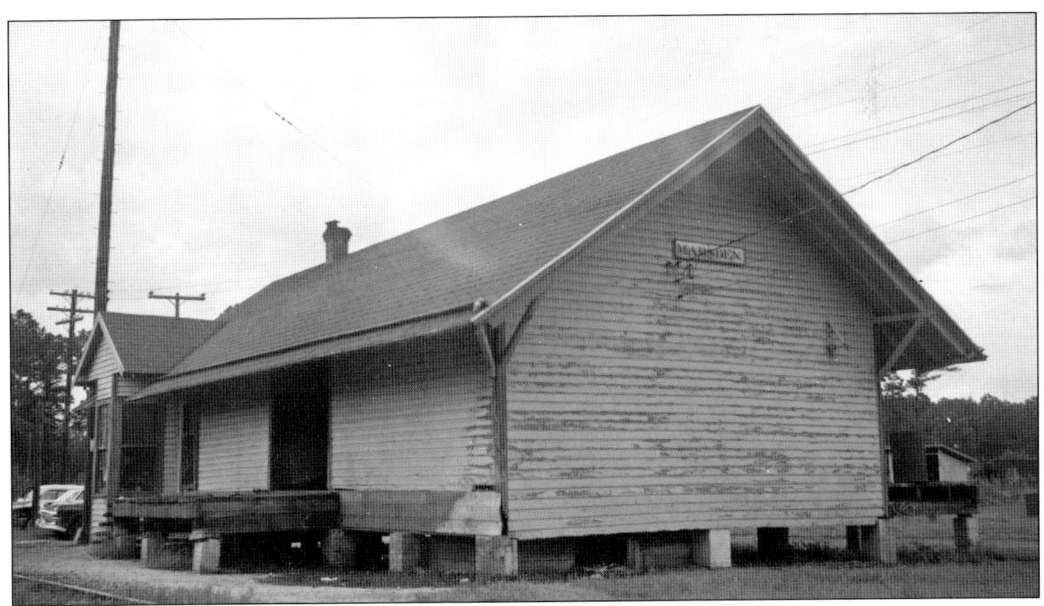

Ever seen a town with a name too hard to pronounce? Norfolk Southern thought so and named their Chocowinity station Marsden, after a railroad official, when the depot was built. This depot was later torn down after the current brick building was completed in 1970. (Photograph by Tom King, courtesy of the King-Marsh collection.)

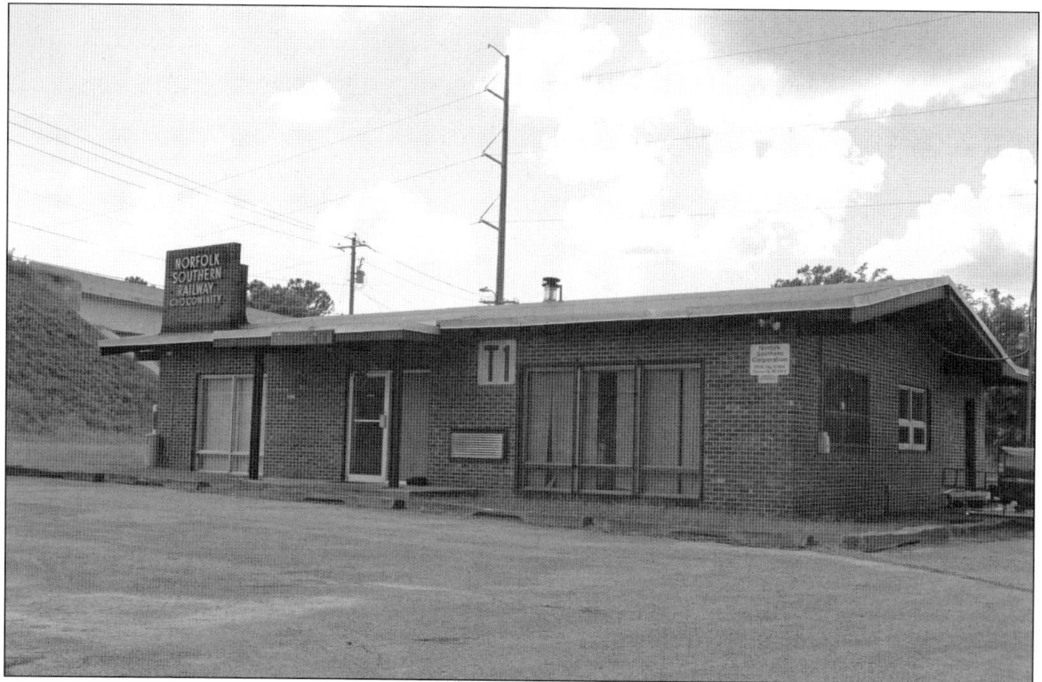

The replacement Chocowinity depot, as still used by Norfolk Southern Corporation today. The lettering on the roof sign was placed there when the depot opened and never removed. It helps the modern operator uses the same name today. (Author's collection.)

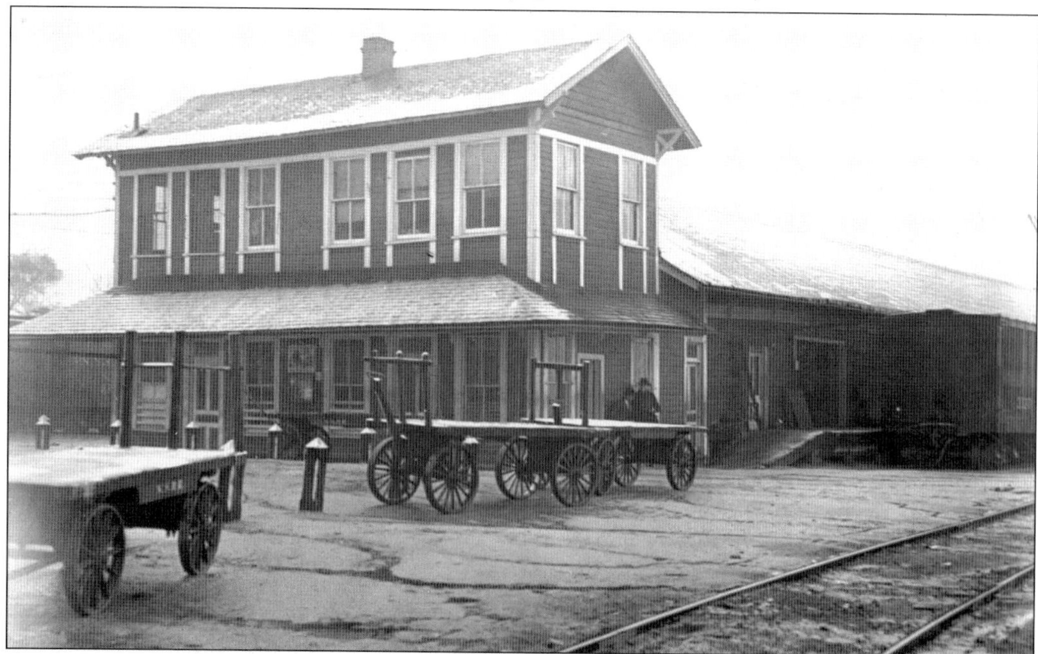

The original depot at Washington, shown in 1910, had a nice two-story station for passengers and offices. In later years, this section was torn down and replaced by an area suited for freight traffic until it closed in 1968. The building was torn down several years ago. (Courtesy of the State Archives of North Carolina.)

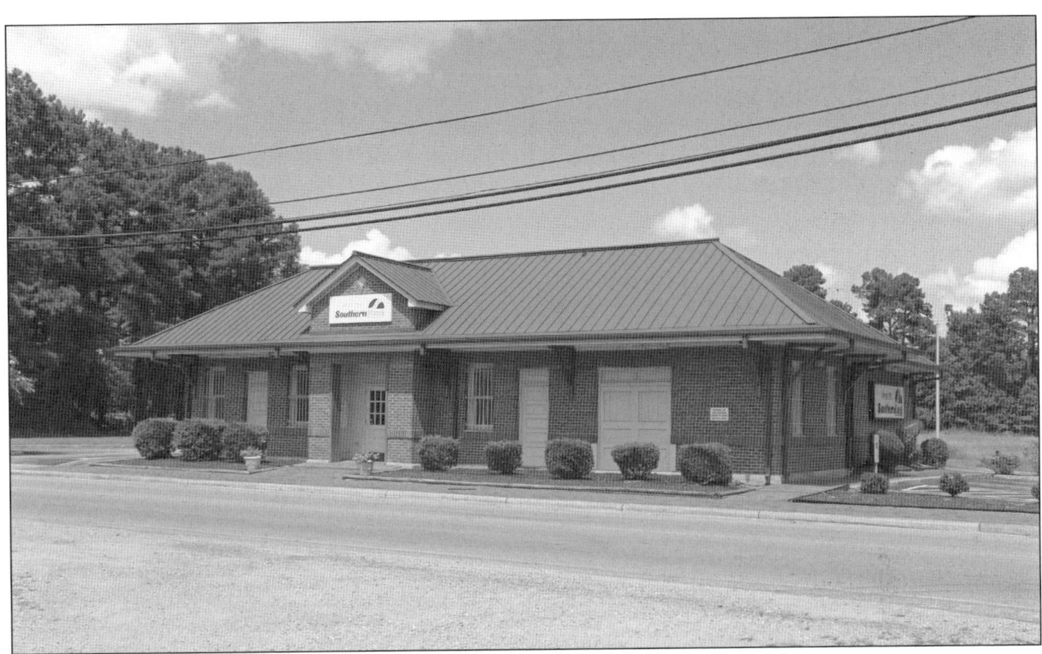

The Plymouth passenger station served both the Norfolk Southern Railway and Atlantic Coast Line (ACL) Railroad during the 1920s, even though the ACL already had their own station in town. In 1952, the NS built a new freight station due to the end of passenger service. The freight station was used by the Southern Railway after the merger but no longer exists today. (Above, author's collection; below, photograph by Tom King, courtesy of the King-Marsh collection.)

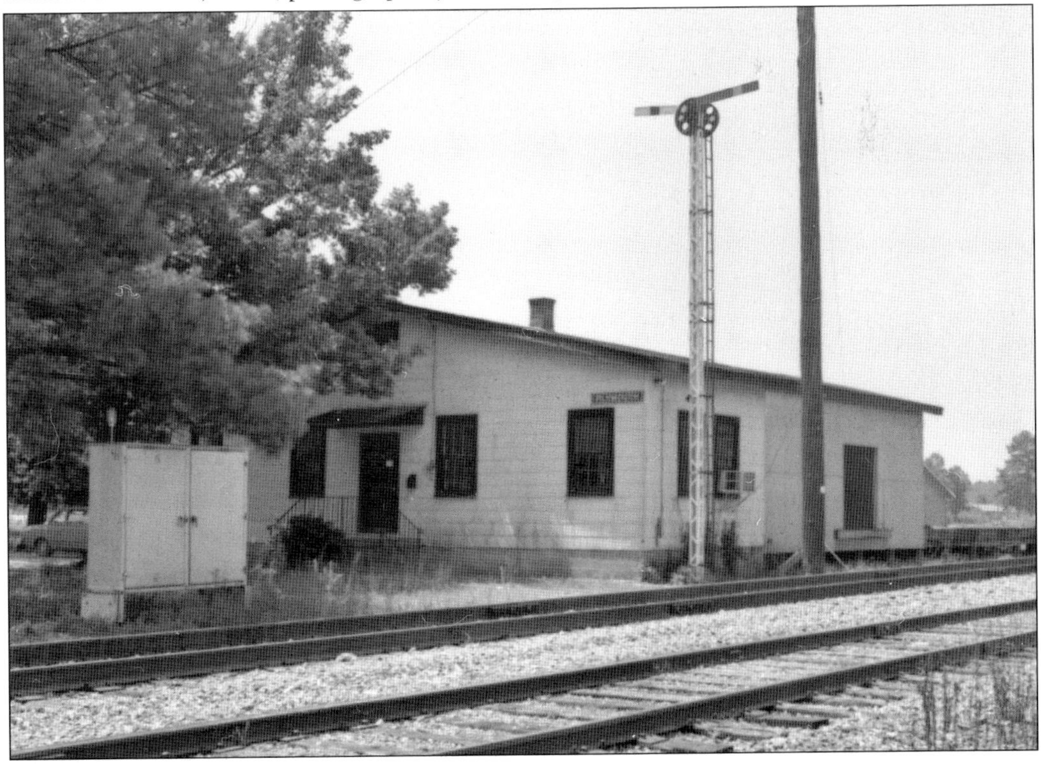

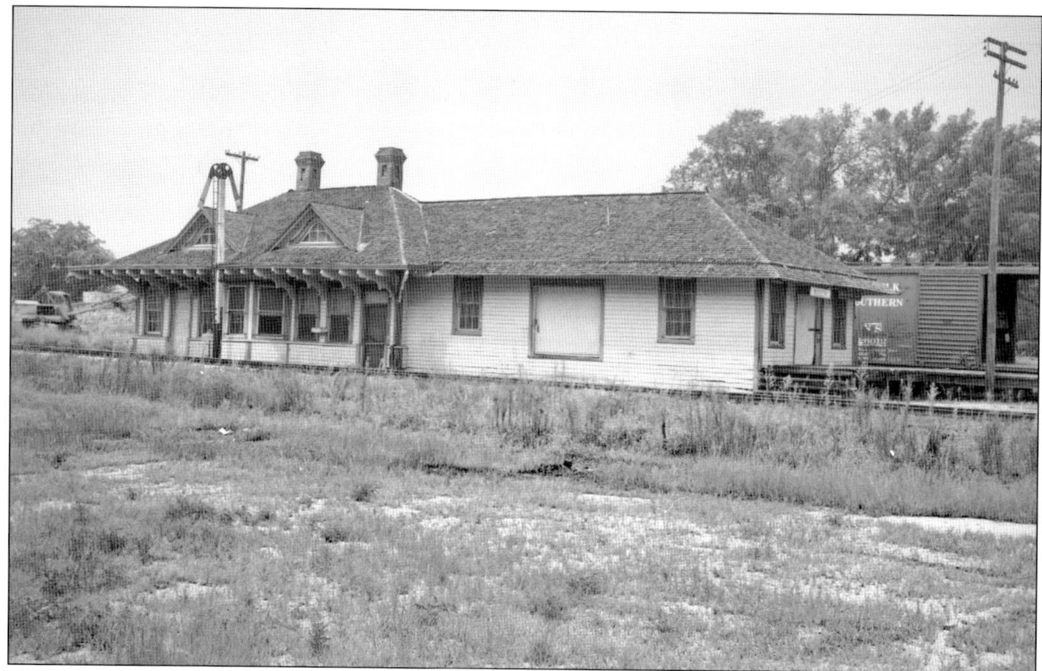

Mackeys was the station located at the south end of the Albemarle Sound. A trestle connecting Mackeys and Edenton was built in 1910 and dismantled in the 1980s. Photographed on August 5, 1965, the only railroad building remaining in Mackeys today is a section foreman's house. (Photograph by Tom King, courtesy of the King-Marsh collection.)

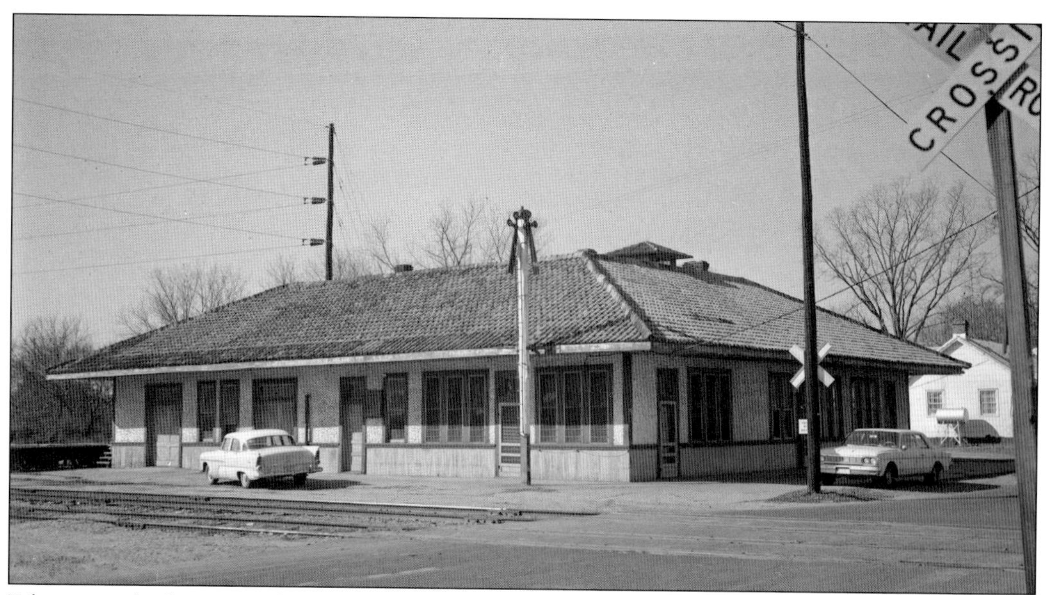

Edenton is the location of a colonial port; the town was chartered in 1722 and named in honor of Gov. Charles Eden. It served as the second capital of the colony from 1722 to 1743. The large depot no longer stands today. (Photograph by Tom King, courtesy of the King-Marsh collection.)

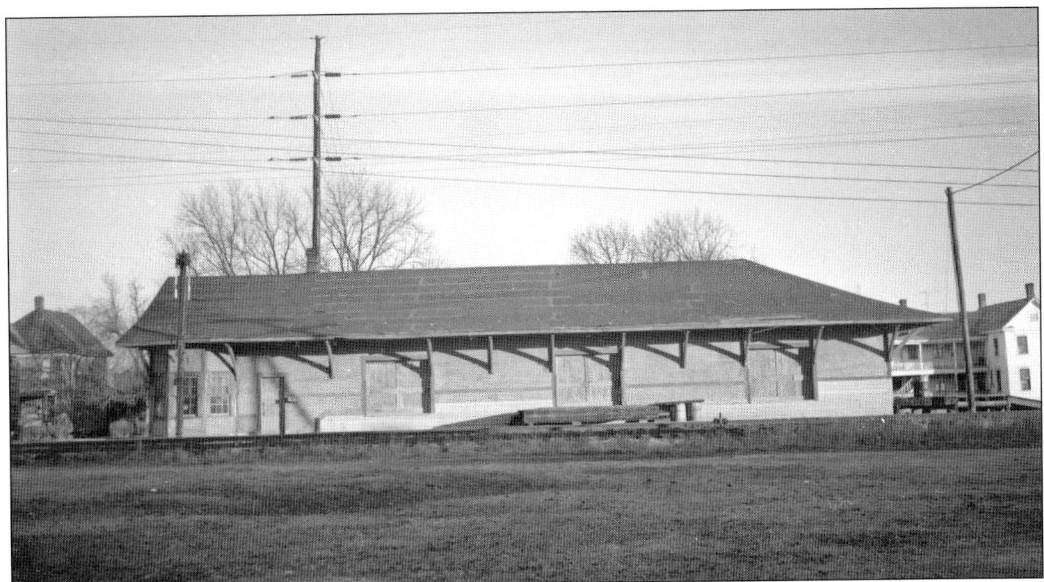

Hertford is known as the hometown of Jim "Catfish" Hunter, an MLB Hall of Fame pitcher who played for teams including the Oakland Athletics and New York Yankees. Dating from 1758, the area was known for its lumber business and takes its name from the Yeoman Indians—"Land of Beautiful Women." (Photograph by Tom King, courtesy of the King-Marsh collection.)

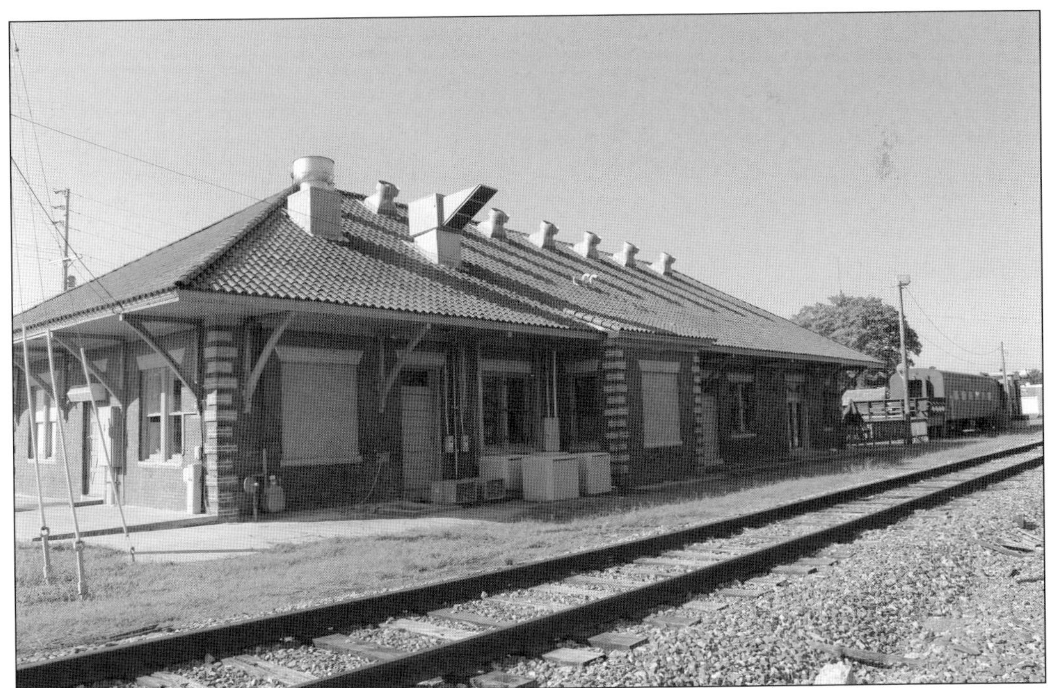

Elizabeth City, located on the Pasquotank River, was founded in 1794 and known as the "Harbor of Hospitality." The depot has been preserved and houses a local business today. (Author's collection.)

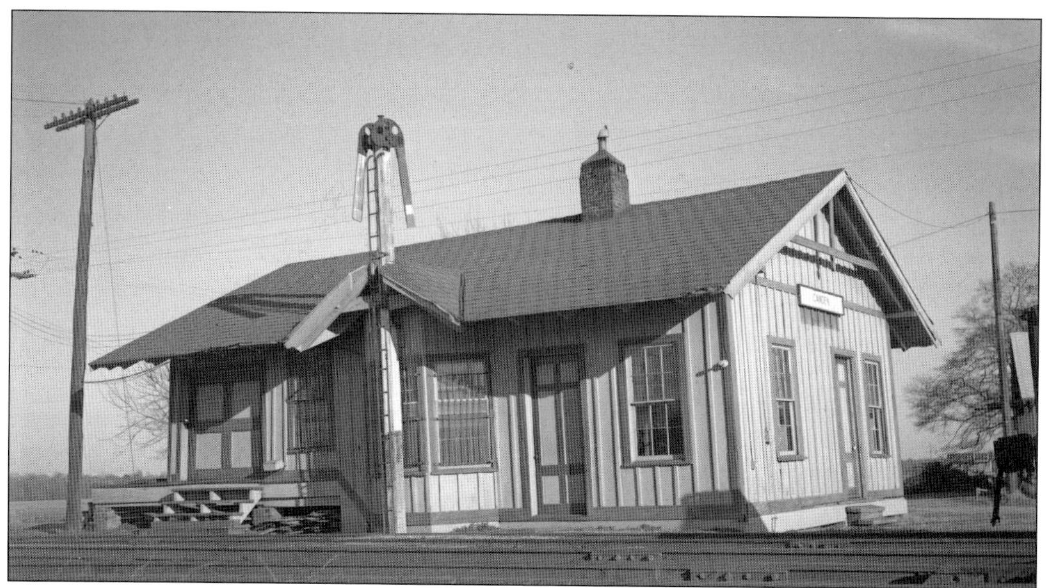

Camden, although unincorporated, is the county seat of Camden County, since it was the first North Carolina consolidated city-county in 2006. The depot, photographed on February 4, 1968, is no longer standing. (Photograph by Tom King, courtesy of the King-Marsh collection.)

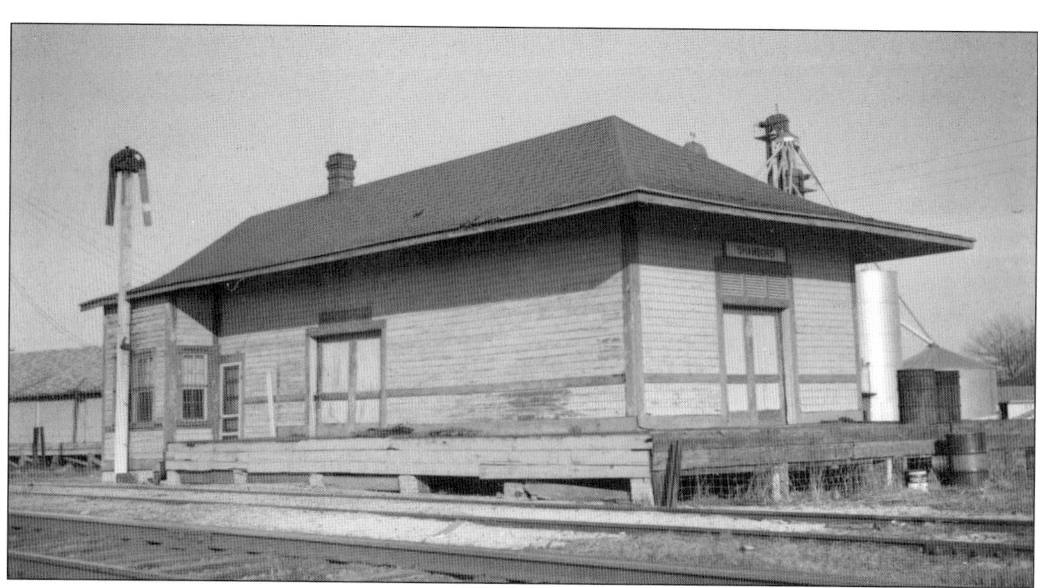

Shawboro, located in Currituck County, is a small community about 20 miles from the Virginia border. The depot, shown in 1968, was later torn down. (Photograph by Tom King, courtesy of the King-Marsh collection.)

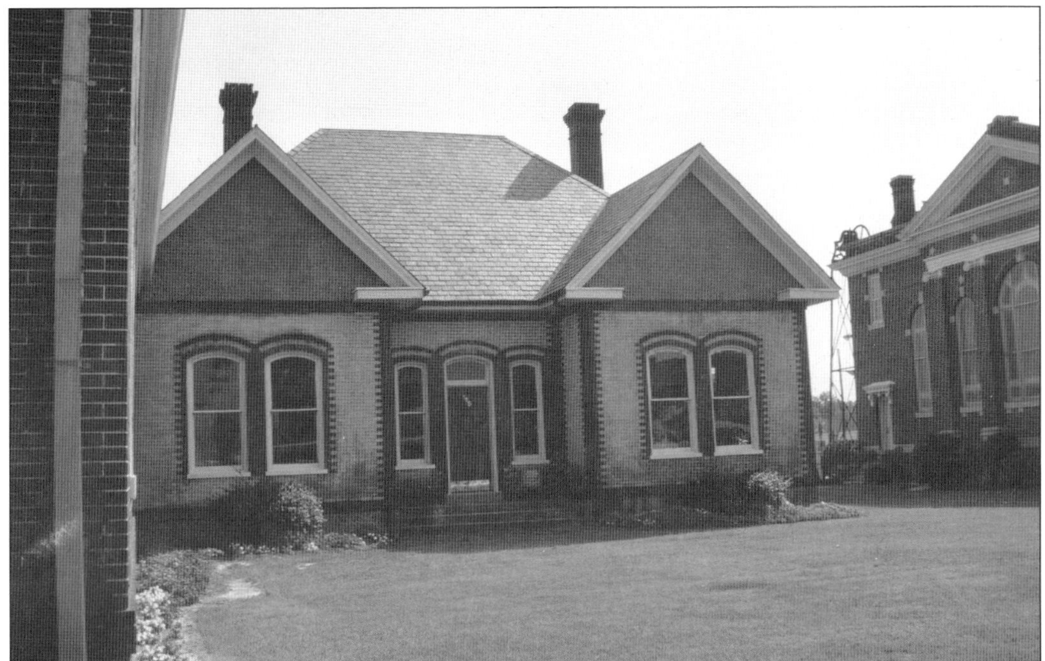

The Aberdeen & Asheboro (A&A) dates to 1889 and operated the whole length between these two towns by 1897. The railroad used this building as their offices between 1906 and 1914, when the line was officially merged into Norfolk Southern. (Author's collection.)

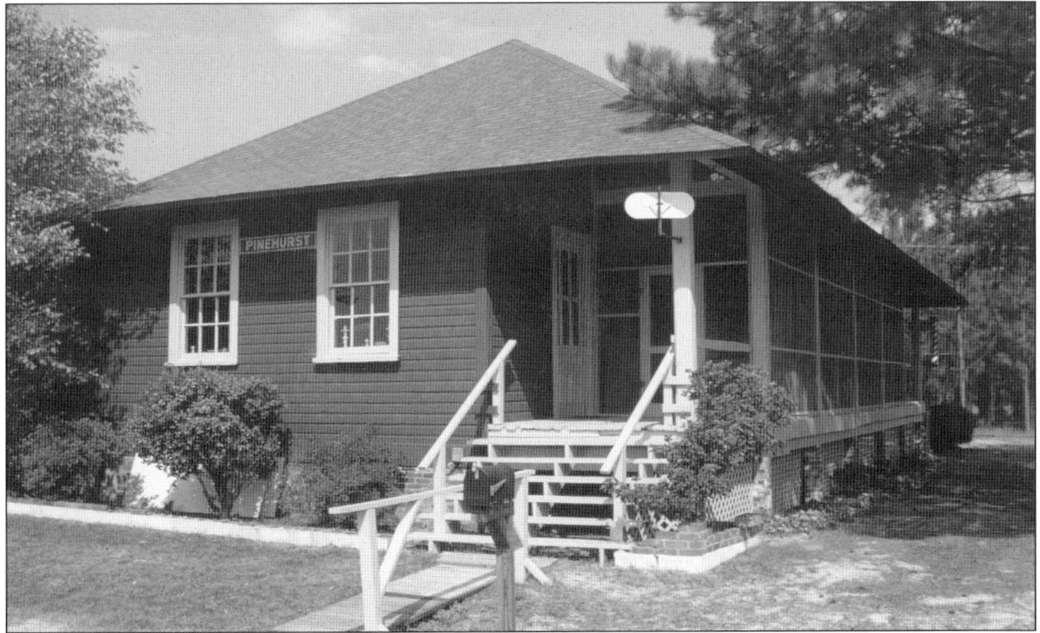

By the beginning of the 20th century, Pinehurst was well on the way to becoming a major golf resort in the sand hills of North Carolina. The town, originally called Tuftstown after the developer, was incorporated in 1890. The Norfolk Southern Railway had direct service to Pinehurst through the A&A Railroad, with several Pullmans usually lined up during the height of the season. The depot, dating to 1900, has been owned by private business for several years. (Author's collection.)

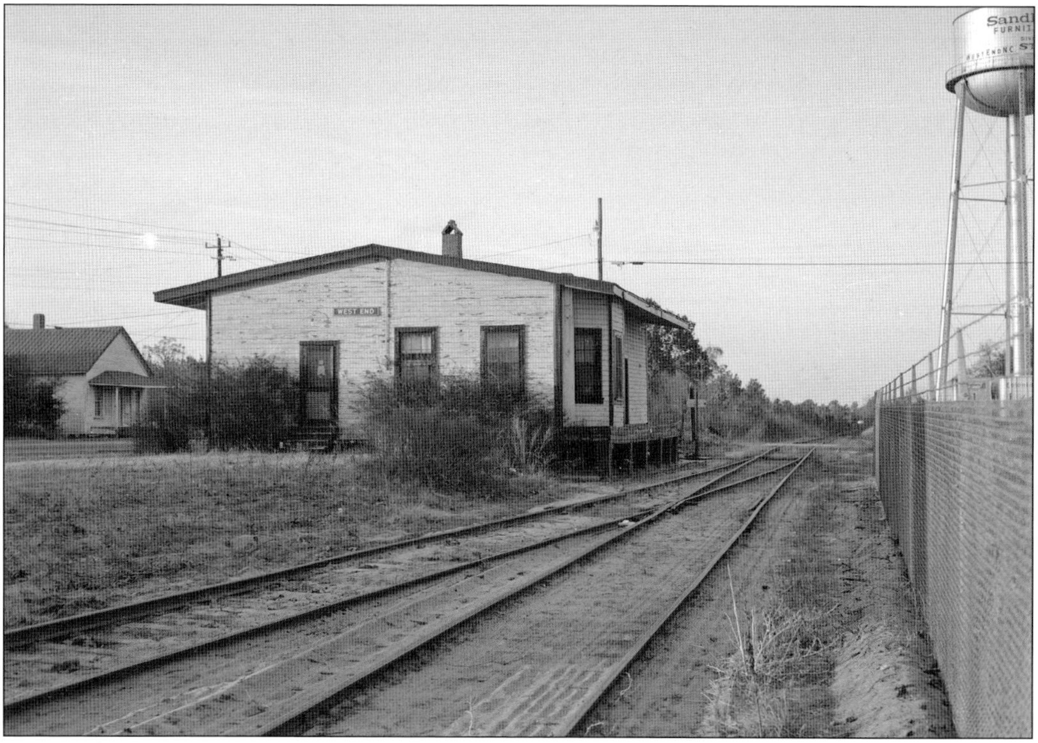

West End was the original terminus of the Aberdeen & West End. A branch to Jackson Springs was constructed from there in 1901. The depot still stands and was recently restored into a residence. (Photograph by Tom King, courtesy of the King-Marsh collection.)

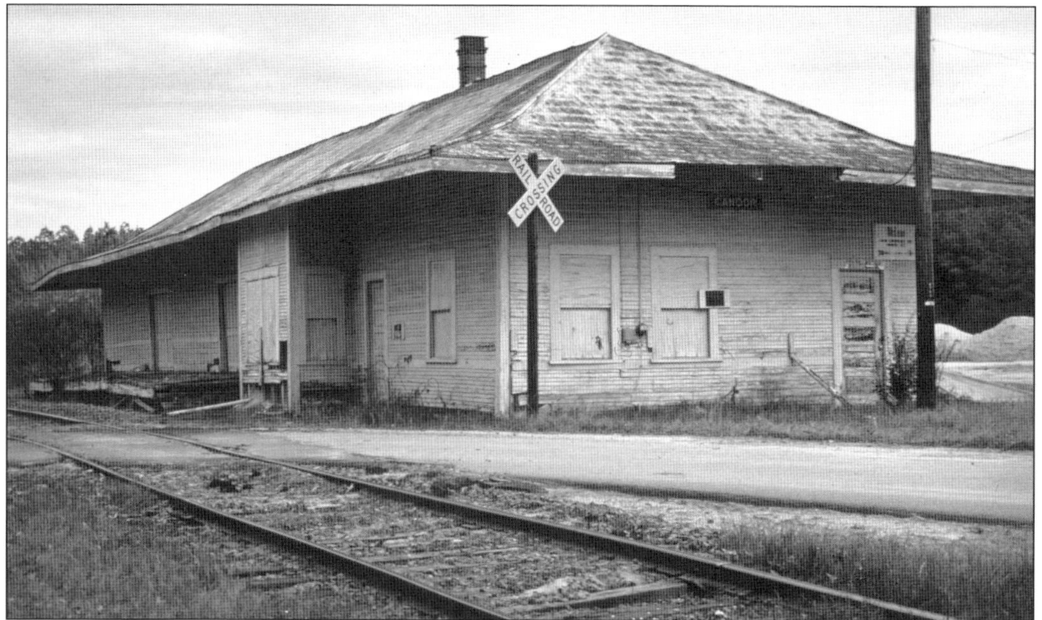

Candor, named for its settlers' honest dealings, is known for the peaches grown in the area, giving them the name "Peach Capital of North Carolina." Today, the AC&W Railway operates their main locomotive shop in Candor, and the depot still stands today. (Author's collection.)

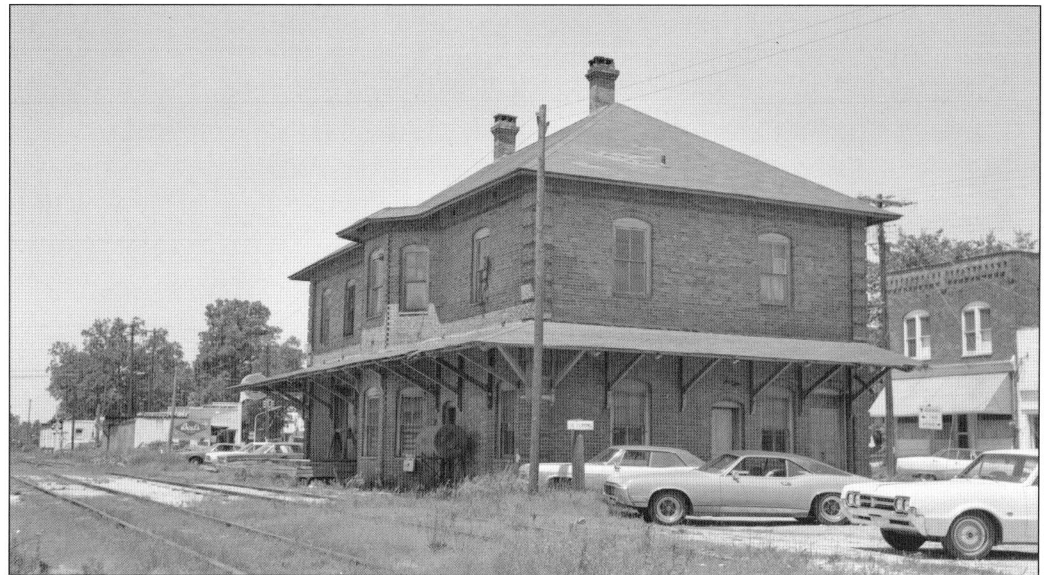

Biscoe was the location of the A&A general offices and shops, but its importance diminished after Norfolk Southern Control. The depot was torn down several years ago. (Photograph by C.K. Marsh, courtesy of the King-Marsh collection.)

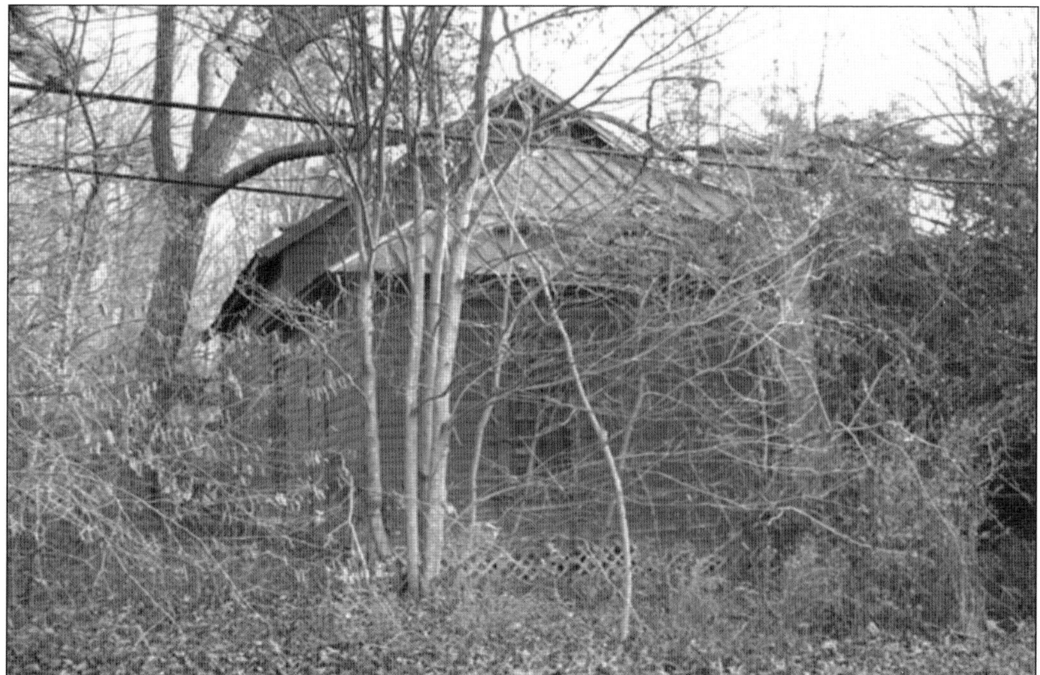

Seagrove is considered the pottery capital of North Carolina, including the North Carolina Pottery Center. It was named for Edwin G. Seagraves, a railroad official during construction. The depot, built in 1890, still stands north of town, owned by one of the local pottery companies. (Author's collection.)

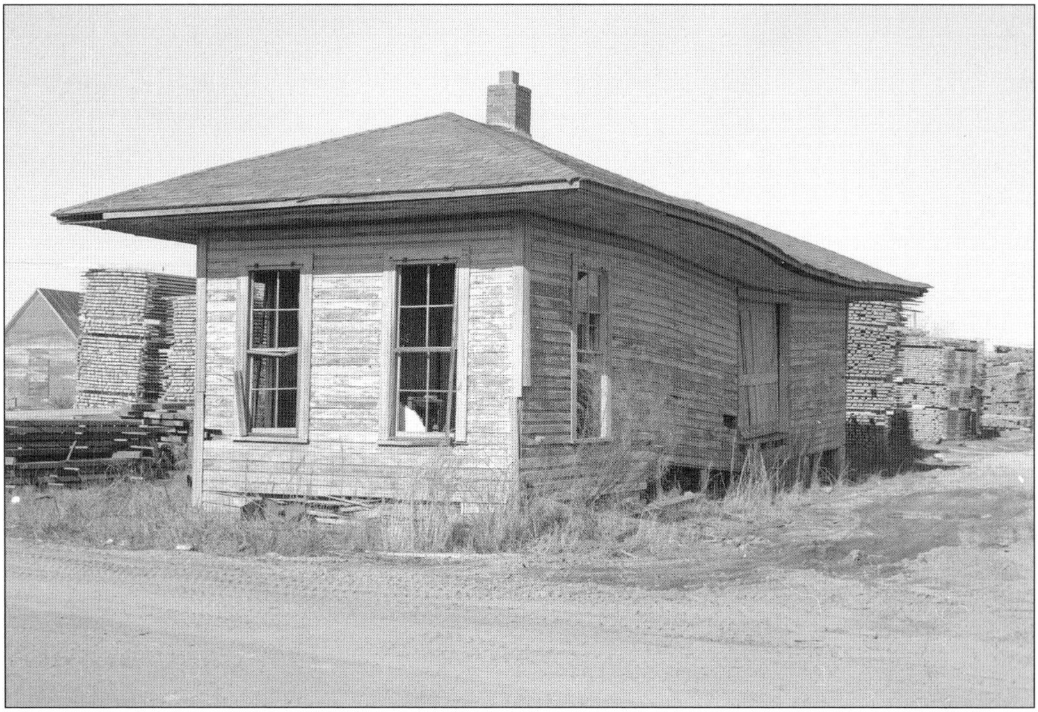

Norman is located on a branch built from Candor to Ellerbe in 1911. The depot, shown almost derelict in 1975, no longer exists today. (Photograph by G.M. McDonald, courtesy of the King-Marsh collection.)

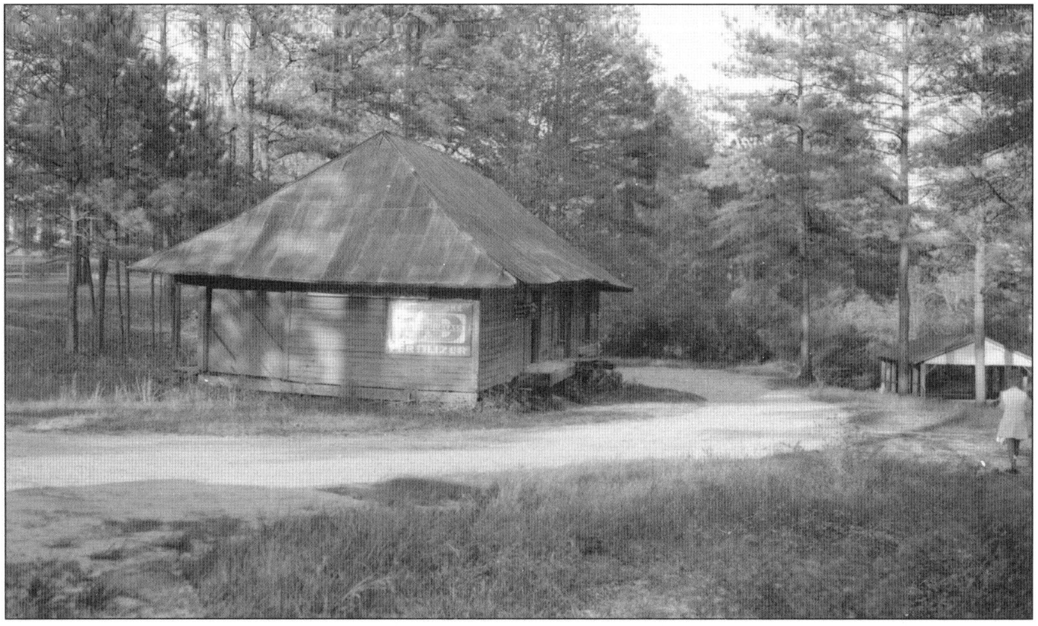

The Jackson Springs Railroad operated a branch line from West End, opening in 1901. The town had a depot and hotel for travelers wanting to be near Pinehurst. The railroad was absorbed into the A&A in 1907. The depot was saved and used for storage by the time this image was captured in 1973. (Photograph by G.M. McDonald, courtesy of the King-Marsh collection.)

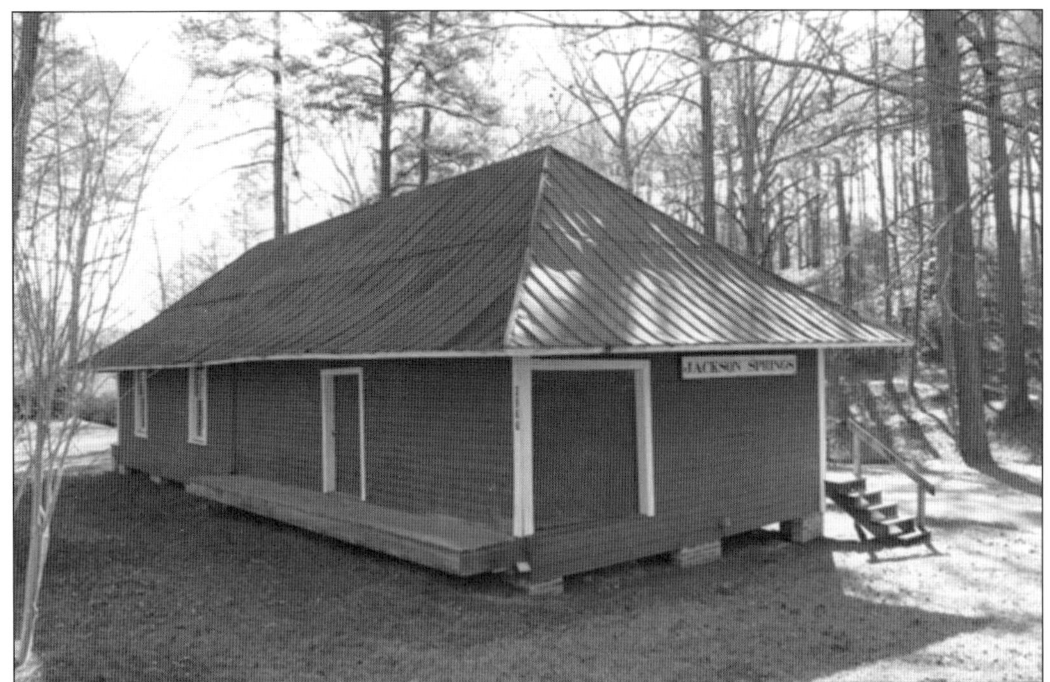

This view of the modern restored Jackson Springs depot shows the red NS depot color. (Author's collection.)

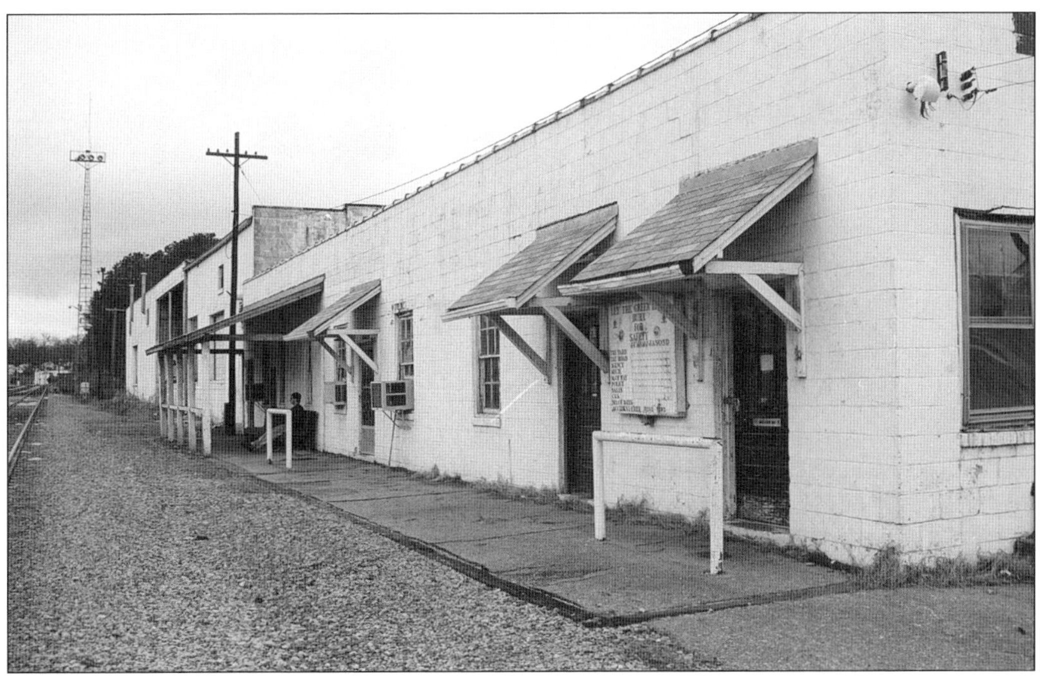

The Glenwood Yard Office in Raleigh, North Carolina, was used by NS after Raleigh Union Station closed for the remainder of their passenger service, ending in 1951. (Author's collection.)

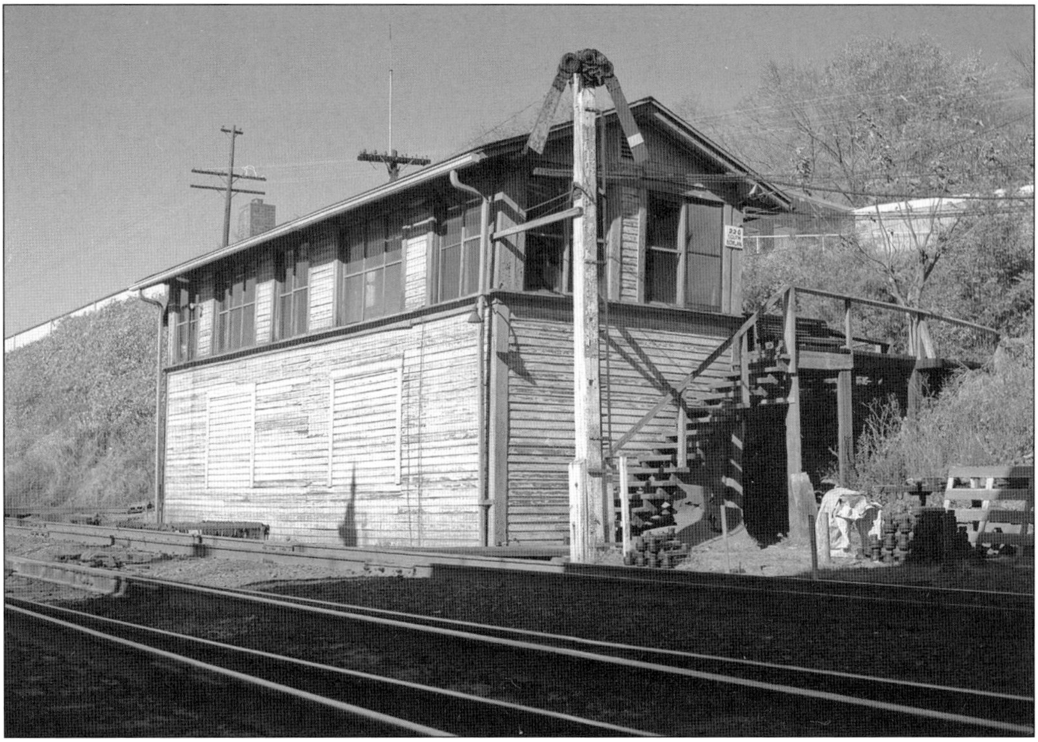

Boylan Tower in Raleigh was the interlocking plant to control trains of the Norfolk Southern crossing the Seaboard Air Line main line. The tower was photographed on November 17, 1973, and continued to be used through the 1980s. (Photograph by Bob Graham, courtesy of the King-Marsh collection.)

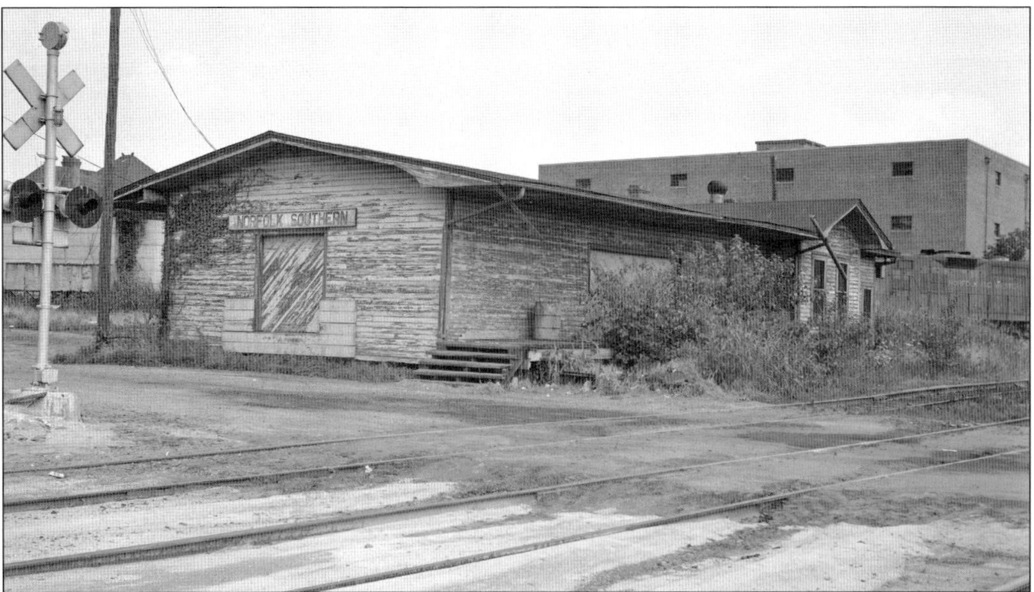

The NS Durham Freight Station was located in the wye of the Norfolk & Western, whose locomotive is shown in the background. Because of the location, this building was erected with angled sides to fit in the curve. (Photograph by C.K. Marsh, courtesy of the King-Marsh collection.)

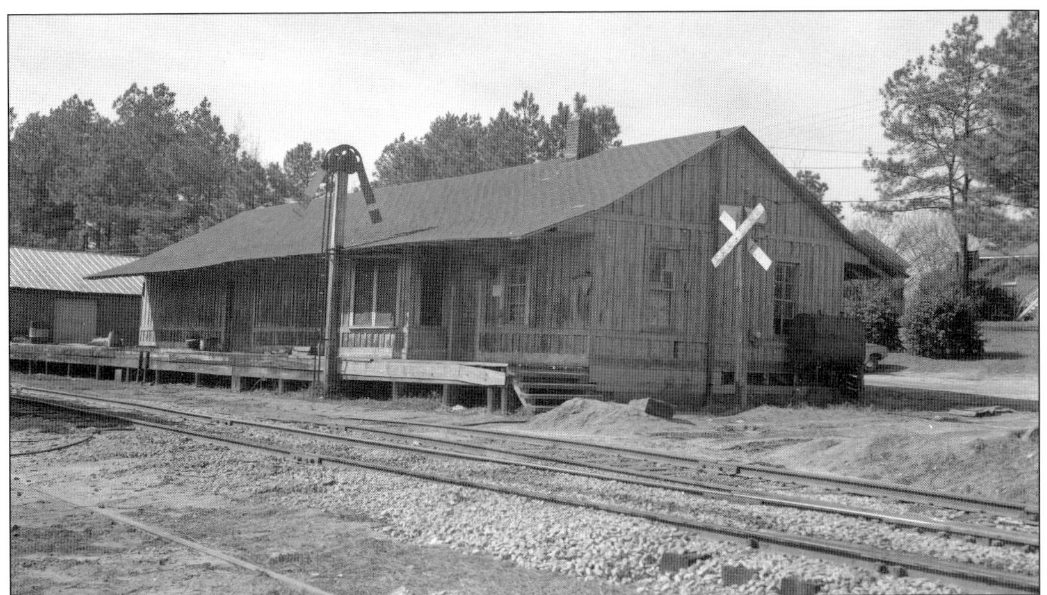

Lillington is located on the NS branch to Fayetteville, opening in 1906. The depot, photographed on February 18, 1973, has been preserved for private business. (Photograph by C.K. Marsh, courtesy of the King-Marsh collection.)

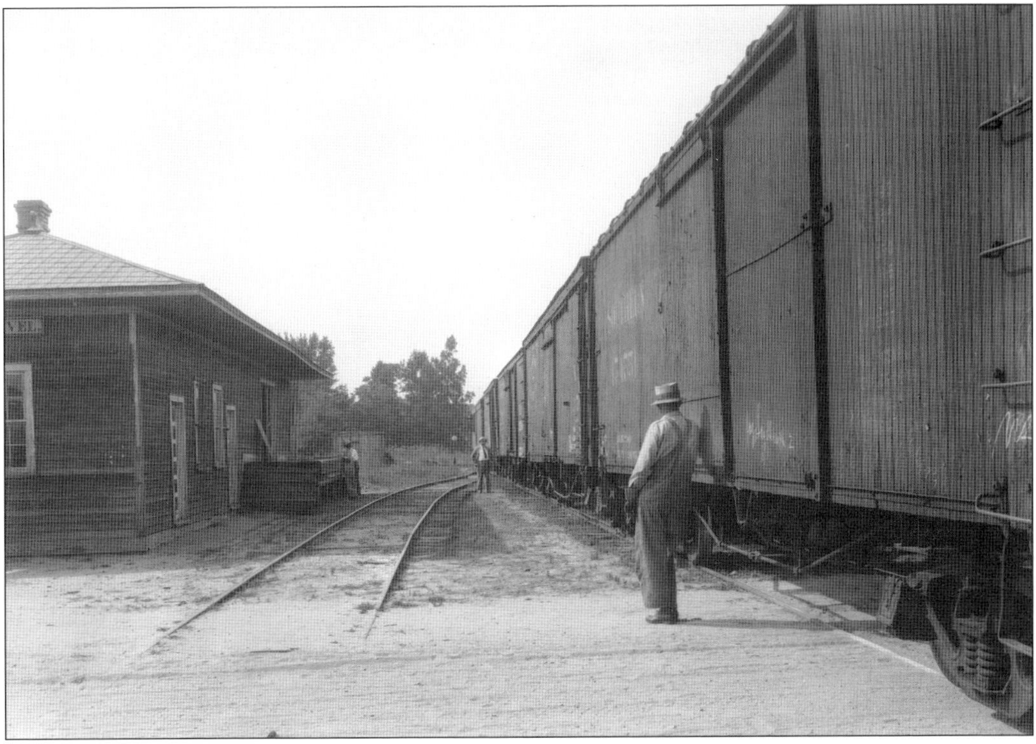

Here is a classic railroad shot at Bunnlevel in 1932, also on the branch to Fayetteville. Originally named Bunn's Level, after a local merchant in 1904, the town was incorporated as Bunnlevel in 1921 but went inactive by the 1950s. The depot no longer stands today. (Courtesy of the State Archives of North Carolina.)

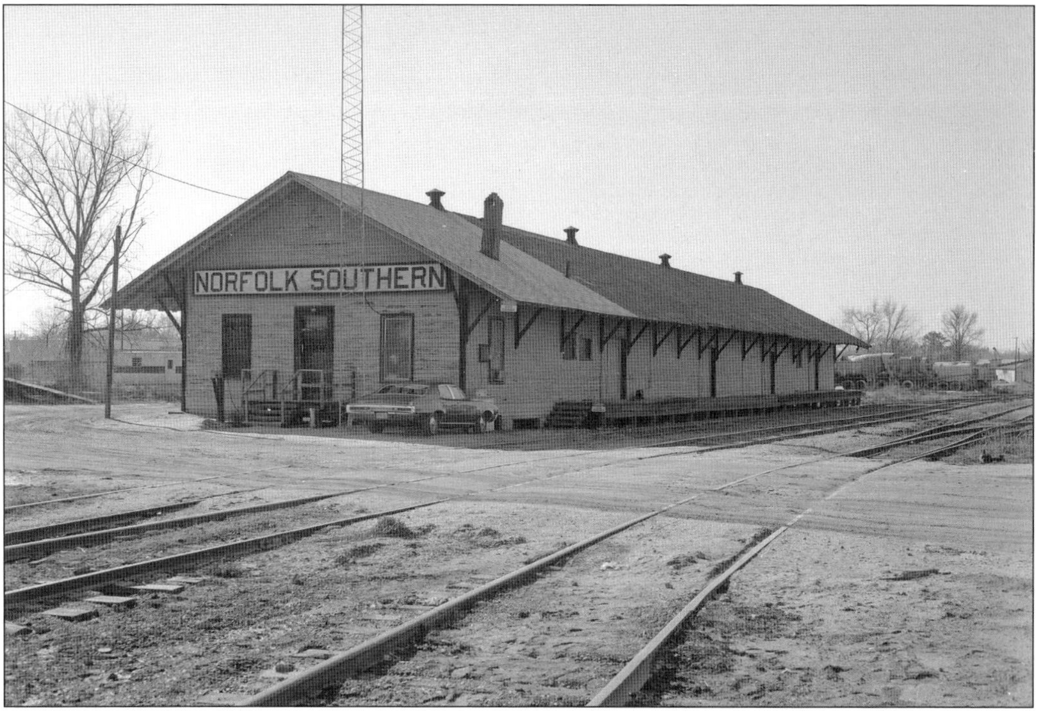

The Norfolk Southern freight depot in Fayetteville is pictured here sometime in the 1970s. The NS interchanged with the Atlantic Coast Line to reach southern cities. (Photograph by Tom Sink, courtesy of the King-Marsh collection.)

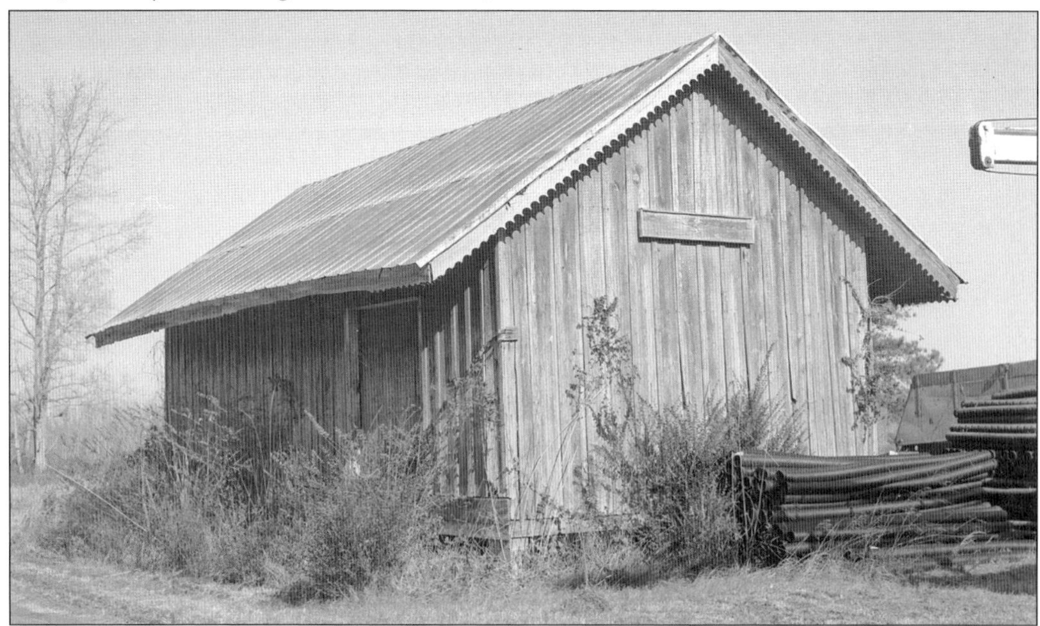

Trotville is a small community located on the former Norfolk Southern route from Edenton to Suffolk, Virginia. This line was completed in 1902 as a narrow-gauge railroad, converted to standard-gauge in 1904, and abandoned on September 24, 1940. The small Trotville depot is shown on December 21, 1975. (Photograph by Tom King, courtesy of the King-Marsh collection.)

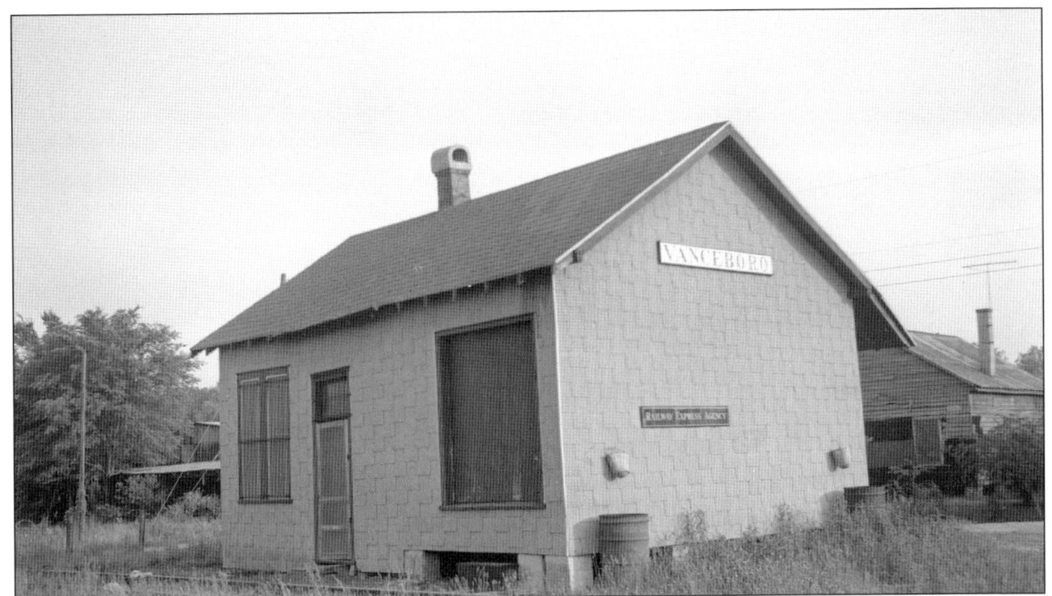

Vanceboro, located on the branch from Washington to New Bern, was completed in 1907. The depot, photographed on May 16, 1965, still has the Railway Express Agency sign, though it is doubtful much freight was shipped from the town. (Photograph by Tom King, courtesy of the King-Marsh collection.)

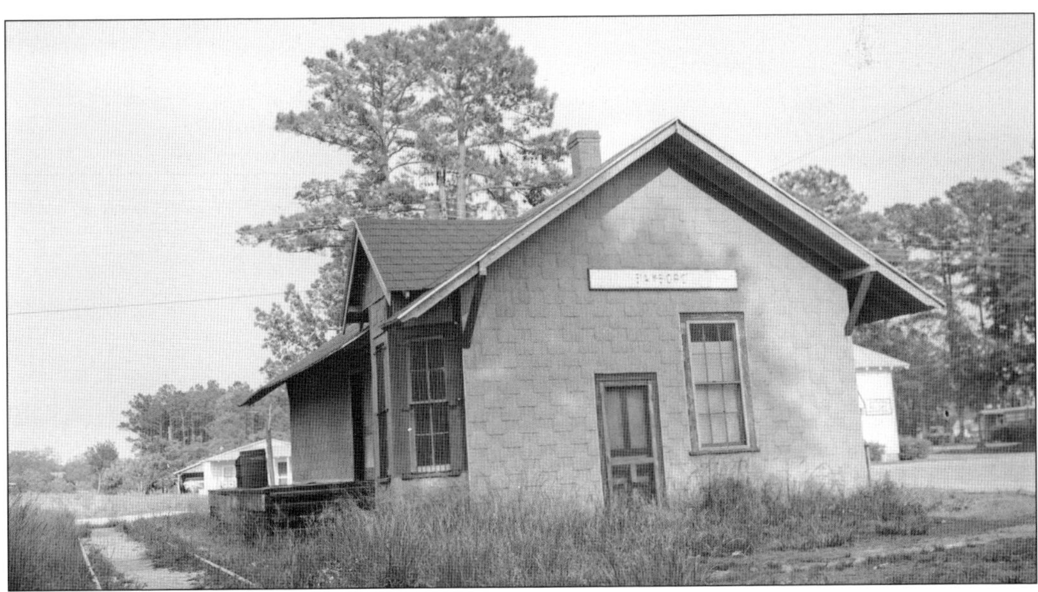

Bayboro is a small community located on the New Bern to Oriental branch, completed in 1910. This depot and Vanceboro appear to have the same siding applied, and both were photographed on the same day. (Photograph by Tom King, courtesy of the King-Marsh collection.)

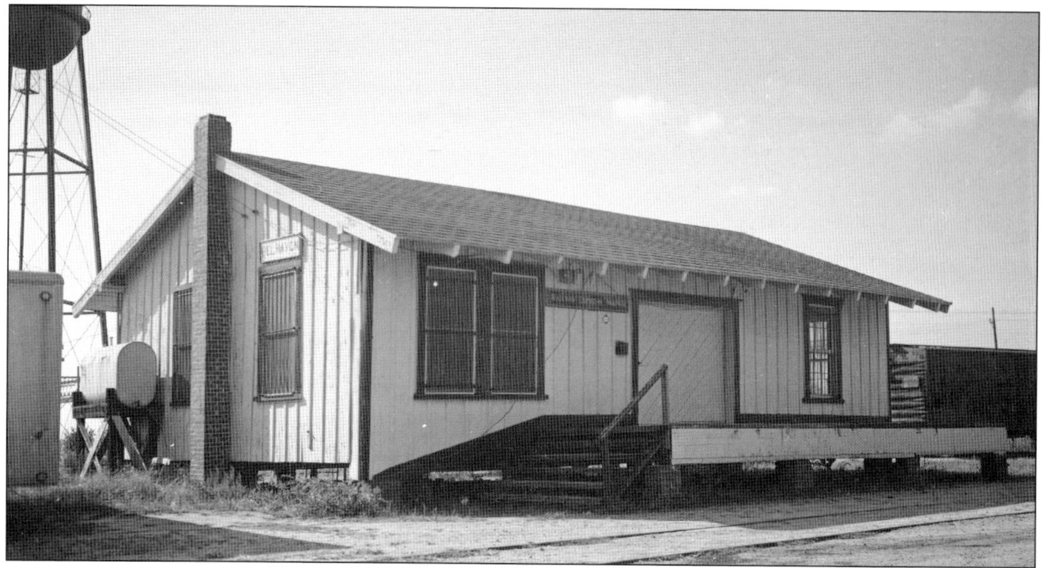

Belhaven is the terminus of the Albemarle & Pantego Railroad, completed in 1887. The Norfolk Southern Railroad took over this line in 1891, gaining equipment and a hotel in Belhaven. The depot still stands today as a community building. (Photograph by Tom King, courtesy of the King-Marsh collection.)

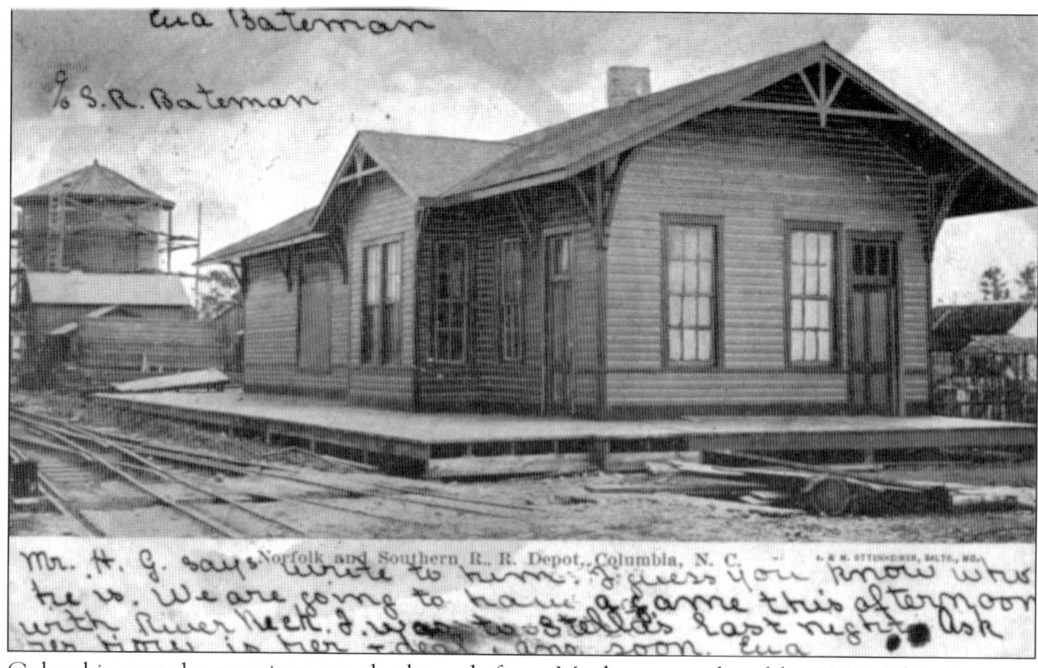

Columbia was the terminus on the branch from Mackey, completed by 1904. This line was eventually abandoned, along with several others, in the 1940s. (Author's collection.)

Four

Union Depots and Short Lines

Several locations in North Carolina had more than one railroad offering passenger service, so a central Union Station would be built to better serve the traveling public. These stations were generally served by three or more railroads, although sometimes a railroad may pull out and construct its own station. Raleigh is an interesting example, where the Seaboard Air Line and Southern Railway both used Union Station but pulled out in 1942, and then constructed their own depots near downtown. Norfolk Southern, which also used the building, moved passenger service to its freight yard until it was discontinued. Most union stations served until the host railroads ended passenger service or when Amtrak took over the service in 1971.

Eastern North Carolina had some interesting short line railroads, like the East Carolina Railway from Tarboro to Hookerton, before service was cut back to Farmville. The Virginia & Carolina Southern Railroad went from Lumberton to Hope Mills and then east to Elizabethtown. Both of these lines were controlled in some part by the Atlantic Coast Line, causing their depots to have a slight resemblance in design.

By far the most interesting was the Atlantic & North Carolina Railroad, constructed in the 1850s to connect the North Carolina Railroad to the ocean. It was controlled by the Norfolk Southern Railway over 30 years, ending in 1935. It connected the important city of Goldsboro to Morehead City, which developed into one of the state's major ports. It has been leased to the Southern Railway and, later, the modern Norfolk Southern Corporation since 1958.

Finally, some of the electric streetcar depots are highlighted. Many times, these were just simple shelters for passengers but were ornate in their own right, made of stone or concrete. Very few of these depots exist today, having been torn down after the streetcar service ended.

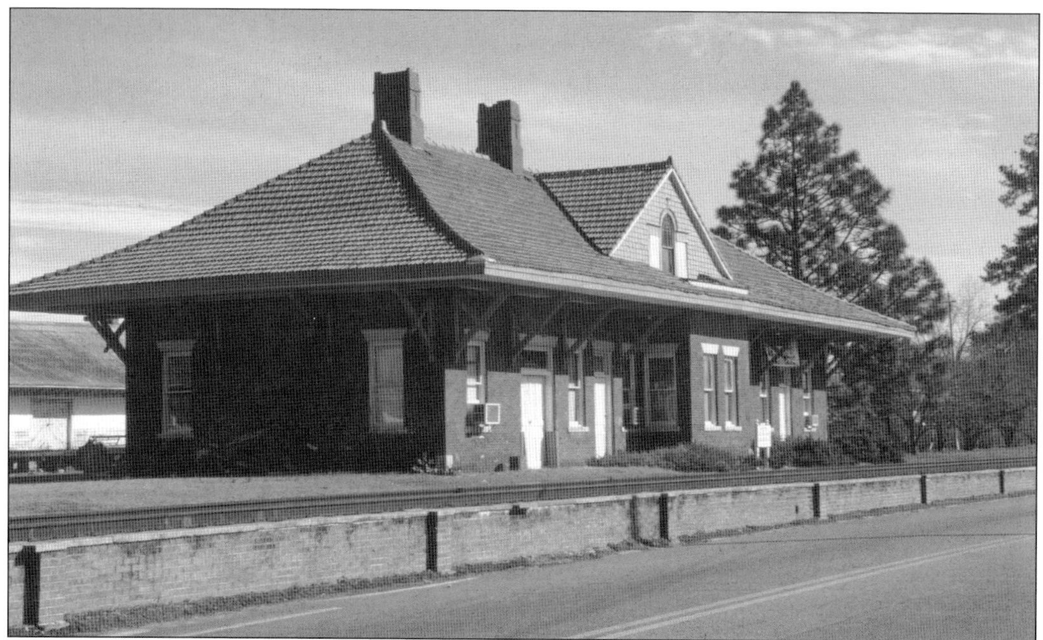

Maxton was serviced by the Atlantic Coast Line from their Parkton branch and the Seaboard Air Line operating between Wilmington and Hamlet. Each railroad had separate freight stations, using union station for passenger service. The building was constructed based on Seaboard plans and serves as a community building today. (Author's collection.)

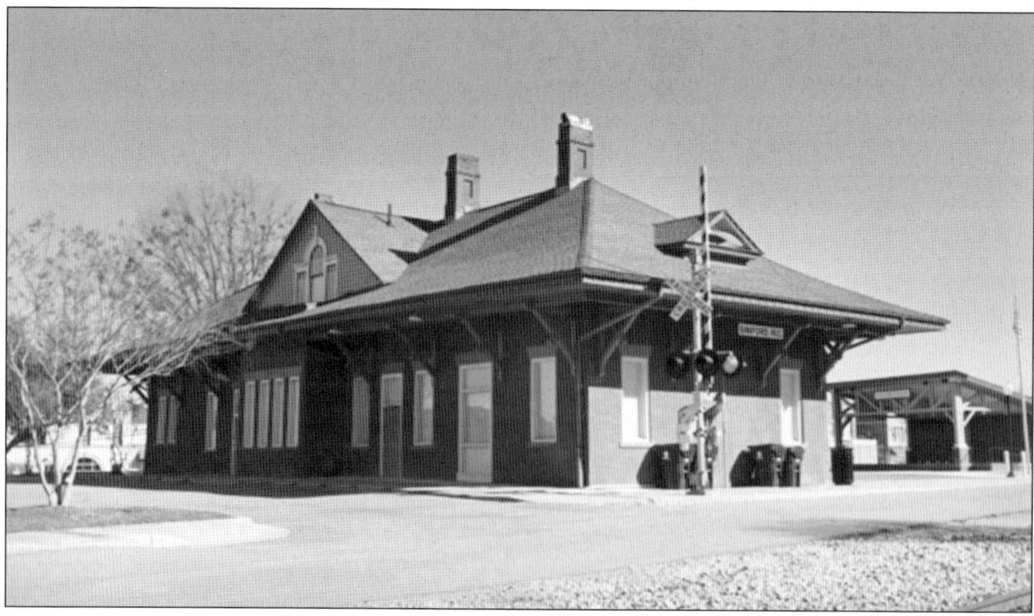

Sanford was the connection of three railroads, though two were originally the same line. Along with the Seaboard Air Line, the Cape Fear & Yadkin Valley served Sanford until 1894, when it was split between the Atlantic Coast Line and Southern Railway. The short line Atlantic & Western Railway is also based in Sanford. The Seaboard-style depot has been preserved and helps tell the railroad history of Sanford, along with 1872 station agent house, known today as the Railroad House. (Author's collection.)

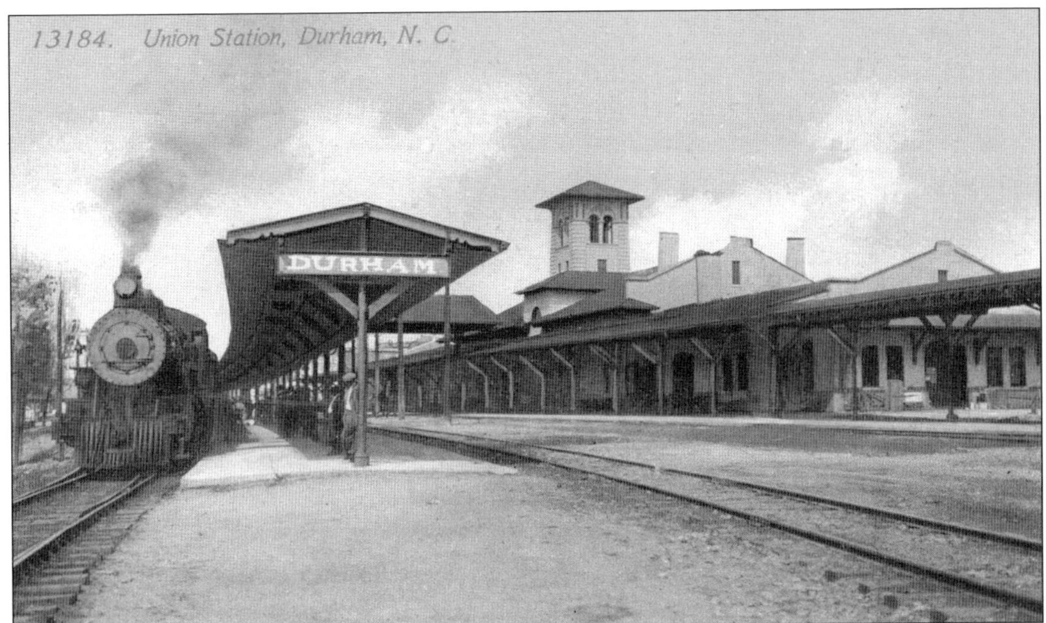

Durham was served by the Southern Railway, Norfolk & Western, and Seaboard Air Line. The station was constructed in 1905, designed by the famous architect Frank Milburn, who constructed several grand stations for the Southern Railway. The building was torn down in 1968 to make room for a new downtown highway loop. (Author's collection.)

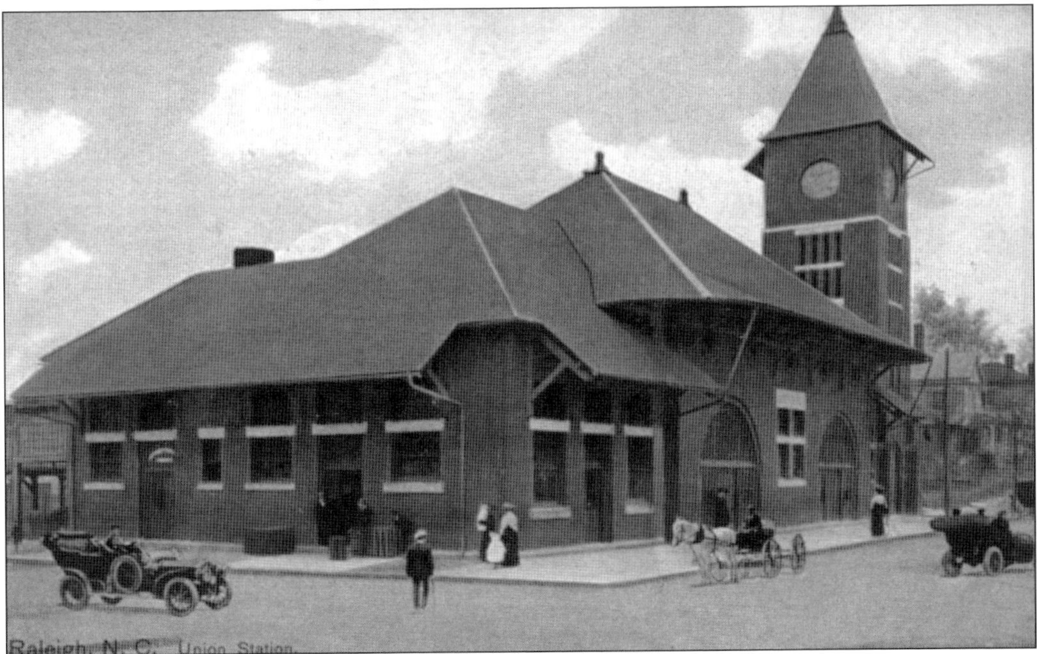

Raleigh Union Station was constructed in 1890 and used by the Seaboard Air Line, Southern Railway, and the Norfolk Southern Railway. Seaboard left first, constructing a new depot in 1942, followed by Norfolk Southern terminated passenger service in 1948, and the Southern moved to its new station in 1950. The building was preserved, hosting different companies through the years at Dawson and West Martin Streets. (Author's collection.)

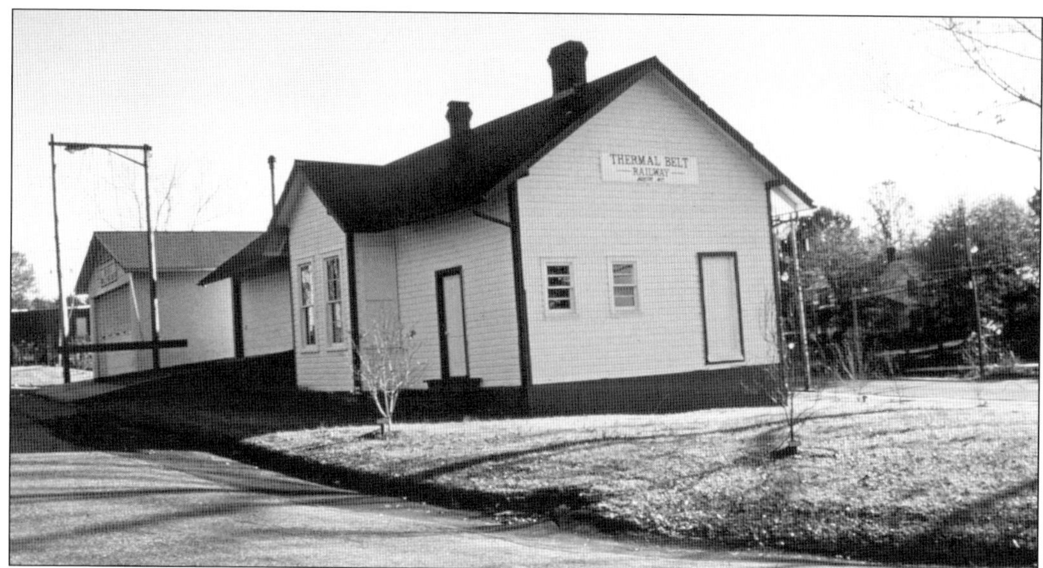

Bostic, a small community near Forest City, had a union station that served the Seaboard Air Line and Clinchfield Railroad, though the station was patterned after Seaboard plans. A small yard was also constructed to interchange freight cars between the two railroads. This building was used as the headquarters for the Thermal Belt Railway during the 1990s, operating between Bostic and Forest City. (Author's collection.)

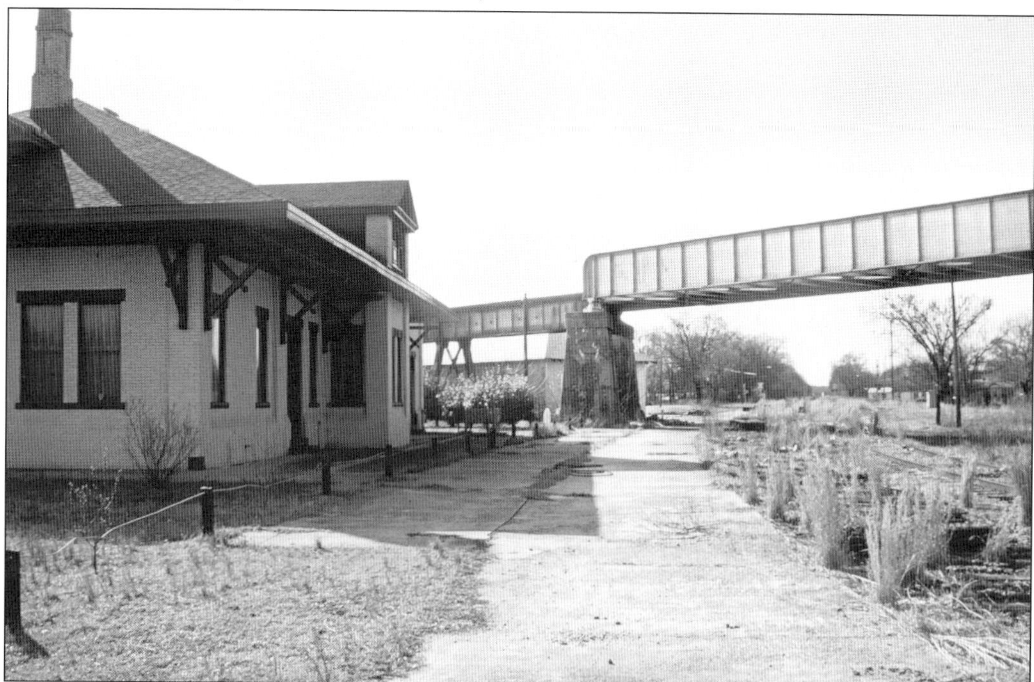

The town of Weldon is named for Daniel Weldon, who owned much of the land in the area. Early residents referred to the area as Weldon's Place until it was officially incorporated on January 6, 1843, three years after the W&W was completed. The Atlantic Coast Line ran across the elevated bridge, while the Seaboard was at ground level, heading to Norfolk. Today, the depot building still stands, serving as the town library. (Author's collection.)

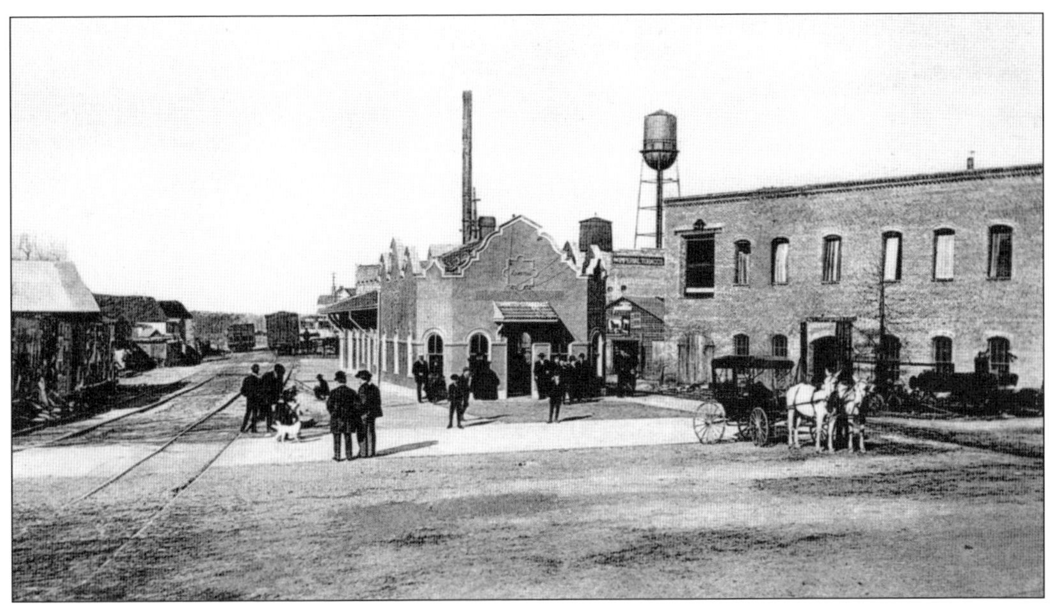

The view above shows the Atlantic & North Carolina depot in Kinston during the 1910s, when the line was under Norfolk Southern Railway control. Norfolk Southern faulted on their lease payment in 1932, causing the railroad to return to independent operation in 1935. Sometime in the 1920s or 1930s, a new Kinston Union Station was constructed, as shown below. The building later became a bus station and was torn down sometime after the 1970s. (Both, courtesy of the State Archives of North Carolina.)

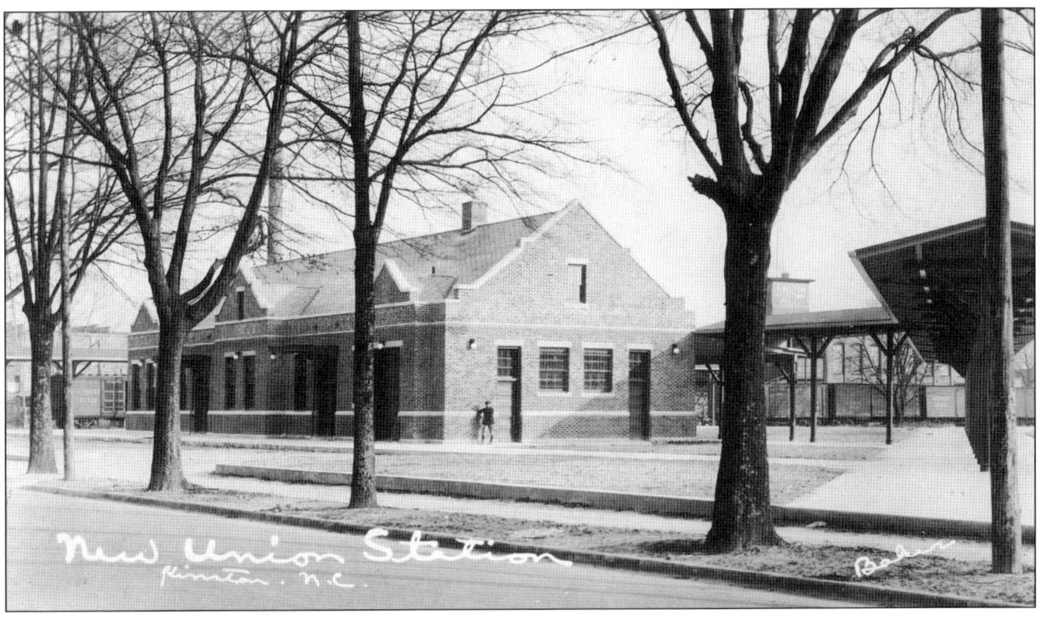

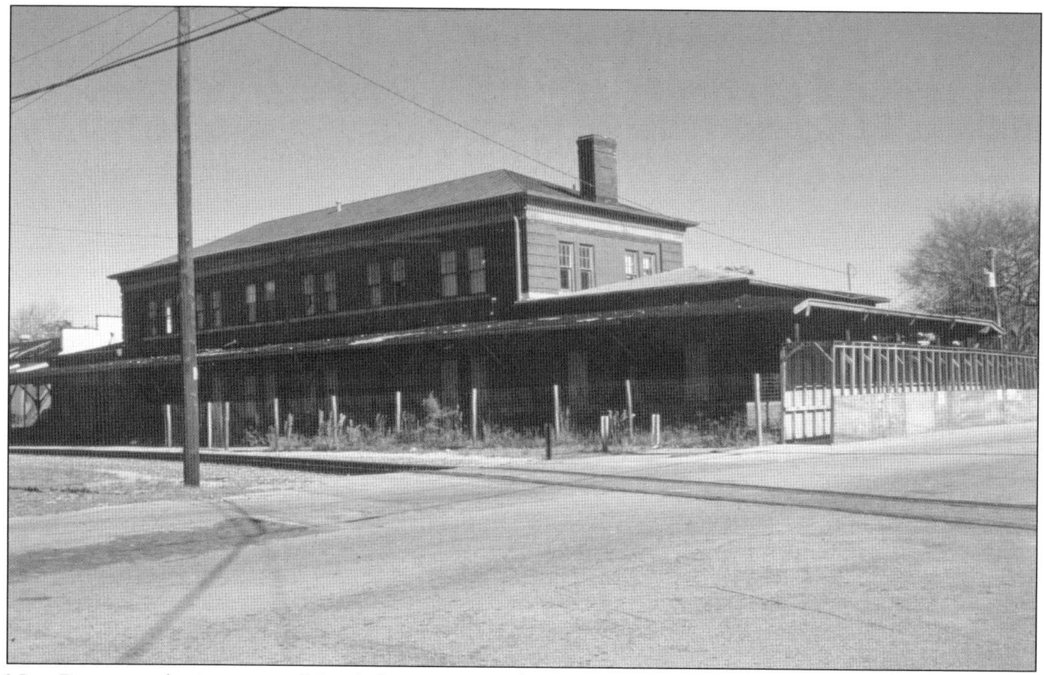

New Bern was the junction of the Atlantic & North Carolina and Atlantic Coast Line Railroads, and this union station was built in 1910. Passenger service from both roads was ended by 1950, and a new revitalization movement in New Bern has begun to restore this building. (Author's collection.)

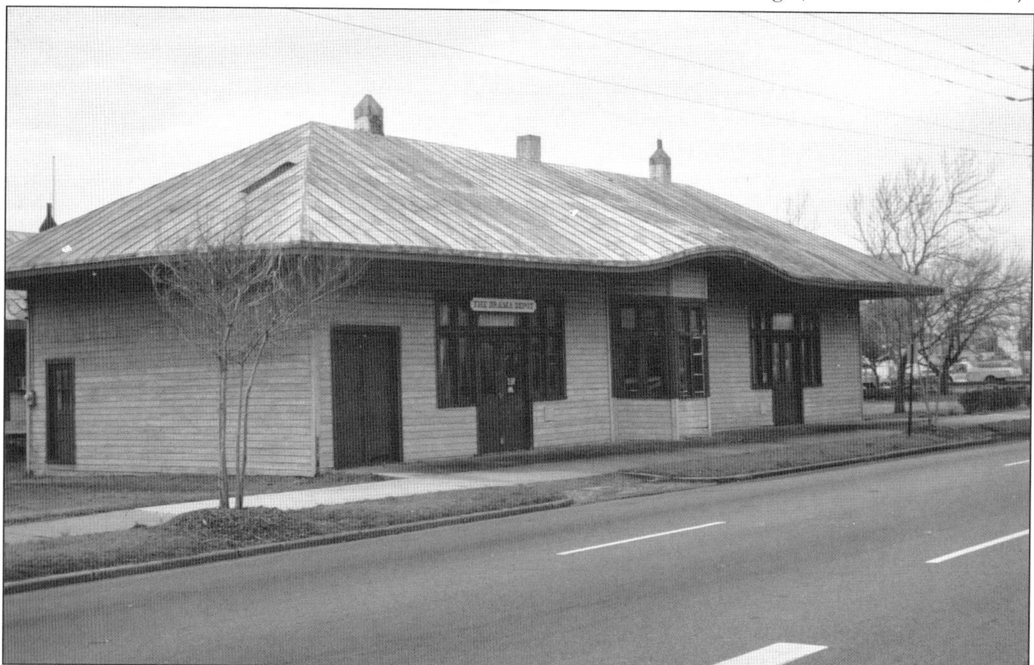

The depot at Morehead City was located originally near the tracks that run through the center of the street. The depot, built by 1910, was moved by the city to Arendell Street in the city park and contains offices for the Downtown Morehead City Revitalization Association. (Author's collection.)

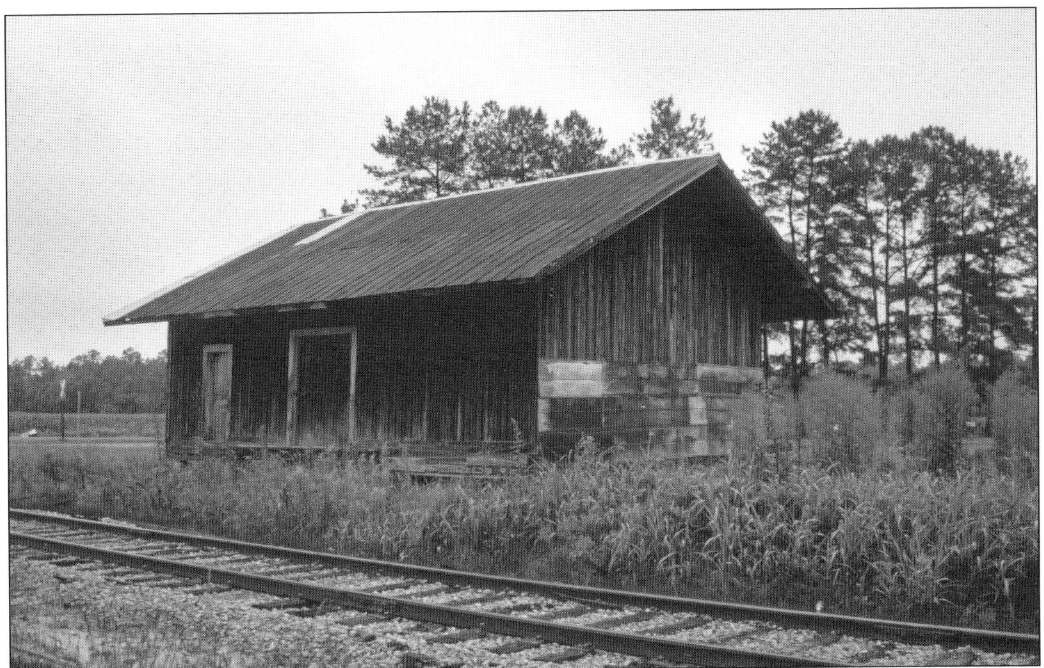

The Aberdeen & Rockfish Railroad was incorporated in 1892, reaching Dundarrach in 1900. Passenger service was operated until 1949, resulting in this depot being sold into private ownership. The depot still stands beside the tracks today. (Author's collection.)

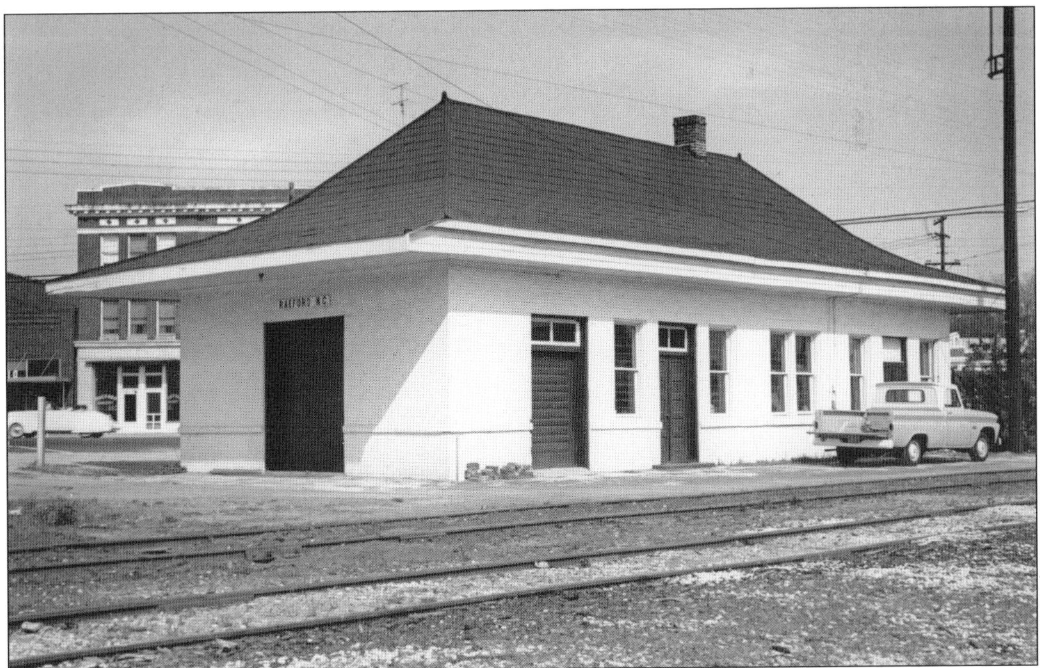

Raeford is located where the A&R and Laurinburg & Southern (L&S) Railroads interchanged freight near the depot shown here on April 20, 1967. The depot still stands today and has a definite Seaboard look, similar to the Aberdeen depot. (Author's collection)

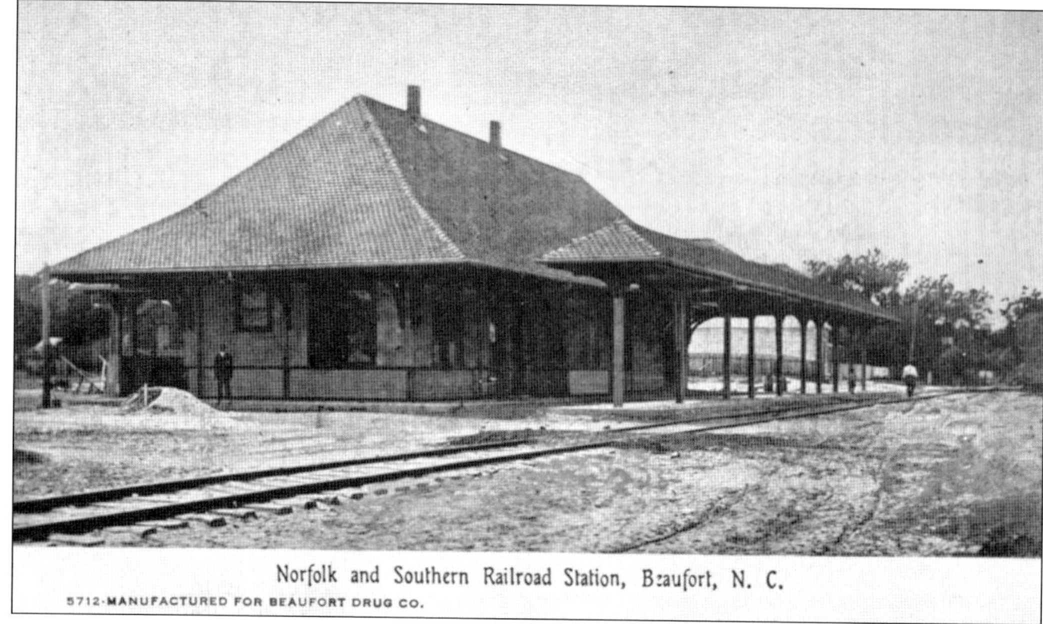
Norfolk and Southern Railroad Station, Beaufort, N. C.
5712-MANUFACTURED FOR BEAUFORT DRUG CO.

Beaufort is located across the sound from Morehead City, under the service of the Beaufort & Morehead Railroad. The Norfolk Southern Railway constructed a large depot in town, reflecting the importance of this coastal community while they controlled this small railroad. The depot has been restored and used by the town. (Above, author's collection; below, Author's collection.)

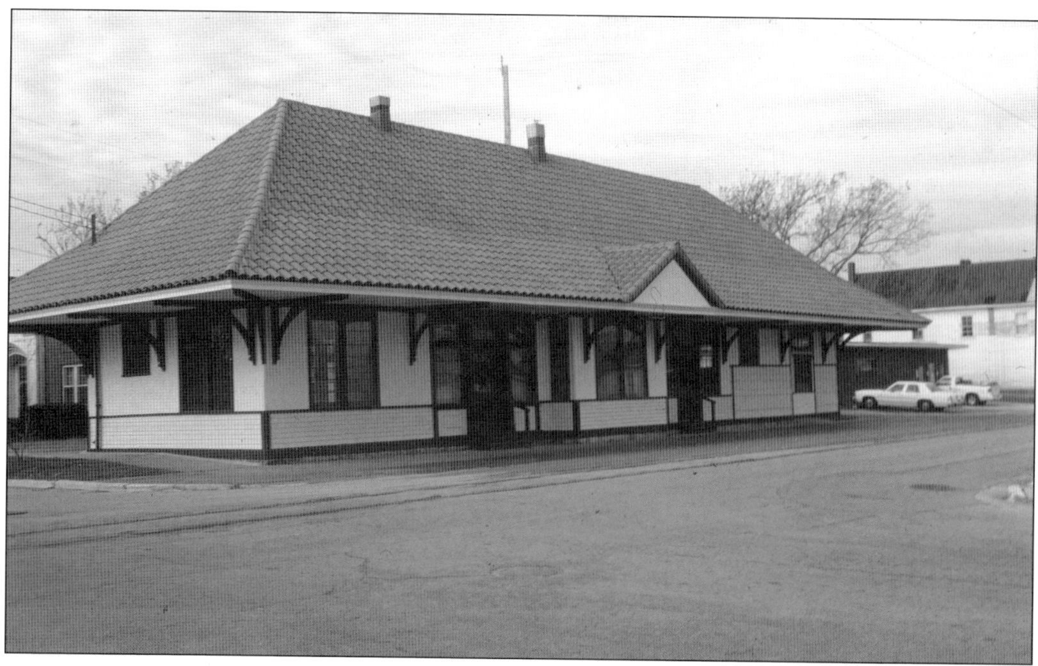

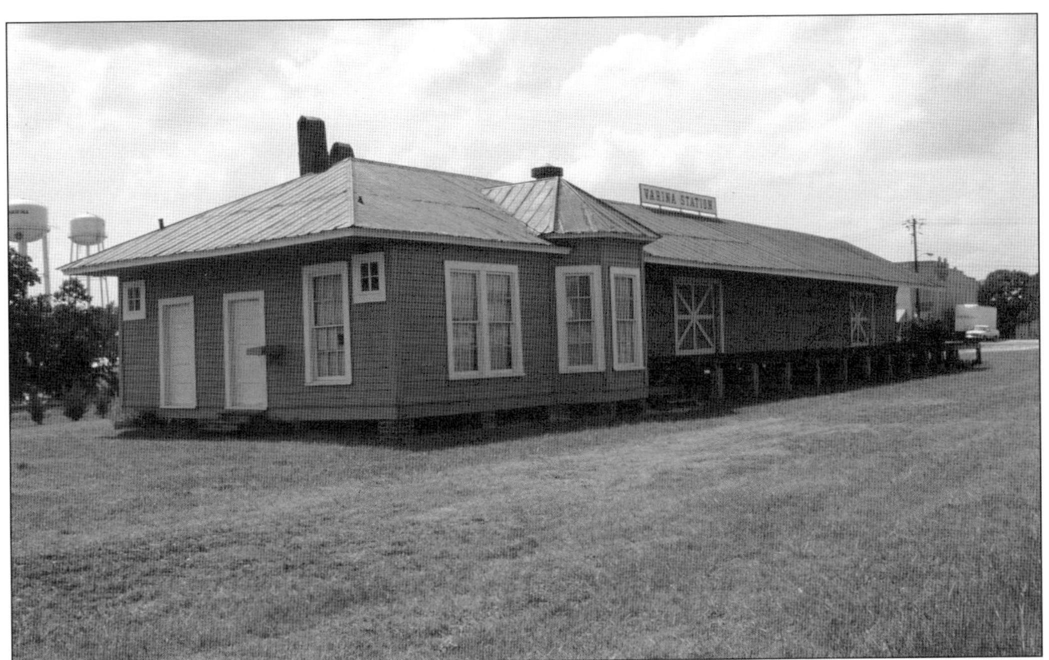

The Durham & Southern (D&S) Railway depot in Varina was originally known as a union station, since it served both the D&S and Norfolk Southern for passenger service. The 1915 depot has undergone a new restoration since this photograph was taken in 1994 and now serves as a private business. (Author's collection.)

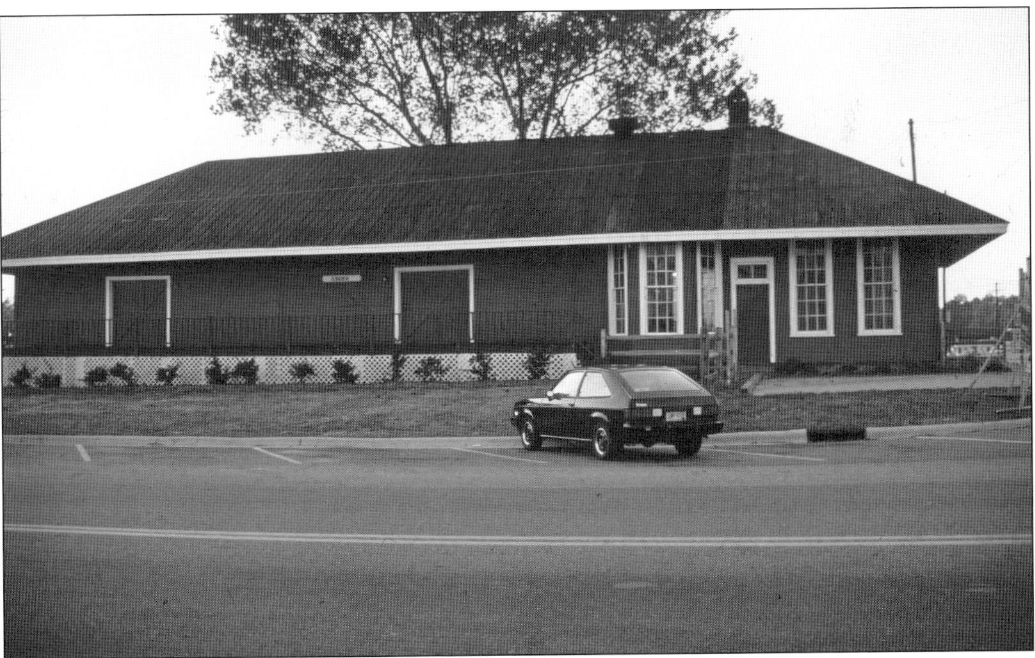

This image of the Angier depot is from 1990, but the building looks basically the same today, housing a private business. The D&S was merged into the Seaboard Coast Line in 1976, and the line from Varina to Erwin was later abandoned. (Author's collection.)

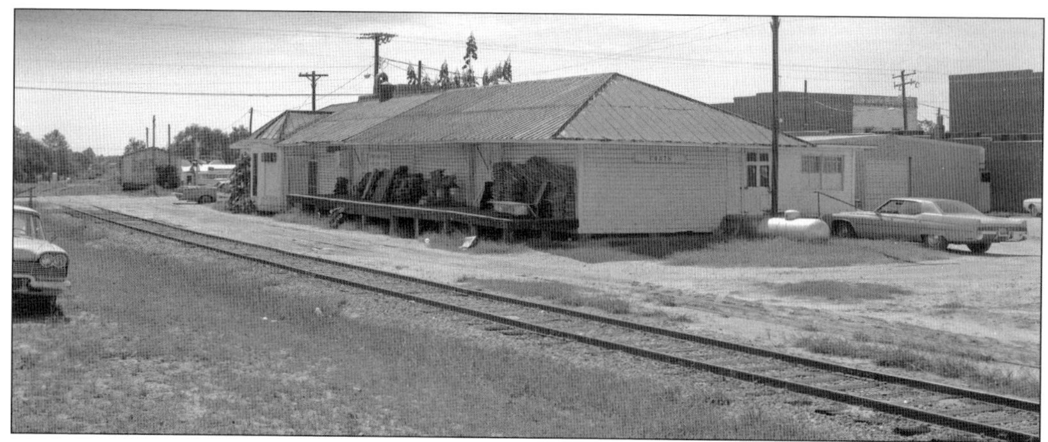

Coats is a town in Harnett County named for James T. Coats, who purchased land and set up a general store. The depot, built by 1915, still stands today as a commercial business. (Photograph by C.K. Marsh, courtesy of the King-Marsh collection.)

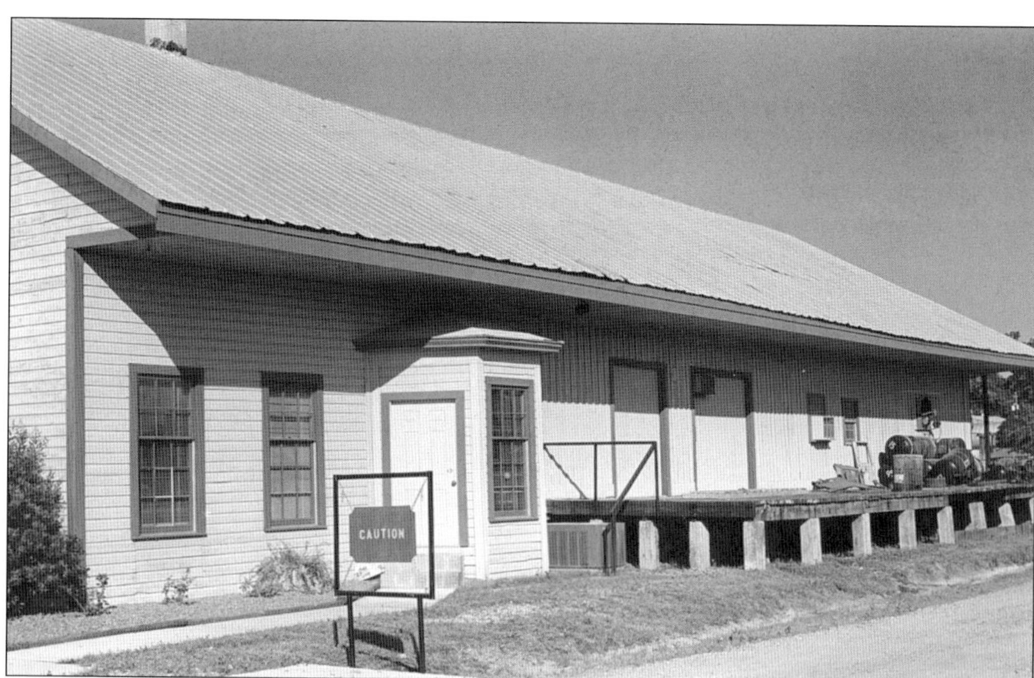

Dunn was the southern terminus for the Durham & Southern, making a connection with the Atlantic Coast Line. Dunn was originally known as Lucknow before changing to Dunn and incorporating in 1887. Dunn was named for Bennett Dunn, who supervised the construction of the ACL line through the area. This depot still stands and is used by a commercial business. (Author's collection.)

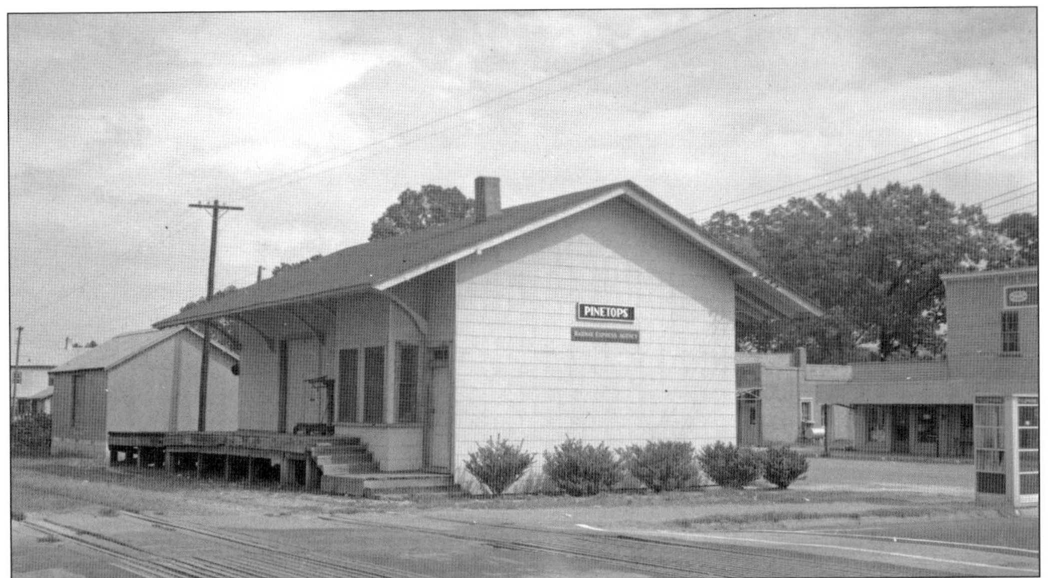

This image of the Pinetops depot on October 20, 1963, was captured while the East Carolina Railway was still in service. This depot was later modified by adding brick to the exterior and converted into the local police department by the early 1990s. (Photograph by Tom King, courtesy of the King-Marsh collection.)

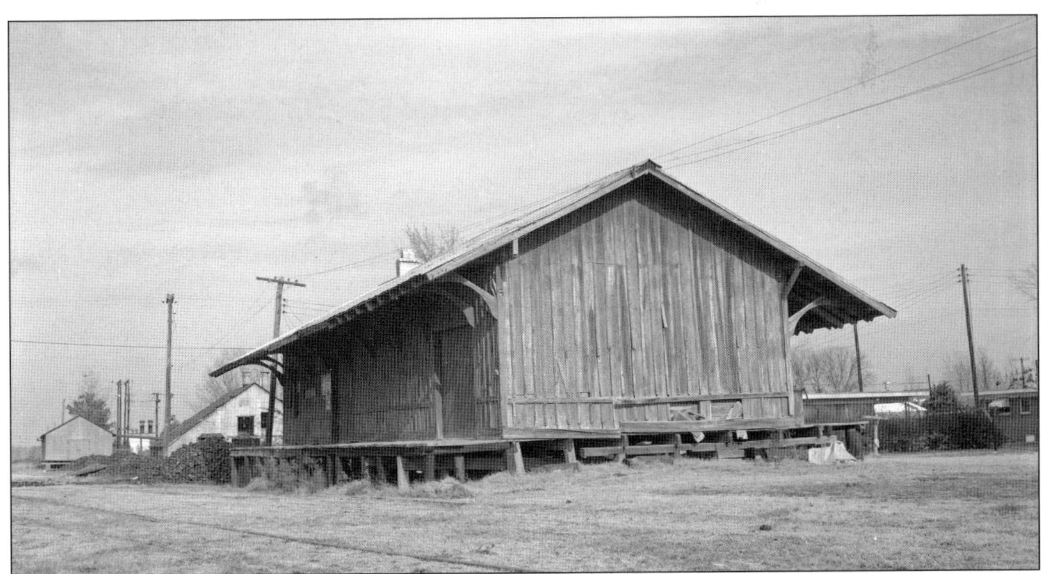

Macclesfield is located in southern Edgecombe County and was started in 1901 by Henry Clark Bridgers, who constructed the East Carolina Railway starting in 1898. The depot was photographed on November 14, 1965, the day before the railroad was shut down. (Photograph by Tom King, courtesy of the King-Marsh collection.)

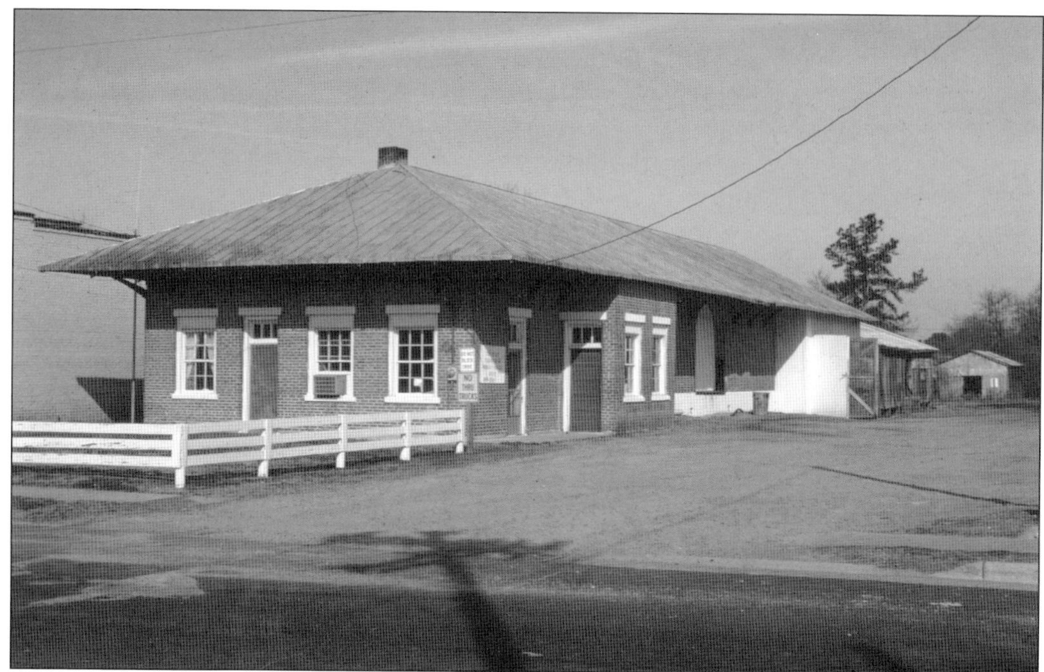

Fountain, located in Pitt County, is reportedly 20 miles from Greenville, Tarboro, Wilson, and Snow Hill. The depot, built by 1910, has been used by the town for several years. (Author's collection.)

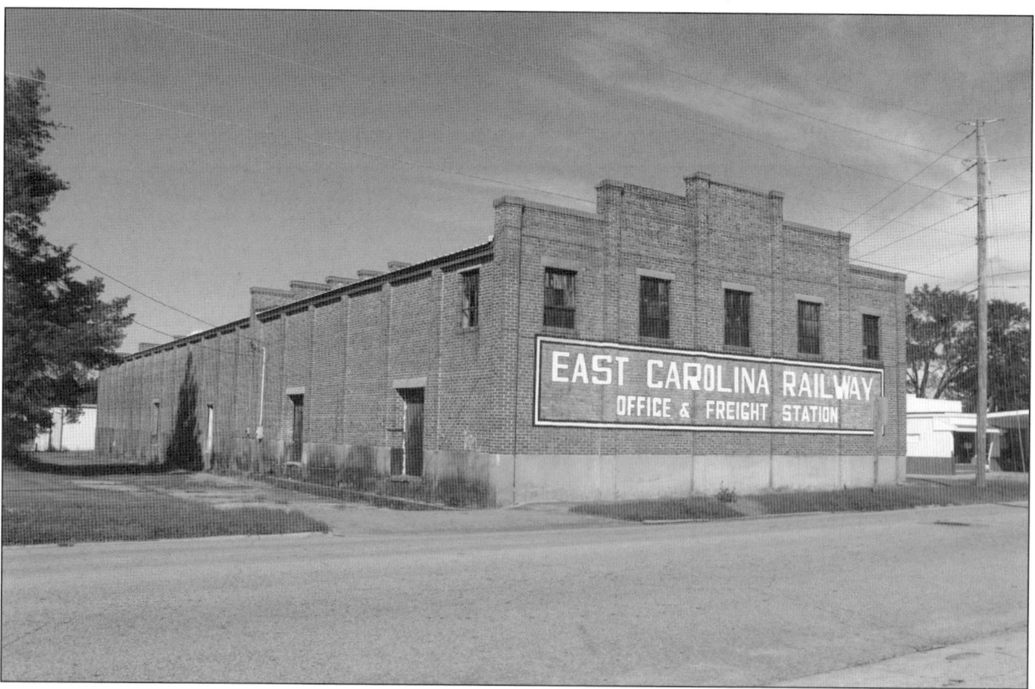

Farmville became the southern terminus of the East Carolina Railway by the 1940s, and it used this brick freight station until the line closed in 1965. Long in private business, the railroad name was repainted a few years ago. (Author's collection.)

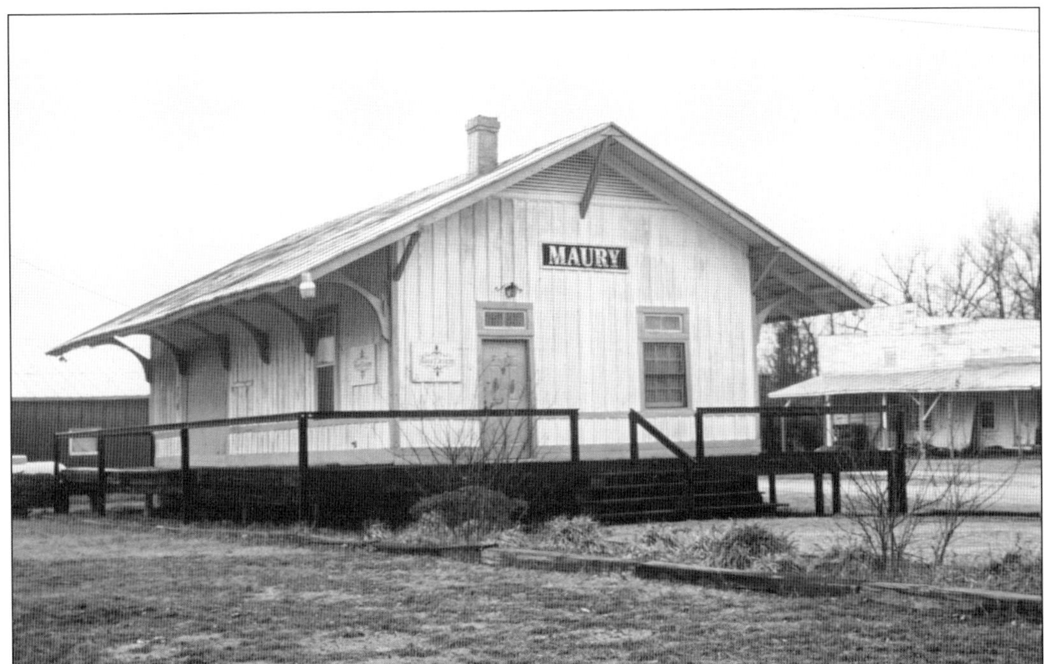

The Maury depot, shown here in 1992, definitely shows the ACL influence and is a sister to the Macclesfield depot. The depot has been maintained fairly well since the line was abandoned in 1933 due to the Great Depression. (Author's collection.)

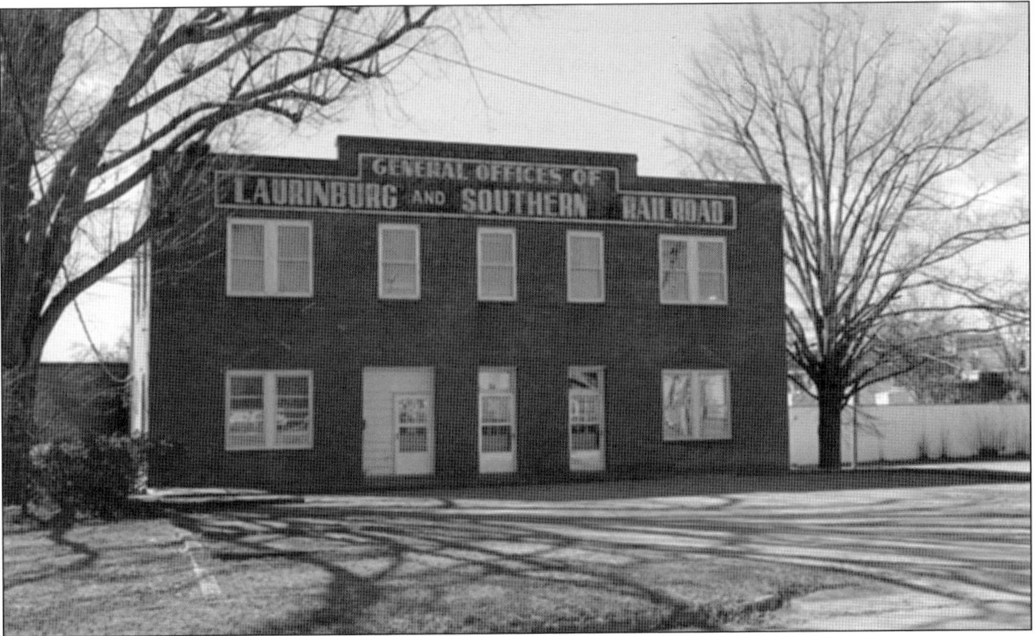

The Laurinburg & Southern (L&S) Railroad has been in operation since March 9, 1909, and built this headquarters building in 1927. Through the 1980s, the L&S operated several short lines in North Carolina, though many have since been abandoned. Gulf & Ohio Railways gained control of the L&S in 1994 and also operates the Nash County and Yadkin Valley Railroads today. (Author's collection.)

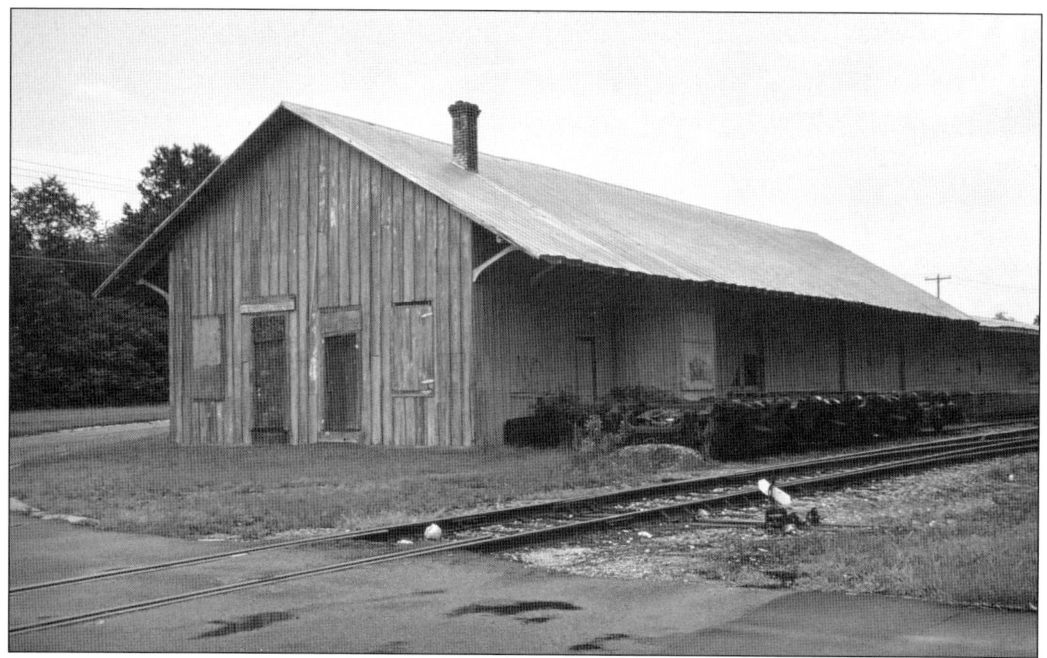

The first L&S depot in Laurinburg was built in 1910 alongside the Seaboard Air Line tracks. The building is similar in design to ACL stations, even though it sits alongside the SAL tracks. The depot has been razed but still looks to be in fair shape during 1996. (Author's collection.)

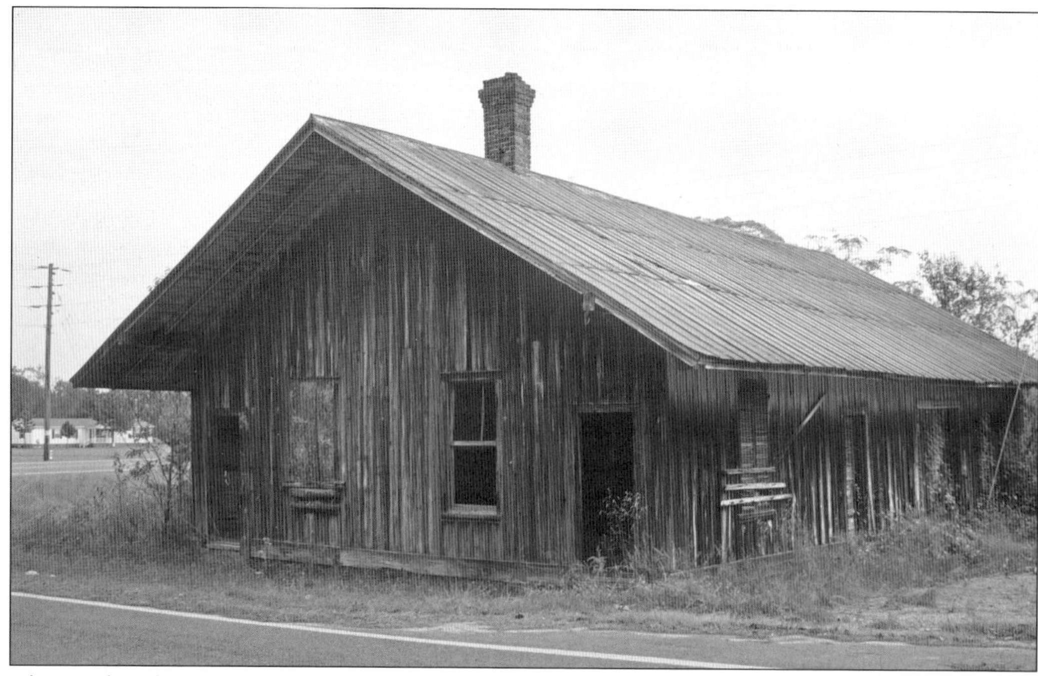

The Rockingham Railroad operated from its namesake city south to Ghio, which was called Scholl by the railroad. This building is all that is left from the railroad, and it has been sitting vacant for several years. (Author's collection.)

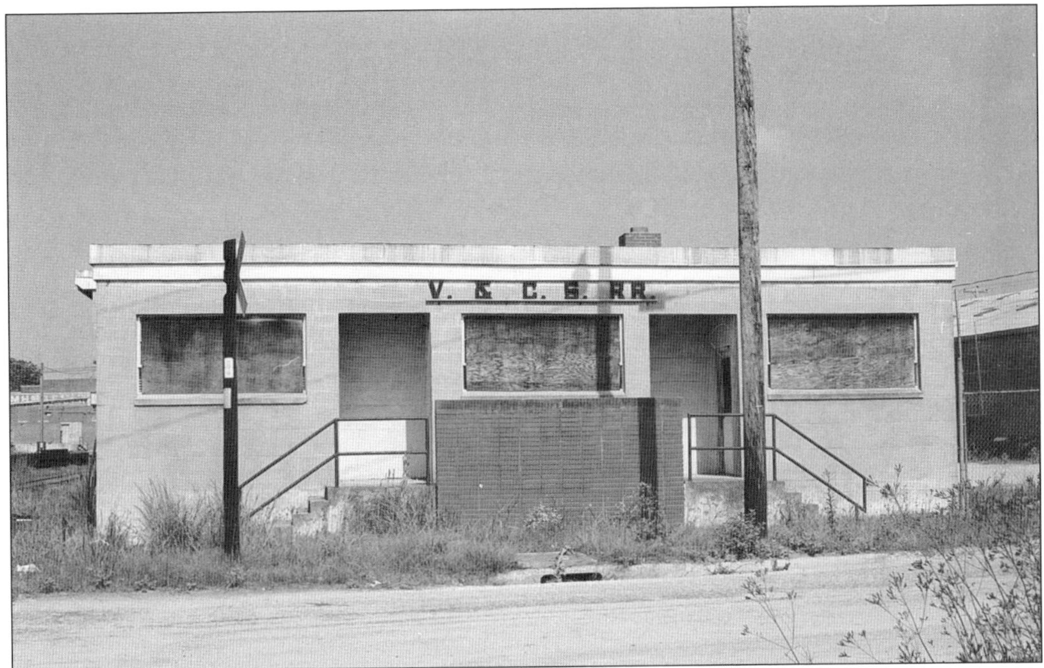

The Virginia and Carolina Southern (V&CS) Railroad was incorporated on March 4, 1906, constructing this office building in Lumberton by 1950. Controlled by the ACL for most of the its corporate life, it regularly ran ex-ACL 4-6-0 locomotives into the 1950s. This building still stands, sans the "V&CS RR" lettering, and appears to be well maintained. (Author's collection.)

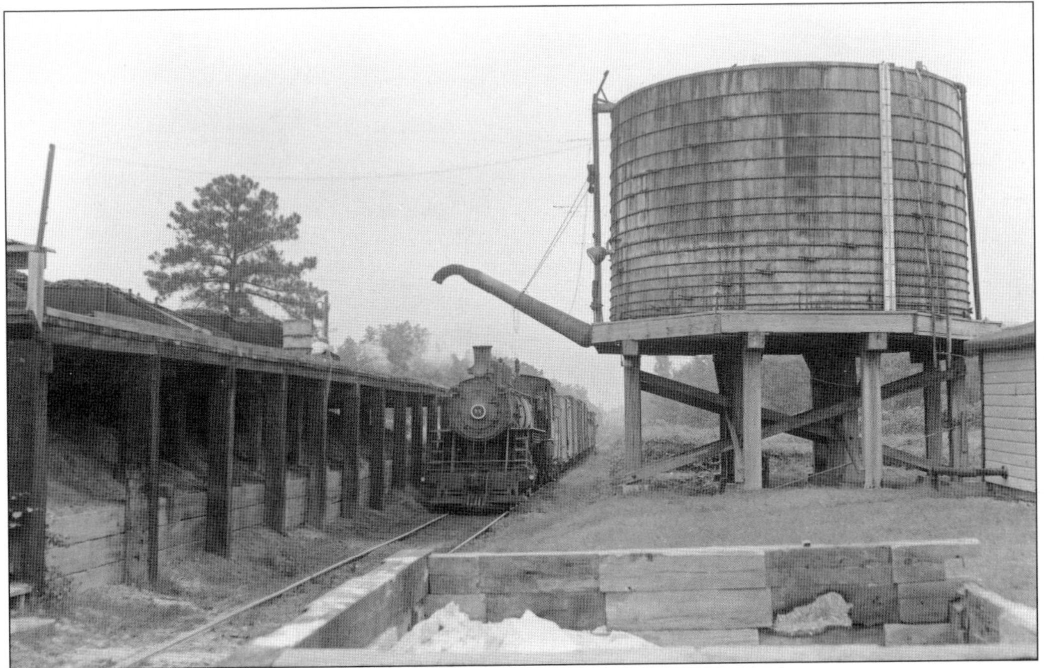

At St. Pauls, the railroad had a small depot (which is longer standing), several freight buildings, and its locomotive service area, as shown here on May 29, 1956. (Photograph by John Krause, author's collection.)

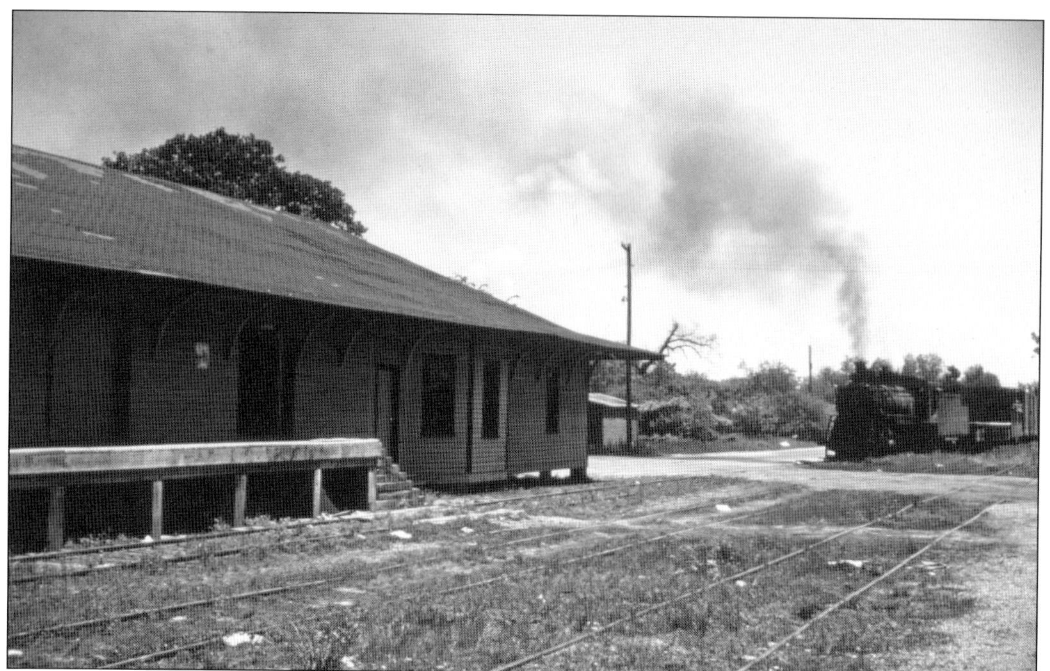

Elizabethtown was the eastern terminus of their line from St. Pauls. This view from April 27, 1957, shows a steam-powered freight ready to head back west. The station still existed in 1964 but was torn down several years ago. (Courtesy of the Brian Ezzelle collection.)

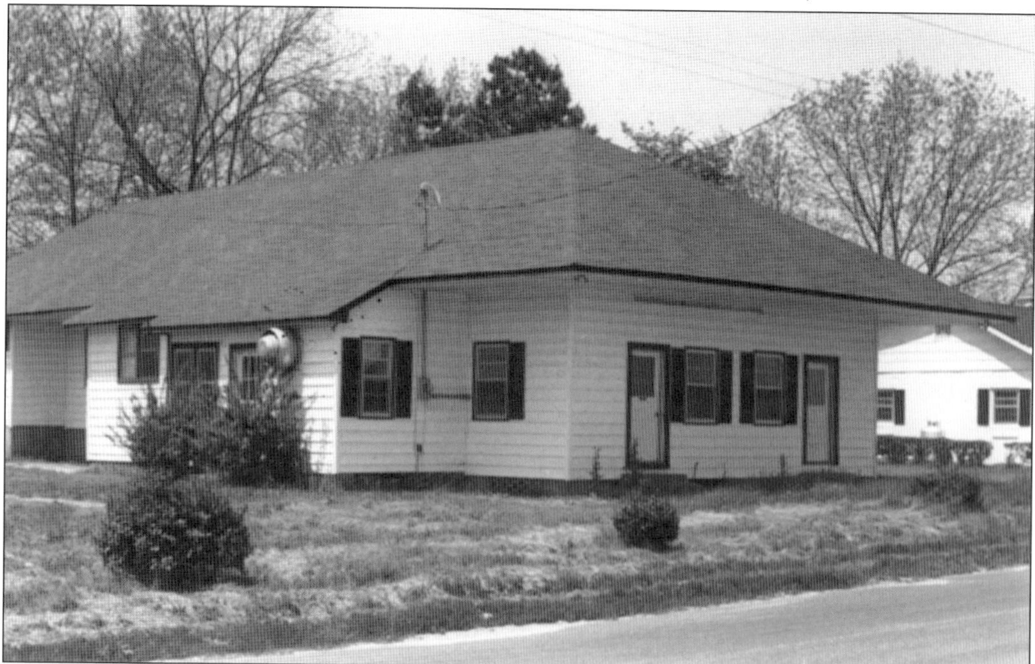

The Maxton, Alma & Southbound Railroad was incorporated on February 21, 1911. Their depot in Rowland has been converted to apartments. The line, operating from Maxton through Raemon to Rowland, was abandoned in 1937, and the rail taken up and sold for scrap. (Courtesy of S. David Carriker.)

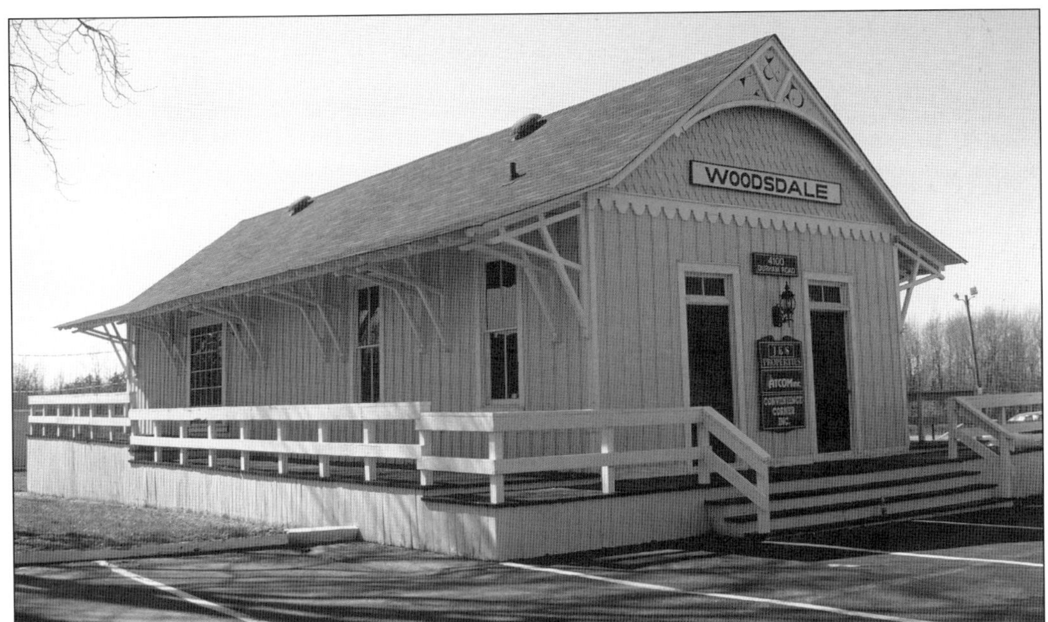

The Woodsdale depot was originally constructed by the Lynchburg & Durham Railroad by 1890, when the 115-mile line was completed into Durham. This line was leased to the Norfolk & Western Railway on March 1, 1892, and later abandoned by Norfolk Southern Corporation. This depot was moved to Roxboro and now is used for private business. (Author's collection.)

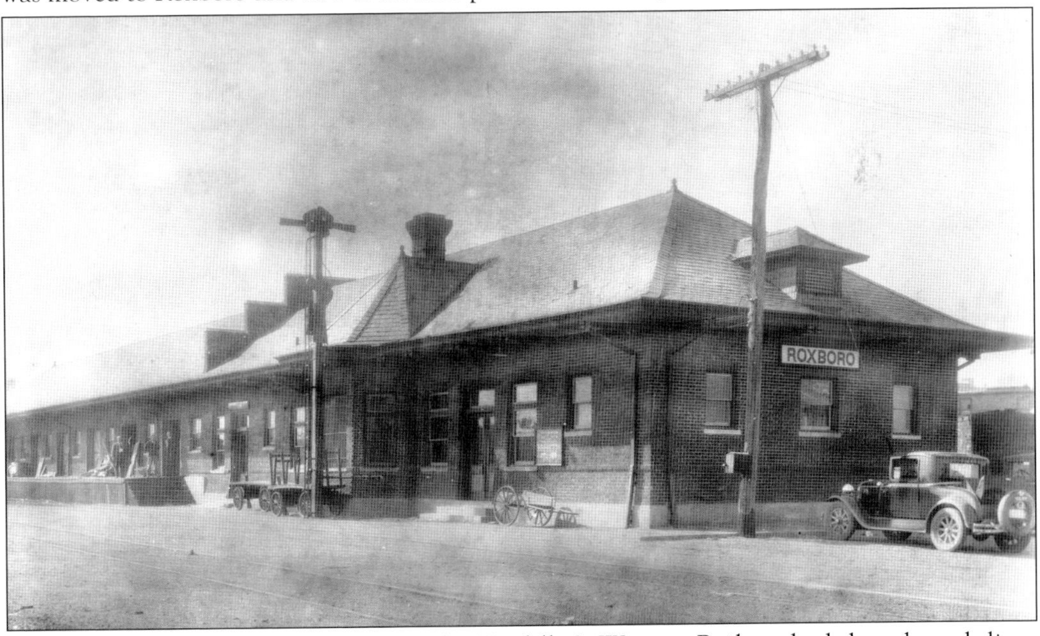

Although not technically a short line, the Norfolk & Western Railway had three branch lines operating in North Carolina and only one in the eastern part of the state. Their line from Keysville, Virginia, went south through Roxboro to Durham. This 1920s-era photograph shows the new Roxboro depot, replacing the original built in 1917. Roxboro was incorporated on January 9, 1855, named for Roxburgh, Scotland. Sadly, this depot no longer exists today. (Courtesy of the State Archives of North Carolina.)

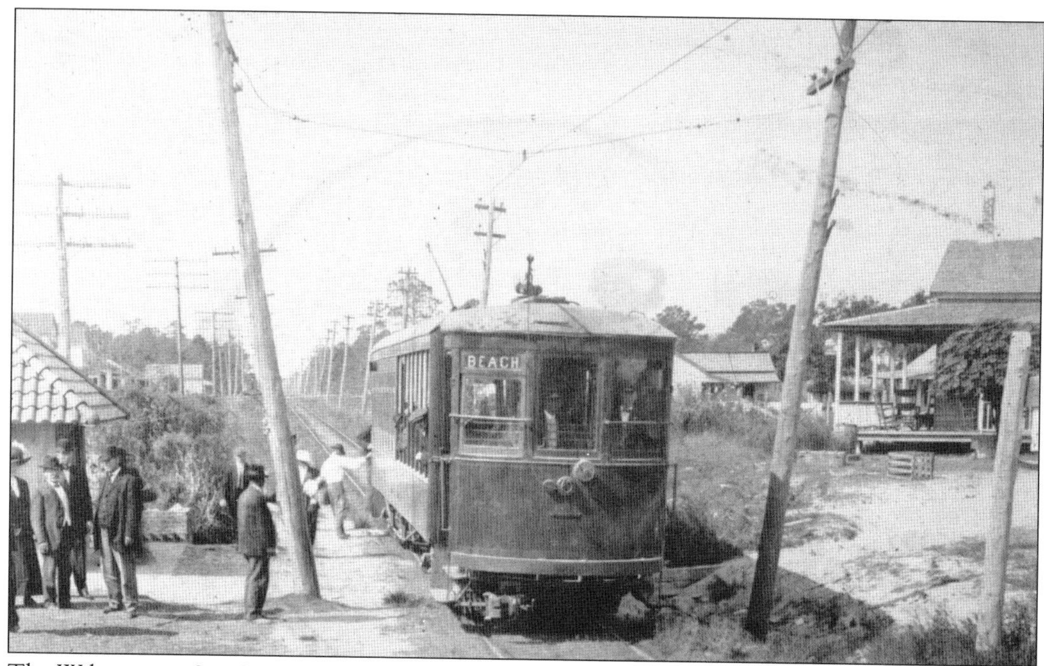

The Wilmington Sea Coast Railroad was chartered in 1887 to construct a rail line from downtown Wilmington to Wrightsville Beach. Originally powered by steam, it was later electrified in 1902. This interurban line operated until 1940, when a road was built to the beach, paralleling this rail line. Today, only the Audubon Trolley stop, similar to the covered structure on the left, remains of this route. (Courtesy of the Hanover Public Library.)

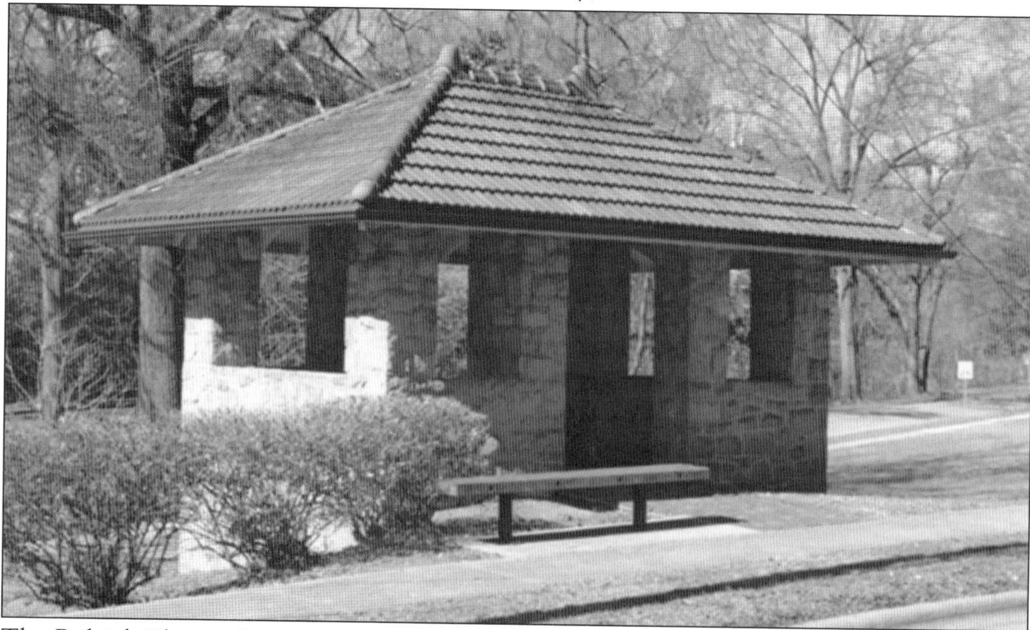

The Raleigh Electric began operating on September 1, 1891, mainly in downtown Raleigh. Carolina Power & Light Company expanded the system to include Glenwood Avenue and the 1912 construction of the 100-acre Bloomsbury Park. This shelter is the only one standing today from the streetcar history of Raleigh. (Author's collection.)

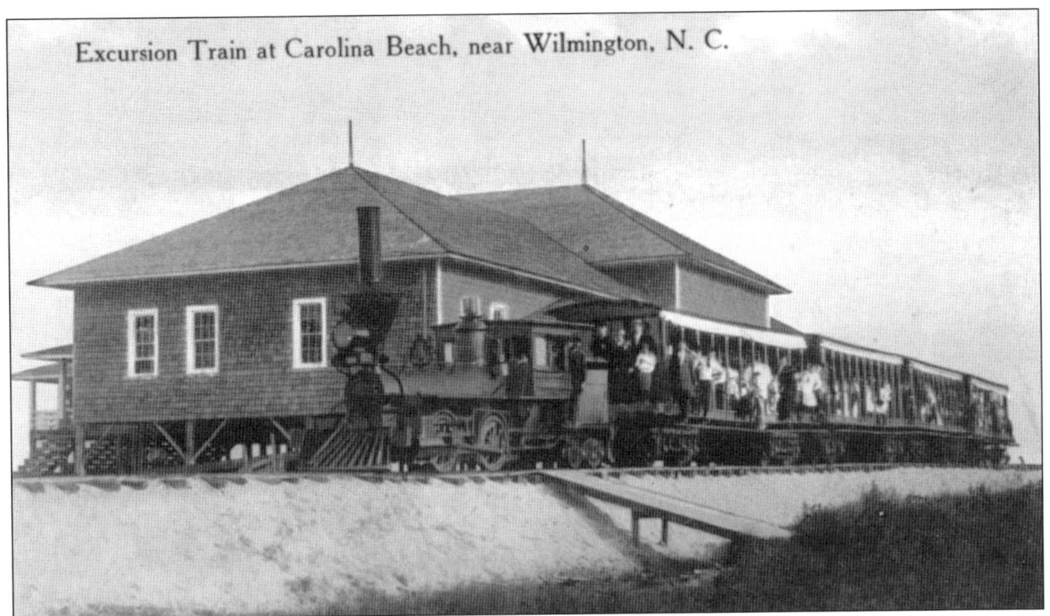

The New Hanover Transit Company offered a combination of ferry and steam train to Carolina Beach during the 1910s. Passengers would take a ferry from Wilmington down to a landing on the Cape Fear River, then load onto the open-air cars for a ride across the sand to the ocean. This service was discontinued in 1919 when the ferry berth burned and was never rebuilt. (Author's collection.)

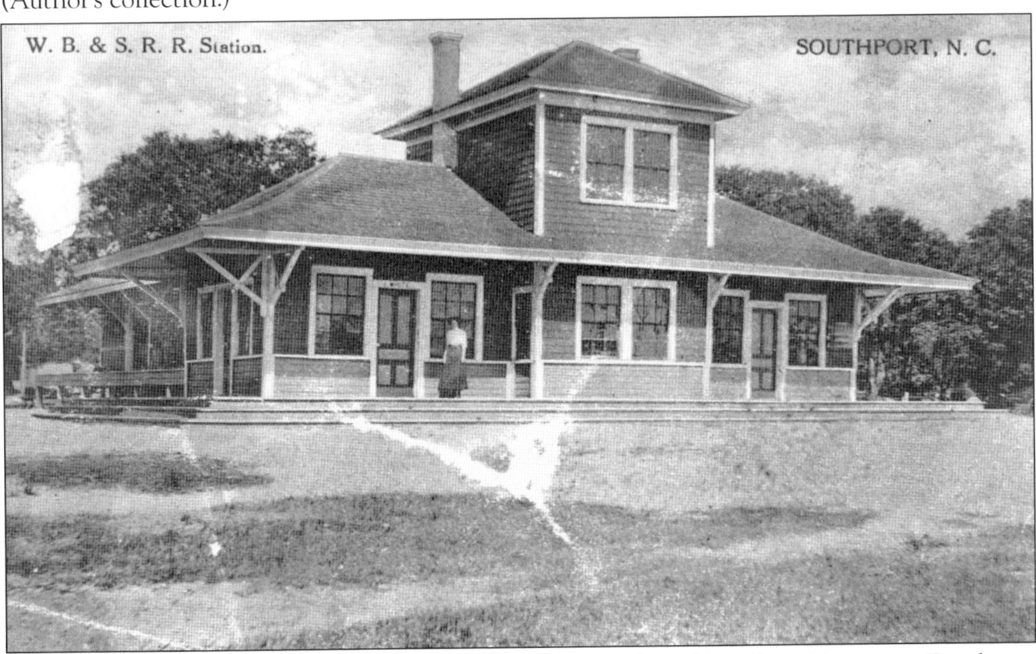

The Wilmington, Brunswick & Southern Railroad operated a rail line from Navassa to Southport until 1941. It constructed this depot in Southport, with trains backing to the station from a wye track. The Sunny Point Military Terminal railroad later used part of the roadbed from the WB&S during construction in the 1950s. The depot was torn down several years ago. (Courtesy of the State Archives of North Carolina.)

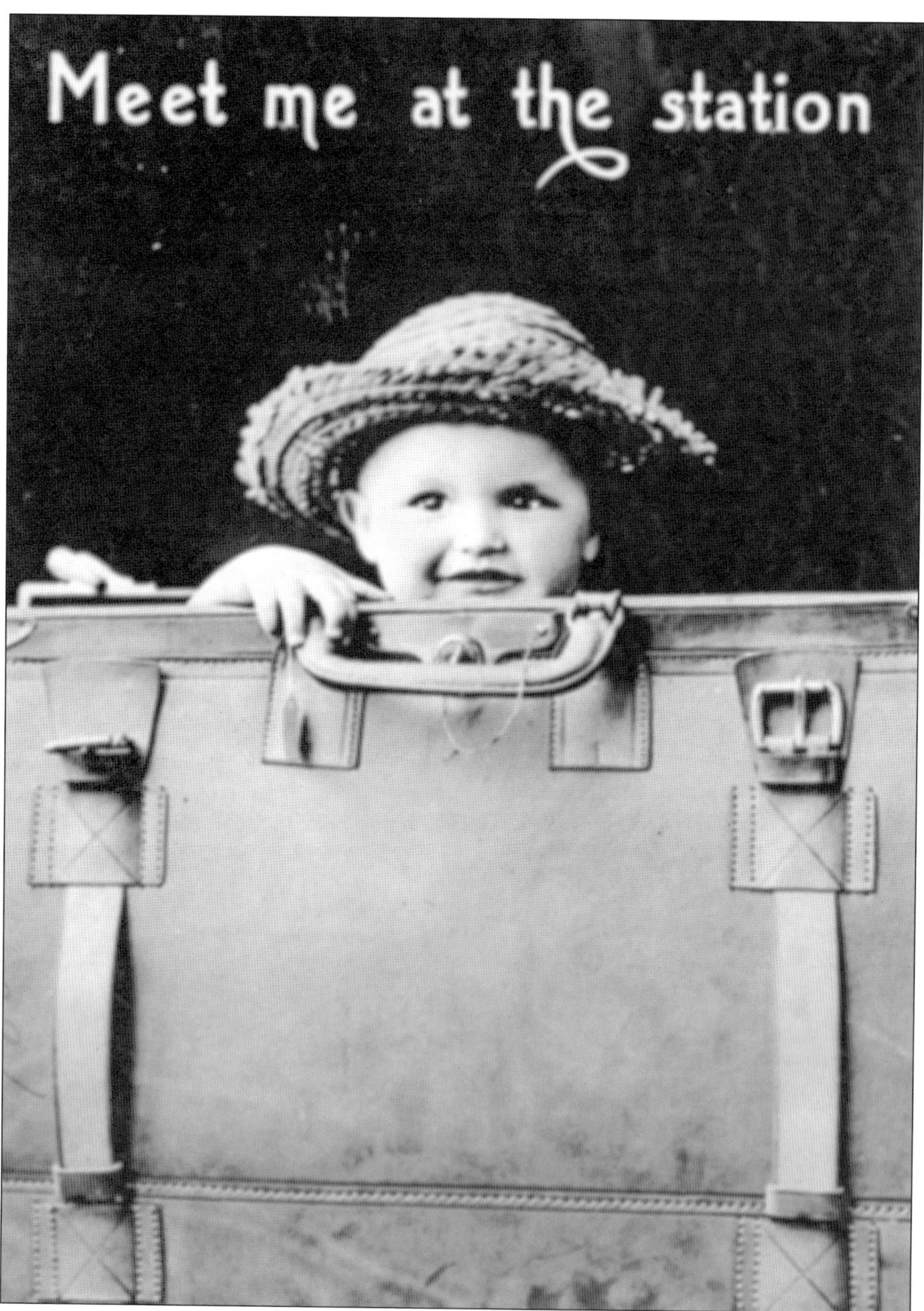

This image, dating from the early 1900s, epitomizes the feeling of many during that time—pack a bag or trunk, meet at a local station, ready to experience the next great adventure! (Author's collection.)

Bibliography

This book seeks to give a concise overview of railroad depots found in eastern North Carolina, but it cannot cover everything that either was or is still remaining across the state. This bibliography has been included for those wanting to conduct more research or need more information to create a driving tour and explore the state for themselves.

Bridgers Jr., Henry C. *East Carolina Railway, Route of The Yellow-hammer.* Tarboro, NC: T&E Publishers of Louisville, Carolina Division, 1973.

Peterson, Art, et al. *A Directory of North Carolina's Railroad Structures.* Raleigh, NC: National Railroad Historical Society, 2001.

Prince, Richard E. *Atlantic Coast Line: Steam Locomotives, Ships and History.* Green River, WY: Richard Prince, 1966.

———. *Norfolk Southern Railroad, Old Dominion Line and Connections.* Published by Richard Prince, Salt Lake City, Utah, 1972.

———. *Seaboard Air Line Railway – Steam Boats, Locomotives and History.* Published by Richard Prince, Salt Lake City, Utah, 1969.

pwrr.org/nstation/index/html

Reisweber, Robert, et al. *The Original Norfolk Southern Railway 1883–1974.* Lewisburg, PA: Garrigues House Publishers, 2007.

Robertson, Bill. *80 Years of Laurinburg and Southern History.* Laurinburg, NC: Bill Robertson, 1989.

Wrinn, Jim and Edward Lewis. *The Road of Personal Service: A Centennial History.* Aberdeen NC: Aberden & Rockfish Railroad, 1992.

www.rrshs.org/N.C./ncrrstruc.htm